CW00952431

SHAKESPEARE ON SCREEN: KING LEAR

The third volume in the re-launched series Shakespeare on Screen is devoted to film versions and adaptations of *King Lear*. Bringing together an international group of scholars, the chapters provide new insights and perspectives on what constitutes 'Learness' in a range of films, TV productions, translations, free retellings and appropriations from around the world. Taking 'screen' in its broader sense, it also covers digital material such as video archives, internet movies and YouTube videos. The volume features an invaluable film-bibliography and accompanying online resources include additional essays and an expanded version of the film-bibliography.

VICTORIA BLADEN is Sessional Lecturer and Honorary Research Fellow in the School of Communication and Arts at the University of Queensland where she has twice received a Faculty award for teaching excellence. She has published four Shakespearean text guides: *Measure for Measure* (2015), *Henry IV Part 1* (2012), *Julius Caesar* (2011) and *Romeo and Juliet* (2010). She co-edited *Supernatural and Secular Power in Early Modern England* (2015) and *Shakespeare on Screen:* Macbeth (2013) as well as *Shakespeare and the Supernatural* (2019). She has also published articles in several volumes of the Shakespeare on Screen series, including *Shakespeare on Screen:* The Tempest *and Late Romances* (Cambridge University Press 2017) and is on the editorial board for the Shakespeare on Screen in Francophonia project in France.

SARAH HATCHUEL is Professor of Film and Media Studies at the University Paul-Valéry Montpellier 3 and President of the Société Française Shakespeare. She has written extensively on adaptations of Shakespeare's plays: *Shakespeare and the Cleopatra/Caesar Intertext: Sequel, Conflation, Remake* (2011), *Shakespeare, from Stage to Screen* (2004), *A Companion to the Shakespearean Films of Kenneth Branagh* (2000), and on television series: *Lost: Fiction vitale* (2013), *Rêves et séries américaines: la fabrique d'autres mondes* (2015). She is general co-editor of the Shakespeare on Screen series and of the online journal *TV/Series*.

NATHALIE VIENNE-GUERRIN is Professor in Shakespeare Studies at the University Paul-Valéry Montpellier 3, Vice President of the Société Française Shakespeare and Director of the Institut de Recherche sur la Renaissance, l'âge Classique et les Lumières (IRCL, UMR 5186 CNRS). She is co-editor-in-chief of the international journal *Cahiers Élisabéthains* and co-director, with Patricia Dorval, of the *Shakespeare on Screen in Francophonia* Database. She has published *The Unruly Tongue in Early Modern England, Three Treatises* (2012) and is the author of *Shakespeare's Insults: A Pragmatic Dictionary* (2016). She is co-editor, with Sarah Hatchuel, of the Shakespeare on Screen series.

'Shakespeare on Screen' is unique in Shakespeare studies. Each volume is devoted to a single Shakespeare play, or a group of closely related plays, and discusses how it has been adapted to the medium of film and television. The series ranges far beyond the Anglo-American sphere, paying serious attention to European perspectives and combining discussion of mainstream Shakespeare cinema with broad definitions of adaptation and appropriation. As a result, each volume redefines the limits of the field and of the play. The series provides the finest writing on screened Shakespeare by scholars of international significance.

Originally published by Presses universitaires de Rouen et du Havre (PURH), Shakespeare on Screen is now extended by Cambridge University Press to provide fresh emphasis on new media, multimedia and the evolution of technologies. A special feature of each volume is a select film-bibliography, which will be augmented by a substantial free online resource.

SHAKESPEARE ON SCREEN: KING LEAR

EDITED BY

VICTORIA BLADEN
SARAH HATCHUEL
and
NATHALIE VIENNE-GUERRIN

CAMBRIDGE
UNIVERSITY PRESS

CAMBRIDGE
UNIVERSITY PRESS

University Printing House, Cambridge CB2 8BS, United Kingdom

One Liberty Plaza, 20th Floor, New York, NY 10006, USA

477 Williamstown Road, Port Melbourne, VIC 3207, Australia

314–321, 3rd Floor, Plot 3, Splendor Forum, Jasola District Centre,
New Delhi – 110025, India

79 Anson Road, #06–04/06, Singapore 079906

Cambridge University Press is part of the University of Cambridge.

It furthers the University's mission by disseminating knowledge in the pursuit of
education, learning, and research at the highest international levels of excellence.

www.cambridge.org
Information on this title: www.cambridge.org/9781108426923
DOI: 10.1017/9781108589727

© Cambridge University Press 2019

This publication is in copyright. Subject to statutory exception
and to the provisions of relevant collective licensing agreements,
no reproduction of any part may take place without the written
permission of Cambridge University Press.

First published 2019

Printed in the United Kingdom by TJ International Ltd. Padstow Cornwall

A catalogue record for this publication is available from the British Library.

ISBN 978-1-108-42692-3 Hardback

Additional resources for this publication at https://www.cambridge.org/gb
/academic/subjects/literature/renaissance-and-early-modern-literature
/shakespeare-screen-king-lear?format=HB.

Cambridge University Press has no responsibility for the persistence or accuracy of
URLs for external or third-party internet websites referred to in this publication
and does not guarantee that any content on such websites is, or will remain,
accurate or appropriate.

*This book is dedicated to all the unaccommodated women
and men of the world at present.*

Contents

Illustrations

Notes on Contributors

SYLVAINE BATAILLE is Lecturer in the English Department at the University of Rouen Normandie and a member of ERIAC (Équipe de Recherche Interdisciplinaire sur les Aires Culturelles). She works on the questions of appropriation, adaptation, translation and reference in sixteenth- and seventeenth-century English literature and in today's popular culture, with a focus on drama TV series and screen adaptations of Shakespeare's plays. She has recently co-written several entries on TV series with Shakespearean echoes for the *Stanford Global Shakespeare Encyclopedia* (to be published online).

VICTORIA BLADEN is Sessional Lecturer and Honorary Research Fellow in the School of Communication and Arts at the University of Queensland where she has twice received a Faculty award for teaching excellence. She has published four Shakespearean text guides: *Measure for Measure* (2015), *Henry IV Part 1* (2012), *Julius Caesar* (2011) and *Romeo and Juliet* (2010). She co-edited *Supernatural and Secular Power in Early Modern England* (2015) and *Shakespeare on Screen: Macbeth* (2013) as well as *Shakespeare and the Supernatural* (2019). She has also published articles in several volumes of the Shakespeare on Screen series, including *Shakespeare on Screen: The Tempest and Late Romances* (Cambridge University Press 2017) and is on the editorial board for the Shakespeare on Screen in Francophonia project in France.

MELISSA CROTEAU is Professor of Film Studies & Literature and the Film Program Director at California Baptist University. For two decades, she has been teaching university courses on early modern British literature and culture, film history and theory, and film adaptation. Dr Croteau has presented papers and given lectures on world cinema, Shakespeare on film and religion in film at numerous international conferences. Her publications include the book *Re-forming Shakespeare: Adaptations and Appropriations of the Bard in Millennial*

Film and Popular Culture (2013); a co-edited volume entitled *Apocalyptic Shakespeare: Essays on Visions of Chaos and Revelation in Recent Film Adaptations* (2009); an edited collection entitled *Reel Histories: Studies in American Film* (2008); and essays on the films *V for Vendetta* (2005) and *Hamlet Goes Business* (1988).

SAMUEL CROWL is Trustee Professor of English at Ohio University, where he has taught since 1970. He has been five times honoured for outstanding teaching and was a leader in the university's curriculum reform efforts in the 1980s. He is the author of six books on various aspects of Shakespeare in performance including *Shakespeare at the Cineplex* (2003), *The Films of Kenneth Branagh* (2006), *Shakespeare and Film* (2008) and *Hamlet* (2014) for the Screen Adaptations series. He has lectured at leading colleges and universities in the United States, Europe and Africa as well as at The Shakespeare Institute in Stratford-upon-Avon, The Folger Shakespeare Library in Washington D.C. and The Shakespeare Guild in New York. At its 200th Commencement in 2015 Ohio University awarded him an Honorary Degree.

JOSÉ RAMÓN DÍAZ FERNÁNDEZ is a Senior Lecturer in English Literature at the University of Málaga (Spain). He has published articles in *Early Modern Literary Studies, The Shakespeare Newsletter* and *Shakespeare Bulletin* and has contributed essays to the collections *The Reel Shakespeare: Alternative Cinema and Theory* (2002), *Almost Shakespeare: Reinventing His Works for Cinema and Television* (2004), *Latin American Shakespeares* (2005) as well as all the volumes in the Shakespeare on Screen series edited by Sarah Hatchuel and Nathalie Vienne-Guerrin. In 2001 and 2006, he co-chaired the 'Shakespeare on Film' seminars at the World Shakespeare Congresses in Valencia and Brisbane. His volume of revenge tragedies by Thomas Kyd, John Webster and John Ford was awarded the Translation Prize by the Spanish Association for Anglo-American Studies in 2007. He has been the principal investigator of a research project on Shakespeare in contemporary culture from 2008 to 2012. He is currently on the editorial board for the Shakespeare on Screen in Francophonia project in France (www.shakscreen.org/) and has also served on the boards of the journals *Shakespeare* (British Shakespeare Association) and *Atlantis* (Spanish Association for Anglo-American Studies).

JACEK FABISZAK teaches cultural history and theory at the Faculty of English, Adam Mickiewicz University, Poznań, Poland. His research interests include English Renaissance theatre and drama and their stage, televisual and filmic transpositions. He has published and given papers at conferences on Shakespeare's plays – one of his major publications in this area is *Polish Televised Shakespeares* (2005). He also applied linguistic and sociological tools in the analysis of drama, which resulted in the publication of *Shakespeare's Drama of Social Roles* (2001), a book that attempts to interpret Shakespeare's last plays in light of the theory of social roles and speech act theory. He co-authored *Szekspir. Leksykon* [Shakespeare. A lexicon] (2003), co-edited *Czytanie Szekspira* [Reading Shakespeare] and wrote on Christopher Marlowe, on both his plays (focusing on imagery) and their screen versions (especially *Edward II*).

SARAH HATCHUEL is Professor of Film and Media Studies at the University Paul-Valéry Montpellier 3 (France) and President of the Société Française Shakespeare. She has written extensively on adaptations of Shakespeare's plays: *Shakespeare and the Cleopatra/Caesar Intertext: Sequel, Conflation, Remake* (2011), *Shakespeare, from Stage to Screen* (2004), *A Companion to the Shakespearean Films of Kenneth Branagh* (2000), and on television series: *Lost: Fiction vitale* (2013), *Rêves et séries américaines: la fabrique d'autres mondes* (2015). She is general editor of the Shakespeare on Screen collection (with Nathalie Vienne-Guerrin) and of the online journal *TV/Series*.

DIANA E. HENDERSON is Professor of Literature and MacVicar Faculty Fellow at the Massachusetts Institute of Technology. She is co-editor of *Shakespeare Studies* and a former President of the Shakespeare Association of America. Her publications include *Passion Made Public: Elizabethan Lyric, Gender and Performance* (1995); *Collaborations with the Past: Reshaping Shakespeare across Time and Media* (2006); *A Concise Companion to Shakespeare on Screen* (2006); and *Alternative Shakespeares 3* (2008), as well as more than forty Shakespeare-related articles. She has worked with the Royal Shakespeare Company, the Actors' Shakespeare Company, the Potomac Theatre Project, the New York Theater Workshop, the Huntington Theater Company, and the Central Square Theater (among others) as consultant, featured speaker or dramaturg. She is a principal collaborator in MIT's Global Shakespeares projects.

PETER HOLLAND was Judith E. Wilson Reader in Drama at the University of Cambridge, then Director of the Shakespeare Institute, Stratford-upon-Avon, and Professor in Shakespeare Studies at the University of

Birmingham, before becoming, in 2002, McMeel Family Professor in Shakespeare Studies in the Department of Film, Television and Theatre at the University of Notre Dame. He has published extensively on Shakespeare and performance and has edited numerous Shakespeare plays, including *A Midsummer Night's Dream* for the Oxford Shakespeare and *Coriolanus* for the Arden Shakespeare 3rd series. He is a General Editor of *Oxford Shakespeare Topics, Great Shakespeareans* and the Arden Shakespeare 4th series. He was, for nineteen years, Editor of *Shakespeare Survey*.

PIERRE KAPITANIAK is Professor of early modern British civilization at the University Paul-Valéry Montpellier 3. He works on Elizabethan drama as well as on the conception, perception and representation of supernatural phenomena from the sixteenth to eighteenth centuries. His publications include *Spectres, Ombres et fantômes: Discours et représentations dramatiques en Angleterre* (2008), *Fictions du diable: démonologie et littérature* (2007) and a translation and edition of the play *The Witch/ La Sorcière* (2012). He is also engaged with Jean Migrenne in a long-term project of translating early modern demonological treatises, and has already published James VI's *Démonologie* (2010) and Reginald Scot's *La Sorcellerie démystifiée* (2015). He is currently working on the trilogy of demonological treatises by Daniel Defoe.

DOUGLAS M. LANIER is Professor of English at the University of New Hampshire, and he served as the Fulbright Global Shakespeare Centre Distinguished Professor in 2016–2017. His essays on Shakespearean appropriation and adaptation have appeared in many journals and essay collections; his monograph, *Shakespeare and Modern Popular Culture*, was published in 2002. He has served as a Trustee of the Shakespeare Association of America, and he was a guest editor of a special issue entitled #bard for *Shakespeare Quarterly* in 2017. He is currently completing two projects: a monograph on film adaptations of *Othello* worldwide and a book on *The Merchant of Venice* for the Arden Language & Writing series.

COURTNEY LEHMANN is the Tully Knoles Professor of the Humanities and Professor of English at the University of the Pacific. She is the 2016 winner of the Distinguished Faculty Award, the highest honour in teaching, research and service at the University of the Pacific. She has published more than forty essays and articles on Shakespeare and cinema in venues ranging from *Shakespeare Quarterly* to *Textual Practice* and is the author of *Shakespeare Remains: Theater to Film, Early Modern to Postmodern* (2002) and *Romeo and Juliet* (2010) for the Screen Adaptations series, and co-author of *Great Shakespeareans: Welles, Kurosawa, Kozintsev, Zeffirelli* (2013). She is the co-editor of several Shakespeare and film anthologies, as well as *The New Kittredge King John* and *Henry VIII*.

LOIS LEVEEN, PhD, is a novelist and literary critic living in Portland, Oregon. Her most recent book, *Juliet's Nurse*, imagines the fourteen years leading up to *Romeo and Juliet*, from the point of view of one of Shakespeare's most fascinating, comic and tragic female characters. A former professor at UCLA and Reed College, Leveen earned degrees in history and literature from Harvard University, the University of Southern California and UCLA. Her scholarly articles and poetry have appeared in numerous academic and literary journals, and she has published pieces on intersections of literature and history in *The New York Times, The Atlantic, The Chicago Tribune, The Wall Street Journal, The Los Angeles Review of Books* and other publications.

RACHAEL NICHOLAS is a PhD researcher in the Department of Drama, Theatre and Performance at the University of Roehampton. Her thesis focuses on how theatre broadcasting changes the way that audiences encounter, experience and value Shakespeare in performance. She has recently contributed chapters to *Shakespeare and the 'Live' Theatre Broadcast Experience* (2018) edited by Pascale Aebischer, Susanne Greenhalgh and Laurie E. Osborne and to *Ivo van Hove: from Shakespeare to David Bowie* (2018) edited by Susan Bennett and Sonia Massai. She is a Co-Chair of the Society of Theatre Research's New Researcher's Network.

ANAÏS PAUCHET is a doctoral student at the University Paul-Valéry Montpellier 3, under the supervision of Sarah Hatchuel (University Paul-Valéry Montpellier 3) and Sylvaine Bataille (University of Rouen). Her thesis focuses on the various forms of references to Shakespeare in English-speaking television series. She has recently co-written several entries on TV series with Shakespearean echoes for the *Stanford Global Shakespeare Encyclopedia* (to be published online).

NATHALIE VIENNE-GUERRIN is Professor in Shakespeare studies at the University Paul-Valéry Montpellier 3, Vice President of the Société Française Shakespeare and director of the Institut de Recherche sur la Renaissance, l'âge Classique et les Lumières (IRCL, UMR 5186 CNRS).

She is co-editor-in-chief of the international journal *Cahiers Élisabéthains* and co-director (with Patricia Dorval) of the Shakespeare on Screen in Francophonia Database (shakscreen.org). She has published *The Unruly Tongue in Early Modern England, Three Treatises* (2012) and is the author of *Shakespeare's Insults: A Pragmatic Dictionary* (2016). She is co-editor, with Sarah Hatchuel, of the Shakespeare on Screen series.

Series Editors' Preface

'Shakespeare on Screen' is a series of books created in 2003 by Sarah Hatchuel and Nathalie Vienne-Guerrin. Until 2013 the books were published by the Presses des Universités de Rouen et du Havre (PURH). Each volume is a collection of essays aiming at exploring the screen versions of one play (or a series of plays – such as the history cycles or the Roman plays) by William Shakespeare.

Volumes published by the Presses des Universités de Rouen et du Havre, available from 'le comptoir des presses d'universités' (www.lcdpu.fr/), are:

Shakespeare on Screen: A Midsummer Night's Dream (2004)
Shakespeare on Screen: Richard III (2005)
Shakespeare on Screen: The Henriad (2008)
Television Shakespeare: Essays in Honour of Michèle Willems (2008)
Shakespeare on Screen: The Roman Plays (2009)
Shakespeare on Screen: Hamlet (2011)
Shakespeare on Screen: Macbeth (2013)

The current volume, *Shakespeare on Screen:* King Lear, is the third volume published by Cambridge University Press to date. The two earlier volumes are:

Shakespeare on Screen: Othello (2015)
Shakespeare on Screen: The Tempest *and Late Romances* (2017)

The series thoroughly interrogates, through a diversity of viewpoints, what Shakespearean films do with and to Shakespeare's playtexts. If one film cannot render all the ambiguities of the playtext, the confrontation of multiple versions may convey a multiplicity of interpretations and produce a kaleidoscopic form of meaning.

Films based on Shakespeare fall into categories whose boundaries are always being transgressed. This collection encourages scholarly examination of what 'Shakespearean film' encompasses. It not only provides readers with diverging explorations of the films but also deploys a wide array of methodologies used to study 'Shakespeare on screen' – including all types of screen (cinema, TV and the computer – with digital productions and internet 'broadcasts') and all kinds of filmic works, from 'canonical' adaptations using Shakespeare's text, to derivatives, spinoffs and quotes.

This series acknowledges Shakespeare as a repository of symbolic power and cultural authority in 'mainstream', English-speaking adaptations, while also showing how the plays' words and themes have travelled to other non-English cultures, and can be transacted freely, no longer connected to any kind of fixed cultural standard or stable meaning. The series shows how Shakespeare's western, northern, English-speaking 'centre' has been challenged or at least revisited through geographical and trans-media dissemination.

The books emphasize new media, multimedia and the constant evolution of technologies in the production, reception and dissemination of Shakespeare on film, especially at a time when so many Shakespearean filmic resources can be accessed online, whether it be on open platforms such as YouTube or cinema/television archives.

Each volume offers a select film-bibliography that is expanded in a free online version on the Cambridge University Press website, where the reader can also access links to new media forms of Shakespeare.

Quotations from Shakespeare's works are taken from the Cambridge editions of the plays.

SARAH HATCHUEL
NATHALIE VIENNE-GUERRIN

Acknowledgements

We first and foremost wish to thank Cambridge University Press for publishing this third volume in the Cambridge Shakespeare on Screen series. We are particularly grateful to Emily Hockley for her support, to Lydia Wanstall for her wonderful work as copy-editor and to José Ramón Díaz Fernández for his very careful proof-reading.

This volume stems from a seminar that we co-chaired at the 2016 World Shakespeare Congress organized in London and Stratford-upon-Avon. It is also the result of a long-term collaborative project with colleagues and friends who have come to constitute a dynamic international community of specialists examining the forms that screen Shakespeare can take.

We wish to express our deepest gratitude to the University Paul-Valéry Montpellier 3 and to the University of Le Havre, to our research centres, the GRIC (Groupe de Recherche Identités et Cultures, EA 4314, Le Havre), the RIRRA 21 (Représenter, Inventer la Réalité, du Romantisme à l'Aube du XXIe siécle, EA 2409, Montpellier) and the IRCL (Institut de Recherche sur la Renaissance, l'Âge Classique et les Lumières, UMR 5186, CNRS Montpellier), to the Centre National de la Recherche Scientifique (CNRS) and to the Société Française Shakespeare, who helped us financially, logistically or morally in this venture, from the initial congress seminar to the publication.

Our thanks also go to the international advisory board of the Shakespeare on Screen series: Pascale Aebischer (University of Exeter), Mark Thornton Burnett (Queen's University of Belfast), Samuel Crowl (Ohio University), Russell Jackson (University of Birmingham), Douglas Lanier (University of New Hampshire), Courtney Lehmann (University of the Pacific), Poonam Trivedi (University of Delhi) and Michèle Willems (University of Rouen).

We warmly thank the contributors to this volume for their unfailing patience, reactivity and support, which have made our work on this book a truly collective venture.

We finally wish to thank wholeheartedly our respective families and friends for letting us spend so much (demanding but fun) time together to prepare this volume.

CHAPTER I

Introduction: Dis-locating King Lear *on Screen*

Victoria Bladen, Sarah Hatchuel and Nathalie Vienne-Guerrin

King Lear presents an anatomy of despair. It charts the descent of a monarch from the height of his powers to a state of abjection. Lear shifts from a position at the centre of his court and family to one at the periphery, vulnerable and exposed on the heath. The country moves from unity to civil war, the court becomes a site of barbarism, and the royal family are ultimately extinguished. As the wheel of fortune turns on its downward trajectory, Lear is revealed as a ruler unable to distinguish truth from surface appearances, authenticity from rhetoric; he has little grasp of statecraft and his actions implode a family, debase a state and disintegrate a nation. Yet Shakespeare elicits our sympathy for this flawed figure who, at his lowest, finally learns something of the responsibility of leadership and the need for empathy. Throughout it all, the word 'nothing' reverberates, striking at the core of human existence and meaning. One of Shakespeare's great tragedies, *Lear* constitutes one of our cultural 'monsters of the deep' (4.2.48 Q1), a reminder of humanity's dark capacities.[1]

Lear continues to speak to us, illuminating the human condition and the contemporary world. Two decades into the twenty-first century, the globe continues to witness and grapple with repressive political regimes; behaviours by political leaders viewed by many as irrational, if not repugnant; the use of state-sanctioned torture; entrenched misogyny and the consequences of patriarchal structures; and mass human displacement, exile and suffering. *Lear* seems more relevant than ever; thus, unsurprisingly, filmmakers have continued to enter into dialogues with the play.

Lear has a rich history on screen, beginning with the silent era, during which adaptations included those directed by William V. Ranous (1909, USA),[2] Gerolamo Lo Savio (1910, Italy)[3] and Ernest Warde (1916, USA).[4] Adaptations have taken a wide variety of forms, including the 1965 French 'dramatique',[5] directed by Jean Kerchbron, and television films, the most recent of which was directed by Richard Eyre for the BBC (2018).

Filmmakers have pushed the boundaries of narrative convention, as in Jean-Luc Godard's 1987 film,[6] and they have utilized the medium of filmed live theatre performance, as in the 2016 production starring Don Warrington (directed for the stage by Michael Buffong and for the screen by Bridget Caldwell).[7]

This volume explores *Lear*'s varied screen afterlives, taking 'screen' in its broader sense, extending beyond the cinematic to include a wide range of digital material (television, live theatre broadcasts, video archives and online movies and fanvids). Of course, complete coverage of *Lear* on screen is beyond the scope of any single volume; however, the essays here – in the print volume and the additional essays in the online resources – offer an extensive engagement with the key issues raised by the various adaptations and appropriations of *Lear*.

This introduction provides a broad overview of *Lear* on screen and offers some critical contexts for the chapters in this volume, highlighting their original contributions to the field. The volume comprises four sections. The first, 'Surviving *Lear*', revisits the canon by offering new perspectives on productions that remain landmarks of screen history, continuing, through their afterlives in video and online archives, to influence more recent adaptations and appropriations, and to invite new scholarly perspectives. The second section, '*Lear* en Abyme', considers the metatheatrical reframing of *Lear* generated through intersections of theatre, screen and forms of 'liveness'. The chapters in the third section, 'The Genres of *Lear*', focus on what happens to *Lear* when Shakespeare's tragedy intersects with the codes of various filmic genres such as comedy, the Western or the road movie. The chapters of the final section, '*Lear* on the Loose', focus on the migration and appropriation processes that *Lear* has gone through and explore cases where *Lear* has wandered from the zone of adaptation into freer retellings and citations. Loosened from its moorings to the hypotext, *Lear* moves into new cultural contexts and geographical locations, creating new perspectives that nevertheless maintain dialogues with Shakespeare's text.

The word 'dislocate' appears only once in the whole Shakespearean corpus, uttered by Albany in Q1 of *Lear*, in a speech in which he imagines his hands would be 'apt enough to dislocate and tear' Goneril's 'flesh and bones' (4.2.64 Q1). The notion of 'dislocation' permeates *Lear* and informs this volume, comprising the ways in which the *Lear* films have explored notions of state disintegration, crisis, vagrancy and geographical displacement; the transposition of the play into various contexts; and fragmentation, with dramatic motifs being dismantled and appropriated in free adaptations. By revisiting 'canonical' versions and radical retellings, trans-lations beyond the Anglophone zones, intermedial explorations of meta-narratives, hybrid genres and the varied nodes of the *Lear* cultural rhizome, by standing up for both 'legitimate' and 'bastard' versions, the volume aims to re-invigorate the current critical field.

Surviving *Lear*: Revisiting the Canon

From the extensive *Lear* on screen oeuvre, three films have emerged as canonical, evidenced by José Ramón Díaz Fernández's film-bibliographies (in print and the extended online version): Grigori Kozintsev's *Korol Lir* (USSR, 1970), Peter Brook's *King Lear* (Great Britain and Denmark, 1971) and Akira Kurosawa's *Ran* (Japan and France, 1985).[8] While scholars may differ in their preferences for what can be considered canonical, if we take the amount of critical literature generated by the films as a measure of impact on the critical field, these three films emerge as landmarks in the *Lear* screen-scape: the three 'legitimate' children issuing from the matrix of Shakespeare's tragedy and nourishing many generations of offshoots. Furthermore, the three films and their directors engage in dialogue with each other, constitut-ing a fascinating cluster of interactions and influences.[9]

Kozintsev's experiences in filming *Lear* suggest that adapting the tragedy for the screen can become an endurance test and experience in survival. In her insightful 2013 chapter on the director, Courtney Lehmann quotes his acknowledgement that 'working on the tragedy was unbearable', and argues that 'the feelings detailed in his film diary paint a picture of a man on the brink of suicide'.[10] Kozintsev both did and did not survive *King Lear*: the film was his swan song and he died in 1973. Yet, as Kenneth S. Rothwell notes, although the play is a source of despair, 'Kozintsev squeezes some hope out of hopelessness by identifying his mad king with the struggles of humanity in general'.[11] The casting of 'the diminutive, softly spoken Jüri Järvet (Yuri Yarvet) as Lear facilitates the film's inter-pretation of *Lear* as the story of a journey towards self-revelation of the human condition' (Figure 1.1).[12]

In Kozintsev's film, the Fool survives: the king is dead, long live the Fool, thus highlighting the play's interlinking of king and Fool. The surviving Fool becomes witness to the apocalypse – however, in the etymological sense of revelation. Rothwell notes that the film is embedded in 'Marxist meliorism rather than in Kottian pessimism'.[13]

Peter Brook's 1971 *King Lear*, the next landmark of the *Lear* canon, constituted a second take on the play. After the heavily abridged Omnibus

Figure 1.1: Yuri Yarvet as Lear in Grigori Kozintsev's *King Lear* (1970)

Figure 1.2: Paul Scofield as Lear in Peter Brook's *King Lear* (1971)

television production Brook directed in 1953 with Orson Welles (Lear) and Natasha Parry (Cordelia), Brook revisited his vision of *Lear*. Shot in 1968, with Paul Scofield in the title role, the film was not released until 1971. This version, highly influenced by Jan Kott's reading of *Lear* as an absurd Beckettian world, provoked a 'profound critical division'.[14] Anthony Davies describes it as a 'drama of faces',[15] while Rothwell sees Lear as a 'talking head' (Figure 1.2).[16] The film cultivates discontinuity and a sense of nihilism, drawing from the key idea of nothingness in a play that could ironically be subtitled 'Much Ado About Nothing'. Brook, on many occasions, uses his camera to make this nothing conspicuous, from the first completely soundless sequence[17] to the last shot of the film that leaves a blank colourless screen. It is, according to Peter Holland (2013), 'an exercise in defamiliarization and distanciation'.[18] In Brook's vision, the viewer is situated in this visible nothingness, but ultimately there are no survivors in this bleak world.

In Akira Kurosawa's *Ran* (1985), the sense of despair is translated but in a more colourful way. *Ran* (meaning 'Chaos' in Japanese) constitutes an adaptation both canonical and cross-cultural.[19] Financed by an international partnership of Japanese and French creditors, and distributed by Orion Pictures in the USA, the film was shaped to appeal to both Japanese and international audiences.[20] Consequently, Kurosawa has been criticized 'for being both not Japanese enough and too unapologetically so'.[21] Yet the immense volume of critical responses to *Ran* evidences its significance to the history of *Lear* on screen.

Kurosawa intersected *Lear*'s plot with the Japanese story of sixteenth-century warlord Motonari Mori, who transferred power prematurely to his sons. *Ran*'s narrative centres on the character of Lord Hidetora Ichimonji, and Lear's daughters become sons. Key shifts include adding a violent past for the Lear figure, responsible for the eye gouging of Tsurumaru, brother of Lady Sué. The 'quiet stoicism' of the blind Tsurumaru functions as a 'potent accusation of Hidetora's past guilt'[22] and the haunting flute that he plays adds to the sense of the past catching up to the present. The overall tenor of the film is, in the words of Mark Thornton Burnett, 'a disquisition about loss, chaos and despair'.[23]

Many critics have noted the striking aesthetics of *Ran*. Judith Buchanan has commented on the irony of the film's title, given that 'a more aesthetically beautiful or ordered film could scarcely be imagined'; she notes its 'vividly schematic use of costume and colour, its appreciation of landscape and its painterly eye'.[24] Long shots predominate in the film, the framing constantly placing human action within a wider context of time and space that undermines human pretensions. Peter Babiak suggests that one interpretation of *Ran* is that 'the frame represents the view of the gods, who are powerless to intervene in human affairs but are deeply affected by them'.[25] While the film is set in a specific historical period, the Sengoku Jidai or 'Age of the Country at War' (c. 1467–c. 1600),[26] Kurosawa's depiction of 'dissipating mist' in the opening and closing shots has the effect of 'situating the diegesis of his film in a mythical, rather than historical past'.[27] Yet the spectres of history remain. Also reflecting on the implications of natural elements, Burnett observes the way that repeated cloud imagery 'conjure[s] the terrifying nuclear emblems of the cessation of World War II'.[28]

The first section of this volume revisits these canonical versions in two ways: by focusing on the filmic treatment of one specific character – the

Fool – across three productions, and by reconsidering *Ran* through the lens of posthumanism. Samuel Crowl's chapter, 'Lear's Fool on Film: Peter Brook, Grigori Kozintsev, Akira Kurosawa', puts what seems marginal at the centre of the picture by focusing on the figure of the Fool in these three canonical versions. This character in *Lear* is one of the potent truth-tellers, who differs from Cordelia and Kent in that the Fool's role sanctions and protects his subversive voice. Brook cast Jack MacGowran, a veteran Beckett actor, as the Fool, thus aligning the production with a bleak and minimalist Beckettian world. Kozintsev's choice evoked the horrors of the Second World War; he commented that his Fool, Oleg Dahl, was 'the boy from Auschwitz whom they forced to play the violin'.[29] Kurosawa's androgynous Kyoami, the only Fool given a name, was played by transvestite actor Shinnosuke Ikehata (Pîtâ) (Figure 1.3). Crowl argues that the character is key to the vision in each of these canonical adaptations: 'Each director uses his conception of the Fool as a means of anchoring Lear's story within a cinematic narrative.'

Critics debate whether there is any dimension of hope in Kurosawa's *Ran*. Kott, writing in the late 1980s, emphasized the apocalyptic emptiness at the end of the film.[30] While most critics read the Buddhist references as stressing the bleakness of human destiny, some have found in them suggestions of the potential for redemption.[31] Melissa Croteau's chapter, 'Wicked Humans and Weeping Buddhas: (Post)humanism and Hell in

Figure 1.3: Lord Hidetora Ichimonji (Tatsuya Nakadai) and the Fool Kyoami (Pîtâ) in Akira Kurosawa's *Ran* (1985)

Kurosawa's *Ran*', approaches these debates through the lens of posthumanism, a concept that challenges various aspects of humanism, within an overall context of care for humanity. In the wake of several critics who have analysed the Noh elements in *Ran*,[32] Croteau argues that Kurosawa presents a vision of hell, consistent with a filmic practice that looks directly at the horrors that humans create, and that he draws from Noh in order to break its schemata, resisting resolution to leave audiences in the limbo of apocalypse. She suggests that if there is any hope to be found in the film, it is likely to be located in the viewer; Kurosawa reminds us that 'we have the power *not* to turn away from suffering'.

Alongside *Lear* in the cinema, a rich history of televisual *Lear*s has unfolded, a history relevant to each of the following sections. In her 2008 article on medium specificity, Katherine Rowe highlights the dichotomy between increasing contemporary media convergence on the one hand, and scholarly tendencies to maintain 'medium-specific rubrics' and intellectual boundaries between different types of media on the other.[33] The digital age has brought the reception contexts for film and television closer together, and the increased quality of television productions has arguably reduced the distinction between screen media in some respects. Nevertheless, differences in production contexts and conditions remain relevant to the history of *Lear* on TV, which extends from the early twentieth century to the 'post-television' era. Anthony Davies describes TV as a 'hybrid medium, more happily accommodating words than visualising a universe'.[34] Alan Kimbrough has observed that 'part of the evolution of television can be charted by paying attention to the shift from aural to visual' in signifying.[35] He also points out the risks of 'limited budget studio sets' becoming 'only distraction when ... subjected to the clarity of the camera' and that stylization can often be more effective.[36] The traditionally intimate space of TV shapes acting styles, requiring actors to convey more with gestures reduced in scope, requiring 'the mastery of minimal effects'.[37] Critics generally agree that '*King Lear* is not an easy play for television'.[38] William Worthen comments, 'Everything about the play attacks the restraint of television; it's a magniloquent, grotesque, cruel spectacle.'[39]

However, Ted Nannicelli has noted the recent 'aesthetic turn' in television studies and argues for an appreciation of the art of television.[40] *King Lear* survives through canonical film versions but also through various TV adaptations, which display a wide variety of aesthetic choices, working within the particular conditions of television to achieve effects resonating with *Lear*'s central themes. Peter Brook's 1953 Omnibus production[41] presents a stark, formal set and Orson Welles as a menacing Lear who tears the map with a knife, foreshadowing the impending violence. The sharp edges of the portcullis at Gloucester's castle, together with the cage into which Kent is cast, enhance the sense of foreboding. Backgrounds of shots recede into darkness, overcoming the constraints of a studio set through lighting appropriate for the play's themes. Dramatic chiaroscuro effects, with Lear's lit, stricken face in contrast to the shadows, make for an effective storm scene. However, the compressed text that excised the Gloucester subplot attracted negative criticism.[42]

Tony Davenall's 1974 production, with Patrick Magee as Lear, presents a medieval setting with colourful costumes and tapestries on the walls. The aesthetic detracts from the effect of menace in some places, and the heath is unconvincing as a threatening space during the storm. Yet subtle signs of the violence to come are conveyed through the use of animal skins on the throne, the vein of fire imagery and the mounted antlers, invoking the hunt, in Goneril's dining hall. Effective lighting used in the hovel creates shadows with the appearance of a cage and, for the blinding of Gloucester, the device of a blank screen aligns us with his point of view, drawing us into his suffering. Some critics found the production insensitive to the medium; for example, Davies found the visualization and theatricality of the play 'cramped' and commented that there was 'little to suggest a gain in wisdom' in Lear.[43]

Jonathan Miller directed his first television Lear in 1975, with Michael Hordern as Lear, then returned to the challenge in 1982, using the same lead actors and production and costume designs.[44] Miller's set used a simple yet effective mise-en-scène, with wooden floorboards and black cloth backdrops. The production spent less of its budget on the set in favour of elaborate costumes that, although almost uniformly black, present a range of textures and details creating an aesthetic recalling seventeenth-century Dutch portraiture. The ensemble shots create visually compelling tableaux, prioritizing more visual choices for the viewer over more 'cinematic' editing.[45] However, in Davies's view, Miller's choice of 'dispensing with the royal dimension' rendered 'the tragedy essentially a domestic one. Lear moves about the room like a father, but not like a king'.[46]

Channel Four's 1983 production, directed by Michael Elliott, starred Laurence Olivier as Lear (Figure 1.4). Its opening set suggested Stonehenge; a high-angle shot shows the court prostrate before Lear, rendering the human figures akin to the circle of stones, and this shot is echoed at the tragic ending with the circle around the bodies of Lear and

Figure 1.4: Laurence Olivier as Lear in Michael Elliott's television *King Lear* (1983)

Cordelia. The Stonehenge aesthetic sets a religious tone, also emphasized at several points when Lear prays. Animal skins on the throne suggest the potential for brutality, as does the animal hide map. The use of realistic detail brought the production closer to the conventions of cinema.[47] However, there was criticism of the attempt 'to apply inappropriate techniques of realism' to the television studio context (Holland) and of the predominance of close-ups (Kimbrough).[48]

In Richard Eyre's 1998 BBC production, Ian Holm's Lear is vicious and unpredictable – one who, as Kenneth Rothwell notes, is 'on the edge of lunacy' from the very beginning.[49] Alexander Leggatt points to the production's emphasis on 'close personal relations' and subtlety of performance that are indebted to its origins in a stage production.[50] The dominant reds of the opening set (echoed at the ending with Cordelia's dress) suggest the intersecting associations of blood, family and violence, while the costuming, varying between the modern and the medieval, creates a *Lear* that is not fixed in time, emphasizing its ongoing relevance. The use of mist, with the shift to a white palette, abstracts the setting, accommodating the limits of a studio set, while also linking with the play's theme of compromised vision.

Channel Four's 2008 production, directed by Trevor Nunn and Chris Hunt, presents Ian McKellen in the title role, who effectively 'charts [Lear's] movement towards madness'.[51] Throughout Shakespeare's play, a central vein of circle imagery resonates with its palimpsest of meanings, encompassing the crown, female genitalia, nothingness and the circularity of events and their consequences. The Nunn/Hunt production emphasizes this with a key moment in the opening scene where McKellen's Lear articulates his violent 'nothing' to Cordelia with his face through the crown, a gesture that returns to haunt him. McKellen repeated this gesture in the 2018 live theatre broadcast of the production directed by Jonathan Munby.

It is in the wake of this long history of TV *King Lear* that the online companion to this volume offers a study of the 2018 *Lear* designed for television.[52] Peter J. Smith's essay, 'Richard Eyre's *King Lear*: a Brexit Allegory', explores the new production directed by Richard Eyre for the BBC, starring Anthony Hopkins as Lear and Emma Thompson as Goneril. The film, Smith shows, presents Lear as a military dictator in a bleak contemporary England of stark inequalities, in which the heath becomes a refugee camp and the hovel a shipping container. Eyre's new vision of *Lear* has links with Edward St Aubyn's *Lear* spinoff novel *Dunbar* (2017), part of the Hogarth Shakespeare series, as well as with the developing fallout from Brexit.

Lear en Abyme: Metatheatre and the Screen

Whereas in theatre the audience has the freedom to look where they please, the televisual and cinematic camera can be 'manipulative, even tyrannical', directing our attention and inviting us 'to interpret a series, rather than a congeries, of events'.[53] The camera decides what we see, thus affecting how we read particular scenes. The second section of the volume, '*Lear* en Abyme', explores various aspects of reflexivity in *Lear* on screen. Sarah Hatchuel's chapter, 'Filming Metatheatre: the "Dover Cliff" Scene on Screen', explores the implications of framing choices in her analysis of the conspicuously metatheatrical Dover cliff scene across various types of productions, cinematic and televisual. She argues that, contrary to Kott's assertion that transposition of the scene to the screen is impossible, television and cinema can 'maintain, and even facilitate, the scene's paradoxes of a *non-space*'. Approaches to the scene range from cutting it completely (Brook 1953; Kozintsev) to a variety of choices including using realistic scenery to reproduce the countryside in the television studio yet revealing no cliff (Davenall), showing a real cliff (Blessed 1999; Eyre 2018), using mist to create ambiguity (Eyre 1998), using close-ups to hide environment and thus sustain the non-space (Miller 1982; Elliott) and using editing and framing techniques to oscillate between certainty and uncertainty (Brook 1971; Blessed). Hatchuel locates agency in the viewers, illuminating the ways in which they must deconstruct the visual discourses to decide how to read the filmic spaces created in the Dover cliff scenes.

Yvonne Griggs, on the eve of the new era of the live theatre broadcast, commented that the 2008 Nunn/Hunt TV production failed to 'transcend its stage origins'.[54] However, negotiations between stage and screen, and the framing of the gaze, have become more complex with the advent of this new intermedial genre. Filmed live theatre, while designed first for a cinema broadcast, anticipates a long televisual and other screen afterlife from the release of DVDs to the broadcast on web platforms, and this phenomenon is attracting increasing critical attention for its intersection of the frames and conditions of theatre, cinema and television.[55]

Rachael Nicholas's chapter, 'New Ways of Looking at *Lear*: Changing Relationships between Theatre, Screen and Audience in Live Broadcasts of *King Lear* (2011–2016)', explores these issues, considering a selection of seven productions of *Lear* distributed digitally between 2011 and 2016, some edited live and others edited in postproduction. She argues that these new models of digital distribution have changed relationships between stage productions of the play, screen adaptations and their audiences, and that filming methods shape and create meaning for screen audiences, particularly in their framing choices in depicting violence. Furthermore, online livestreaming, in combination with linked social media, fosters new forms of social engagement and audience dialogue with social and political issues raised by the play.

The evolving relationship between the theatre and new media is precisely the focus of the third and last season of Canadian TV series *Slings & Arrows* (2003–2006), in which the fictional New Burbage Theatre Festival mounts *Lear* for a younger generation, staging it as disrespectfully as the old king is treated in the play, stripping Shakespeare 'of his majesty and high seriousness' (Figure 1.5).[56] The choice of *Lear* as the play-within-the-season functions to display, as Laurie Osborne states, 'the threat that television – and by extension commercialism – poses to theater', all the more so since the stage production experiences many setbacks, including the revelation that the ageing actor playing Lear, Charles Kingman, is dying. Lear's journey thus allows for a reflection on theatre having to compete 'with younger, sexier media' and operating within 'a performance universe of increasingly multiple media options'.[57] Lois Leveen's chapter, 'Re-Shaping Old Course in a Country New: Producing Nation, Culture and *King Lear* in *Slings and Arrows*', explores how the television series mediates the impermanence of both live theatre and life itself: a year after the series ended, William Hutt, the actor playing Kingman, died of cancer. As Hutt's live performances as Lear at the Canadian Stratford Festival had not been recorded, his scenes in the series stand as his theatrical legacy, in

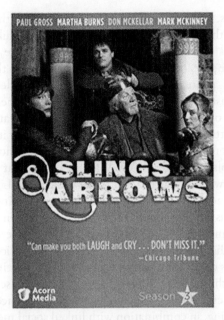

Figure 1.5: Poster for the third season of television series *Slings & Arrows* (2003–2006), focusing on a stage performance of *King Lear*

a specific context where Canadian cultural identity is fostered and (de) constructed.

The Genres of *Lear*

Works that fall short of an 'adaptation' and abandon the language of the playtext may nevertheless manifest various echoes of *Lear*, ranging from sustained engagement to the slightest of citations (as in Peter Weir's 1989 *Dead Poet's Society* where, during the final confrontation of father and son just prior to the son's suicide, the repeated 'nothing' evokes the bleakness of *Lear*). However, as Douglas Lanier poses in the 2017 *Shakespeare/Not Shakespeare* volume, 'How do we tell Shakespeare from "not Shakespeare"? Where to place the slash?'[58]

Gilles Deleuze and Félix Guattari's conception of artistic relations between works as rhizomes, networks spreading horizontally and resisting cultural hierarchies of source and influence, is a valuable metaphor that has inspired recent theoretical conceptions of Shakespearean appropriation, as in the work of Lanier.[59] As well as the organic metaphor of the rhizome, another key metaphor has been that of haunting, as outlined in the work of Maurizio Calbi, indebted to Jacques Derrida's theories.[60]

Adding to these conceptual paradigms, at the 'Tragedies on Screen: the Case of *King Lear*' seminar at the 2016 World Shakespeare Congress, from which this volume stems, the term 'Learness' was suggested as a fruitful neologism to register intertextual correlations and exchanges with *Lear*.[61] The idea of 'Learness' facilitates considering a work on a spectrum between imagined poles of adaptation and appropriation, yet without needing to precisely pinpoint its location. Similarly, Thomas Cartelli and Katherine Rowe in 2007 identified the 'Lear-effect' as the dislodging of a patriarchal figure from his position of authority, leading to feelings of loss and the desire to redeem terrible mistakes; in parallel, the 'Cordelia-effect' may satisfy the need for forgiveness and compensate for the 'Goneril/Regan' functions.[62]

Genre becomes a significant factor in the transposition of *Lear* into new contexts. Screen adaptations and appropriations have reconfigured Lear as the intransigent head of empires or families through engagement with a variety of movie genres, including the gangster film, the Western, melodrama, romance and road movie. The conventions of the gangster film share with *Lear* rise-and-fall trajectories, issues of loyalty and betrayal, the displacement from the traditions of a motherland (i.e. Ireland, Italy) and a sense of belonging to a (mafia) family ruled by a patriarch. Examples include Joseph Mankiewicz's *House of Strangers* (1949), Francis Ford Coppola's *The Godfather* trilogy (1972, 1974, 1990) and the TV series *The Sopranos* (HBO, 1999–2007). The influence is always reciprocal, as Yvonne Griggs argues: '*King Lear* cannot only be reconfigured as gangster epic but can also reshape the codes and conventions of the gangster genre'.[63]

The genre of the Western meets the world of *Lear* in its promotion of vengeful masculinity, chaotic violence and the idea of a wild frontier. Edward Dmytryk's *Broken Lance* (1954) has thus been deemed a Learesque Western in its elegy of a dying world and its representation of an authoritarian and successful ranch owner (played by Spencer Tracy), who is betrayed by the three sons of his first marriage. He eventually finds support in Joe, the son of his second marriage, who suffers racial discrimination because his mother is Native American.

In Uli Edel's *King of Texas* (2002) (Figure 1.6), which takes place in the nineteenth century, shortly after the proclamation of the Republic of Texas, John Lear, a wealthy cattle baron, banishes his daughter Claudia and divides his property between Susannah and Rebecca, only to be rejected by them and to die ultimately alongside his youngest daughter.

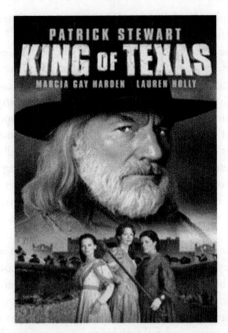

Figure 1.6: Poster for Uli Edel's Western, *King of Texas* (2002), with Patrick Stewart
as John Lear

Pierre Kapitaniak's chapter, 'Negotiating Authorship, Genre and Race in
King of Texas (2002)', explores the production contexts and multiple
authorship generated by the 'creative cartel' behind *King of Texas*, as well
as the film's engagement with *Lear* and its replacement of class issues with
racial ones resulting from the historical and cultural transposition of *Lear*
to the American Western.

Beyond the gangster and Western genres, *Lear* has also been transposed as
melodrama. When Louis Feuillade filmed the single-reel *Le Roi Lear au
village* (1911), he transposed the story to a small provincial town in France,
shooting on location and using natural light to create a pessimistic, realist
melodrama about, as Rowe puts it, the 'contemporary bourgeois fears of
downward mobility'.[64] Perhaps more surprisingly, *Lear* has been transposed
to the romance genre. Several adaptations follow in the tradition that began
with the Restoration period of offering happy endings to Shakespeare's
tragedies. British romances indebted to *Lear* include *Second Generation*
(Channel 4, UK, 2003), a TV serial remake of *Lear* set in England and
India in the 1990s. Mr Sharma, a dying businessman who left Calcutta for

London in the 1960s to create an Indian-food empire, has trouble raising his three daughters. Conflicts arise between and among generations since the characters all present diverse ways of 'performing cultural belonging and hybridity'.[65] The title points to two types of movement: migration issues faced by culturally hybrid citizens and the circulation of *Lear* itself to portray family tensions in popular culture. As Alessandra Marino argues, the series can be seen as a 'second-generation tape' of the play, a copy calling into question 'the concept of purity as related to the nation and to the concealment of minority histories on the part of the national narrative'.[66]

In a similar way, Sangeeta Datta's English film *Life Goes On* (2009) (Figure 1.7), which mixes the codes of heritage films and Bollywood cinema, follows the six days experienced by Sanjay Banerjee, an ageing and respected Hindu physician living in London with his three adult daughters, between the unexpected demise of his wife Manju and her funeral. Sanjay divides his wealth between his daughters (one is training to be an actress and is rehearsing the part of Cordelia) and ends up wandering in a storm at night on (Hampstead) Heath, until the final

Figure 1.7: Poster for Sangeeta Datta's *Life Goes On* (2009), with Sharmila Tagore as Manju

reconciliation, which can occur thanks to the innovative decision of focusing on the mother figure. As Kinga Földváry remarks, this 'creates unions above all divisions' and 'heals all wounds'.[67] Diana Henderson's chapter, 'Romancing *King Lear*: *Hobson's Choice*, *Life Goes On* and Beyond', reassesses versions that provide a happy ending to the tale. She examines how *Lear*, instead of being 'monumentalized', is used to comic, romantic, empathetic and redeeming ends, notably through (proto)feminist critique of male domination.

The rhizome metaphor of intertextuality, with its resistance to hierarchy, renders Shakespeare particularly adaptable to feminist agendas.[68] Courtney Lehmann reflects that, since Mary Pickford, female filmmakers have generally 'produced, directed, and distributed their Shakespeare pictures *outside* the Hollywood system'.[69] An exception is Jocelyn Moorhouse's 1997 screen adaptation of Jane Smiley's novel *A Thousand Acres*: when senile and abusive Larry Cook decides to split his thousand-acre farm in Iowa between his daughters, the land is turned into a symbol of the exploited female 'body-in-pain', in a system that perpetuates the 'mutual degradation of both habitat and humanity'.[70] Henderson's chapter argues that David Lean's 1954 *Hobson's Choice* anticipates later feminist reworkings such as *A Thousand Acres*, and that *Hobson's Choice* has been relatively marginalized, perhaps, she suggests, because of its comic genre.

Another genre with which *Lear* has been brought into dialogue is the American road movie.[71] Douglas M. Lanier's chapter, '"Easy *Lear*": *Harry and Tonto* and the American Road Movie', analyses Paul Mazursky's *Harry and Tonto* (1974), a road movie dramatizing the experience of an older man who, exiled from his home, travels through America, suggesting a congruence between Lear's 'unaccommodated man' and those outside the American cultural mainstream (Figure 1.8). Lanier suggests that the vehicle of *Lear* enables a broadening of this specific genre beyond youth culture. *Lear* also accommodates a specifically American sensibility through the genre of the road movie, revealing in the process why the play, and its darkly tragic dimensions, have been such inhospitable territory for American film adaptation.

Lear on the Loose: Migrations and Appropriations of *Lear*

Lear has migrated beyond the Anglophone world and has been appropriated in a variety of different cultural contexts. Yasujiro Ozu mobilized the tragic motifs of *Lear* in *Tokyo Story* (1953) to portray the 'disintegration of traditional family structures in contemporary Japan' and to challenge

Figure 1.8: Harry (Art Carney) and his cat in Paul Mazursky's *Harry and Tonto*
(1974)

the country's militarism during the Second World War.[72] Even the Egyptian TV series *Dahsha* [*Perplexity*] (2014) adapted *Lear* to the context of Egypt's 2011 revolution to raise issues of widespread poverty, marginalized women, stigmatized illegitimate children and the ongoing dependence upon patriarchal leadership.[73]

In Indian cinema, identity politics has been expressed most significantly through quotations and citations of *Lear*. In *36 Chowringhee Lane* (1981), directed by Aparna Sen, for instance, Violet Stoneham, an Anglo-Indian teacher who chooses to remain in postcolonial Calcutta instead of going back to Britain, appears as an 'unhomed ... relic of the British Raj'.[74] Shakespeare's *Lear* appears as her main source of inspiration, stability and solace in life. Her age, loneliness and self-pity, together with her sense of betrayal by friends, mirror aspects of *Lear*. In Rituparno Ghosh's *The Last Lear* (2007), a film indebted not only to *King Lear* but to *36 Chowringhee Lane*, Harish Mishra is a domineering Anglophile theatre practitioner obsessed with Shakespeare. *King Lear* is not only recited and performed but Mishra echoes Lear himself. Even when Mishra loses his memory and mind, he can still remember Shakespeare's text. *Lear* interacts with postcolonial Indian cinema through forms of pre-Independence nostalgia that prevent the characters, who stand as hybrid vestiges of the past, from moving forward. However, Shakespeare's vitality in postcolonial India, the films suggest, should be ensured by a new generation that is not necessarily Anglophile, through Indian teachers (*36 Chowringhee Lane*) or Indian people (*The Last Lear*).

In his chapter, 'Relocating Jewish Culture in *The Yiddish King Lear* (1934)' for this volume, Jacek Fabiszak examines *The Yiddish King Lear*, directed by Harry Tomashefsky in 1934, based on a play in Yiddish by Jacob Gordin. He outlines the historical and production contexts of the film and its engagement with *Lear*, arguing that Gordin and then Thomashefsky and Joseph Seiden, producer of the 1934 film, transposed and indigenized *Lear* to the needs of Yiddish-speaking audiences in New York.

Lear has crucially been mobilized to emphasize issues of political disenfranchisement and dispossession. *Romani Kris* (1997), directed by Bence Gyöngyössy, uses the play to reveal Hungarian state policies towards poor minorities. The film's folk-music score, Hungarian dialect and images of camps illuminate, as Mark Thornton Burnett points out in a 2014 article, the 'plight of Roma groupings that are dispossessed, prioritizing motifs of depopulation and displacement', where the whole of Hungary stands in for the 'heath'.[75] When Lovér, the Lear-like chief, has to leave his encampment, destroyed by the government to force the gypsy population into apartments, he divides the financial compensation between his two eldest daughters and rejects his youngest (who ends up alive and happy). *Romani Kris* failed to secure mainstream distribution; thus it reflexively stands as a Shakespeare film displaced to the margins, reminding us of the commercial factors and limitations that govern our access to the Shakespearean screen oeuvre.

The potential survival of Shakespeare is interrogated in Kristian Levring's Danish film *The King Is Alive* (2000), where a group of tourists are stranded in the Namibian desert after their bus runs out of gas. In order to distract themselves from their situation, they stage *King Lear*. A stage actor, the oldest member of the group, reconstructs the play from his own faulty memory, foregrounding the act of adapting a text, while the tourists soon use the play's dialogues in their everyday speech. The text mirrors their lives and circulates in unpredictable ways, challenging and rewriting the *Lear* script and emphasizing the idea of personal appropriation. For Maurizio Calbi, *Lear* is here revealed not only to resuscitate and survive in a spectral way, but to help survival (so the title indicates) through the play's evocation of 'dis-adjustment' and bare life.[76] As Jennifer Bottinelli suggests, *Lear* is thus 'deconstructed and then reconstructed as a frenzied commentary on filial and spousal rivalry, race, and spectatorship'.[77] *The King Is Alive* predominantly follows the constraining rules of the Dogme 95 manifesto, challenging Hollywood's artificially composed shots through a documentary-like, 'natural' style that offers an impression of unplanned and unexpected shooting. Through an uncanny staging in the desert, the film points to its instability and to the play's unfinished, multiple and forever-reinvented status (from Q1 to Q2 to F), but also reflexively comments on 'mounting a production without resources, even as it puts itself through a comparable process of self-limitation'.[78]

Courtney Lehmann's chapter in this section, 'The Trump Effect: Exceptionalism, Global Capitalism and the War on Women in Early Twenty-first-century Films of *King Lear*', raises not only aesthetic issues linked to the film but also dire ideological ones. She claims that early twenty-first-century spinoffs, such as *The King Is Alive*, *King of Texas* and Don Boyd's *My Kingdom* (2001), situate the play in a world in which the state of exception is universal and the predatory instincts of late capitalism have been globalized. *Lear* becomes a vehicle for new forms of racism and sexism in the developed world, with the wounded female body being the privileged object of predation, punishment and pointless sacrifice.

Lear is a play renowned for its misogyny. So what happens when Lear becomes female? Victoria Bladen's chapter, 'Looking for Lear in *The Eye of the Storm*', focuses on the Australian film *The Eye of the Storm* (2011), directed by Fred Schepisi, adapting Patrick White's *The Eye of the Storm* (1973), both of which enter into dialogues with *Lear*. Elizabeth Hunter (Charlotte Rampling) has Lear's vanity and selfishness, yet she also has a quasi-mystical awareness of the more profound dimensions to life, rendering the equivalent of the heath scene (a tropical Queensland storm) a transcendent experience. Bladen explores the 'Learness' of the film, how it resonates with the play in some respects, while other facets signal journeys away that nevertheless bring new insights, making the film a typical paradoxical example of both Shakespeare and not Shakespeare.

The Shakespeare/Not Shakespeare continuum becomes more complex with the format of the television series, screened over a longer period of time than the more contained format of the film. The chapter by Sylvaine Bataille and Anaïs Pauchet, 'Between Political Drama and Soap Opera: Appropriations of *King Lear* in US Television Series *Boss* and *Empire*', explores two shows with an evolving relation with *Lear*. Both *Boss* (Starz, 2011–2012) and *Empire* (Fox, 2015–) translate Lear's madness from the start: Tom Kane (Kelsey Grammer), the corrupt mayor of Chicago in *Boss*, and Lucious Lyon (Terrence Howard), the African-American CEO of Empire Entertainment in *Empire*, are both diagnosed with an incurable neurological disease. If *Boss* is a 'post-television' appropriation of the play, using

Lear for cultural cachet, *Empire* appears as a reaction against this trend, unapologetically looking back towards television before the rise of cable channels and paying tribute to prime-time soap opera in a form of nostalgia for television as a domestic medium.

Pushing at the extreme end of the Shakespeare/Not Shakespeare spectrum is Jean-Luc Godard's 1987 *King Lear*, which arguably remains the most *avant-garde* and challenging of Shakespearean screen explorations. A fragmented, self-interrupting, metacinematic work, an anti-movie framed within the film that might have been made, it involves Don Learo, an elderly Mafia chief, and Cordelia, his daughter. For Peter S. Donaldson, the film features 'Lear as God(ard)father', in line with Godard's long-standing interest in American gangsters[79] and a rebellious kind of filmmaking, conducted against mainstream commercial goals.[80] Although this version does not include Gloucester's sons, it asserts, Edmund-like, 'filial rights despite illegitimacy, by turns denying paternity and appropriating the riches of the paternal text', while trifling, Edgar-like, 'with despair, toying with madness, disguising itself, enacting redemption in burlesque'.[81] Godard's work on *Lear* allows the director to reflect on both the dispersion of paternal inheritance and the limits of an artist's control over cultural legacy, audience reception and the future artistic uses of his work. This entails that, for Godard, (in)authenticity in the connection between father/source and child/adaptation seems hardly measurable. The 'father' text of *Lear* adapted by a 'father' artist is decentred and displaced onto a child-film that affirms independence and the denial of its origin. This *Lear*, essentially through disjunctions of voice and gaze, protests not only against 'the restrictively commercial circumstances of its own production' but also against the limitations of language itself',[82] revealing the impossibility of making movies within a profit-driven framework and of finding visual equivalents for words – ending in a vertigo of nothingness. In his afterword to this volume, Peter Holland revisits Godard's 'not'-making of *Lear* as an excavation of the issues and challenges of approaching *Lear* on screen, serving as a fruitful analogy for the critical endeavours of this collective book and as a means to envisage new perspectives for film versions in the future.

At the end of the volume, José Ramón Díaz Fernández presents a select film-bibliography, providing a chronological outline of *Lear* adaptations and derivatives on screen, together with the essential critical reading in the field, which will help readers – both students and scholars – to find their way in the abundant afterlives of the play on screen. A monumental extended version of this film-bibliography is available online, which allows for regular updates and ongoing research. The film-bibliography notably shows how lively *Lear* has been on the small screen. This TV Shakespeare is explored in the three online resources that accompany this volume: Alexa Alice Joubin's contribution on '*King Lear* on the Small Screen and its Pedagogical Implications', Janice Valls-Russell's essay on 'Harry Cleven's *Les Héritières* (2008): *King Lear* in Prime-time Corsica' and Peter J. Smith's review of Richard Eyre's 2018 *Lear* for BBC2.[83] These contributions are illustrations of what dis-location can do to and with the play in an era when, according to Joubin, a 'user-centric culture supplants the reader-centric experience'.[84] As the history and ongoing process of *Lear* on screen illustrates, dislocation generates and inspires, whether it be the fragmentation of the play into video clips that can be watched on ever smaller and more itinerant screens, the transplantation of the play into an insular context or its transposition into current-day London. The various dislocations that *King Lear* evokes and invites are the condition of its being free and alive: migration *is* life.

Notes

1. J. L. Halio (ed.), *The First Quarto of King Lear* (Cambridge: Cambridge University Press, 1994); all subsequent references will be to J. L. Halio (ed.), *The Tragedy of King Lear* (Cambridge: Cambridge University Press, 1992), unless otherwise specified.
2. On open access at www.youtube.com/watch?v=IHr3dXP-7BE (accessed 23 November 2018).
3. On open access at vimeo.com/161213927 (accessed 23 November 2018).
4. On open access at www.dailymotion.com/video/x2142vk (accessed 23 November 2018).
5. Available at www.ina.fr/video/CPF86651306 (accessed 23 November 2018).
6. On open access at www.youtube.com/watch?v=OL7Ii-6Rdpc (accessed 23 November 2018).
7. Clips available via BBC 'Shakespeare Lives' at www.bbc.co.uk/events/ehw2m b/play/agf2rz/p04oh5ys (accessed 23 November 2018).
8. J. L. Halio, in his 1992 Cambridge edition of the play, describes the three films as 'the most notable' (Halio, *Lear*, 55). Similarly, Yvonne Griggs isolates the three films into a 'canon' in a section entitled 'East Meets West: *King Lear* and the Canon' in her *Shakespeare's 'King Lear': the Relationship between Text and Film* (London: Methuen Drama, 2009), 39–99. In his 2016 chapter 'Screening the Tragedies: *King Lear*', MacDonald P. Jackson selects what he considers 'the four best-known screen versions, two for television and two for cinema', namely Jonathan Miller's BBC TV production (1982) and Michael Elliott's version for Granada TV (1983) on the one hand, and Brook's and Kozintsev's films on the other hand, before briefly discussing 'others' in a last section ('Screening the

Tragedies: *King Lear*, in M. Neill and D. Schalkwyk (eds.), *The Oxford Handbook of Shakespearean Tragedy* (Oxford: Oxford University Press, 2016), 607–23.

9. C. Lehmann, 'Grigori Kozintsev', in M. T. Burnett, C. Lehmann, M. H. Rippy and R. Wray, *Welles, Kurosawa, Kozintsev, Zeffirelli*, vol. XVII of *Great Shakespeareans* (London and New York: Bloomsbury, 2013), 117.

10. *Ibid.*, 117, quoting G. Kozintsev, *King Lear: the Space of Tragedy*, trans. M. Mackintosh (Berkeley, Los Angeles and London: University of California Press, 1977), 131.

11. K. S. Rothwell, *A History of Shakespeare on Screen: a Century of Film and Television*, 2nd edition (Cambridge: Cambridge University Press, 2004), 179.

12. Griggs, *King Lear*, 66.

13. Rothwell, *A History*, 178.

14. A. Davies, *Filming Shakespeare's Plays: the Adaptations of Laurence Olivier, Orson Welles, Peter Brook and Akira Kurosawa* (Cambridge: Cambridge University Press, 1988), 143–4.

15. *Ibid.*, 144.

16. Rothwell, *A History*, 144.

17. On the 'complete absence of sound', see Peter Holland's chapter on Peter Brook, in P. Holland (ed.), *Brook, Hall, Ninagawa, Lepage*, vol. XVIII of *Great Shakespeareans* (London and New York: Bloomsbury, 2013), 35.

18. *Ibid.*, 37.

19. For comprehensive outlines of Kurosawa's biography and the positioning of *Ran* in the context of his oeuvre, see M. T. Burnett, 'Akira Kurosawa', in M. T. Burnett, C. Lehmann, M. H. Rippy and R. Wray, *Welles, Kurosawa, Kozintsev, Zeffirelli*, vol. XVII of *Great Shakespeareans* (London and New York: Bloomsbury, 2013), 54–91; and J. Buchanan, 'Cross-cultural Narrative Rhymes: the Shakespeare Films of Akira Kurosawa', in her *Shakespeare on Film* (Harlow: Pearson Longman, 2005), 71–89.

20. P. E. S. Babiak, *Shakespeare Films: a Re-evaluation of 100 Years of Adaptations* (Jefferson: McFarland, 2016), 76.

21. E. C. Brown, 'Akira Kurosawa', *Shakespeare Bulletin* 34 (2016), 497.

22. Buchanan, *Shakespeare on Film*, 81.

23. Burnett, 'Akira Kurosawa', 54.

24. Buchanan, *Shakespeare on Film*, 80.

25. Babiak, *Shakespeare Films*, 77.

26. R. Hapgood, 'Kurosawa's Shakespeare Films: *Throne of Blood, The Bad Sleep Well*, and *Ran*', in A. Davies and S. Wells (eds.), *Shakespeare and the Moving Image: the Plays on Film and Television* (Cambridge: Cambridge University Press, 1994), 235.

27. Babiak, *Shakespeare Films*, 70.

28. Burnett, 'Akira Kurosawa', 80.

29. G. Kozintsev, *The Space of Tragedy*, 72.

30. J. Kott, *The Bottom Translation: Marlowe and Shakespeare and the Carnival Tradition*, trans. D. Miedzyrzecka and L. Vallee (Evanston: Northwestern University Press, 1987), 150.

31. J. Collick, *Shakespeare, Cinema and Society* (Manchester and New York: Manchester University Press, 1989); K. D. Nordin, 'Buddhist Symbolism in Akira Kurosawa's *Ran*: a Counterpoint to Human Chaos', *Asian Cinema* 16.2 (2005): 242–54.

32. K. McDonald, *Japanese Classical Theater in Films* (Rutherford: Fairleigh Dickinson University Press, 1994); D. Richie, *The Films of Akira Kurosawa*, 3rd expanded edition (Berkeley and Los Angeles: University of California Press, 1996); S. Prince, *The Warrior's Camera: the Cinema of Akira Kurosawa*, revised and expanded edition (Princeton: Princeton University Press, 1999); Collick, *Shakespeare, Cinema and Society.*

33. K. Rowe, 'Medium-Specificity and Other Critical Scripts for Screen Shakespeare', in D. E. Henderson (ed.), *Alternative Shakespeares 3* (London and New York: Routledge, 2008), 29.

34. A. Davies, '*King Lear* on Film', in J. Ogden and A. H. Scouten (eds.), '*Lear' from Study to Stage: Essays in Criticism* (Madison: Fairleigh Dickinson University Press, 1997), 261. On televisual Shakespeare, see S. Hatchuel and N. Vienne-Guerrin (eds.), *Shakespeare on Screen: Television Shakespeare: Essays in Honour of Michèle Willems* (Mont-Saint-Aignan: Publications des Universités de Rouen et du Havre, 2008); S. Wells, 'Television Shakespeare', *Shakespeare Quarterly* 33.3 (1982): 261–77; W. B. Worthen, 'The Player's Eye: Shakespeare on Television', *Comparative Drama* 18 (1984): 193–202; and H. R. Coursen, *Watching Shakespeare on Television* (Rutherford: Fairleigh Dickinson University Press, 1993).

35. R. A. Kimbrough, 'Olivier's *Lear* and the Limits of Video', in J. C. Bulman and H. R. Coursen (eds.), *Shakespeare on Television: an Anthology of Essays and Reviews* (Hanover and London: University Press of New England, 1988), 120.

36. *Ibid.*, 117.

37. Worthen, 'The Player's Eye', 196. See also Michael Hordern, quoted in Wells, 'Television Shakespeare', 274.

38. H. R. Coursen, *Shakespeare in Space: Recent Shakespeare Productions on Screen* (New York: Peter Lang, 2002), 168.

39. Worthen, 'The Player's Eye', 197.

40. T. Nannicelli, *Appreciating the Art of Television: a Philosophical Perspective* (London: Taylor & Francis, 2016), 1–2.

41. On open access at www.youtube.com/watch?v=qpjvDQ_Ib-4 (accessed 24 November 2018).

42. M. H. Rippy, 'Orson Welles', in M. T. Burnett, C. Lehmann, M. H. Rippy and R. Wray, *Welles, Kurosawa, Kozintsev, Zeffirelli*, vol. XVII of *Great Shakespeareans* (London and New York: Bloomsbury, 2013), 44; F. W. Wadsworth, '"Sound and Fury"–*King Lear* on Television', *Quarterly of Film, Radio, and Television* 8 (1954): 260.

43. Davies, '*King Lear* on Film', 261–2.

44. On differences between the two versions, see H. Fenwick, 'The Production', in P. Alexander et al. (eds.), '*King Lear': the BBC TV Shakespeare* (London: British Broadcasting Corporation, 1983), 19–34.

45. A. Davies, 'Revisiting the Olivier *King Lear* on Television', in S. Hatchuel and N. Vienne-Guerrin (eds.), *Shakespeare on Screen: Television Shakespeare: Essays in Honour of Michèle Willems* (Mont-Saint-Aignan: Publications des Universités de Rouen et du Havre, 2008), 84; H. M. Cook, 'Two *Lears* for Television: an Exploration of Televisual Strategies', *Literature/Film Quarterly* 14 (1986): 179–80.
46. Davies, '*King Lear* on Film', 264.
47. A. Leggatt, *King Lear*, 2nd edition (Manchester and New York: Manchester University Press, 2004), 135.
48. P. Holland, 'Two-Dimensional Shakespeare: *King Lear* on Film', in A. Davies and S. Wells (eds.), *Shakespeare and the Moving Image: the Plays on Film and Television* (Cambridge: Cambridge University Press, 1994), 60–1; Kimbrough, 'Olivier's *Lear*', 119.
49. Rothwell, *A History*, 265.
50. Leggatt, *King Lear*, 144.
51. H. R. Coursen, *Contemporary Shakespeare Production* (New York: Peter Lang, 2010), 170.
52. Available at www.imdb.com/title/tt7473890/?ref_=nv_sr_1 (accessed 24 April 2018).
53. J. Schlueter, *Dramatic Closure: Reading the End* (Madison: Fairleigh Dickinson University Press, 1995), 115; Worthen, 'The Player's Eye', 194.
54. Griggs, '*King Lear*', 191–2.
55. See P. Aebischer, S. Greenhalgh and L. E. Osborne (eds.), *Shakespeare and the 'Live' Theatre Broadcast Experience* (London: Bloomsbury, 2018).
56. K. Fedderson and J. M. Richardson, '*Slings & Arrows*: an Intermediated Shakespearean Adaptation', in D. Fischlin (ed.), *OuterSpeares: Shakespeare, Intermedia, and the Limits of Adaptation* (Toronto: University of Toronto Press, 2014), 208.
57. L. E. Osborne, 'Serial Shakespeare: Intermedial Performance and the Outrageous Fortunes of *Slings & Arrows*', *Borrowers and Lenders: the Journal of Shakespeare and Appropriation* 6.2 (Fall/Winter 2011): www.borrowers.uga.edu/783090/show.
58. D. M. Lanier, 'Shakespeare/Not Shakespeare: Afterword', in C. Desmet, N. Loper, J. Casey (eds.), *Shakespeare/Not Shakespeare* (Cham: Palgrave Macmillan, 2017), 295.
59. G. Deleuze and F. Guattari, *A Thousand Plateaus: Capitalism and Schizophrenia* (Minneapolis: University of Minnesota Press, 1987); Desmet, *Shakespeare/Not Shakespeare*, 3; D. M. Lanier, 'Shakespeare Rhizomatics: Adaptation, Ethics, Value', in A. Huang and E. Rivlin (eds.), *Shakespeare and the Ethics of Appropriation* (New York: Palgrave Macmillan, 2014), 21–40.
60. M. Calbi, *Spectral Shakespeares: Media Adaptations in the Twenty-First Century* (New York and Basingstoke: Palgrave Macmillan, 2013).
61. Our thanks to Lois Leveen, who suggested the term 'Learness' at the 'Tragedies on Screen: the Case of *King Lear*' seminar, World Shakespeare Congress, 2016.

62. T. Cartelli and K. Rowe, *New Wave Shakespeare on Screen* (Cambridge and Malden: Polity Press, 2007), 154.
63. Griggs, '*King Lear*', 111.
64. Rowe, 'Medium-Specificity', 39.
65. A. Marino, 'Cut'n'mix *King Lear*: *Second Generation* and Asian-British Identities', in C. Dente and S. Soncini (eds.), *Shakespeare and Conflict: a European Perspective* (Basingstoke and New York: Palgrave Macmillan, 2013), 172.
66. *Ibid.*, 177–9.
67. K. Földváry, 'Postcolonial Hybridity: the Making of a Bollywood *Lear* in London', *Shakespeare* (British Shakespeare Association) 9 (2013), 311.
68. C. Lehmann, 'A Thousand Shakespeares: from Cinematic Saga to Feminist Geography or, The Escape from Iceland', in B. Hodgdon and W. B. Worthen (eds.), *A Companion to Shakespeare and Performance* (Malden and Oxford: Blackwell, 2005), 606.
69. *Ibid.*, 590.
70. *Ibid.*, 590.
71. Griggs, '*King Lear*', 62–79.
72. R. Oya, 'Filming "The Weight of This Sad Time": Yasujiro Ozu's Rereading of *King Lear* in *Tokyo Story* (1953)', *Shakespeare Survey* 66 (2013), 55.
73. N. M. Ibraheem, 'Abd al-Raḥīm Kamāl's *Dahsha*: an Upper Egyptian *Lear*', *Critical Survey* 28.3 (Winter 2016): 67–85.
74. R. M. García-Periago, 'English Shakespeares in Indian Cinema: *36 Chowringhee Lane* and *The Last Lear*', *Borrowers and Lenders: the Journal of Shakespeare and Appropriation* 9.2 (Fall/Winter 2015): www.borrowers.uga.edu/1634/show.
75. M. T. Burnett, 'Capital, Commodities, Cinema: Shakespeare and the Eastern European "Gypsy" Aesthetic', *Shakespeare Jahrbuch* 150 (2014), 147–8.
76. Calbi, *Spectral Shakespeares*, 40.
77. J. J. Bottinelli, 'Watching Lear: Resituating the Gaze at the Intersection of Film and Drama in Kristian Levring's *The King Is Alive*'. *Literature/Film Quarterly* 33 (2005), 102.
78. Buchanan, *Shakespeare on Film*, 222.
79. P. S. Donaldson, *Shakespearean Films/Shakespearean Directors* (Boston and London: Unwin Hyman, 1990), 198.
80. S. Bennett, 'Godard and Lear: Trashing the Can(n)on', *Theatre Survey* 39 (1998): 7–19.
81. Donaldson, *Shakespearean Films*, 189.
82. A. Walworth, 'Cinema *Hysterica Passio*: Voice and Gaze in Jean-Luc Godard's *King Lear*', in L. S. Starks and C. Lehmann (eds.), *The Reel Shakespeare: Alternative Cinema and Theory* (Madison and Teaneck: Fairleigh Dickinson University Press, 2002), 60.
83. See one of the first reviews of the film at www.theguardian.com/tv-and-radio/2018/may/28/bbc-king-lear-review-anthony-hopkins?CMP=share_btn_fb and the trailer at www.youtube.com/watch?v=utsDahZ42ys (accessed 29 May 2018).

84. Joubin refers to V. M. Fazel and L. Geddes's 'Introduction' to *The Shakespeare User: Critical and Creative Appropriations in a Networked Culture* (New York: Palgrave, 2017), 3.

WORKS CITED

Aebischer, P., S. Greenhalgh and L. E. Osborne (eds.), *Shakespeare and the 'Live' Theatre Broadcast Experience* (London: Bloomsbury, 2018).

Babiak, P. E. S., *Shakespeare Films: a Re-evaluation of 100 Years of Adaptations* (Jefferson: McFarland, 2016).

Bennett, S., 'Godard and Lear: Trashing the Can(n)on', *Theatre Survey* 39 (1998): 7–19.

Bottinelli, J. J., 'Watching Lear: Resituating the Gaze at the Intersection of Film and Drama in Kristian Levring's *The King Is Alive*', *Literature/Film Quarterly* 33 (2005): 101–9.

Brown, E. C., 'Akira Kurosawa', *Shakespeare Bulletin* 34 (2016): 496–9.

Buchanan, J., *Shakespeare on Film* (Harlow: Pearson Longman, 2005).

Burnett, M. T., 'Akira Kurosawa', in M. T. Burnett, C. Lehmann, M. H. Rippy and R. Wray, *Welles, Kurosawa, Kozintsev, Zeffirelli*, vol. XVII of *Great Shakespeareans* (London and New York: Bloomsbury, 2013), 54–91.

'Capital, Commodities, Cinema: Shakespeare and the Eastern European "Gypsy" Aesthetic', *Shakespeare Jahrbuch* 150 (2014): 146–60.

Calbi, M., *Spectral Shakespeares: Media Adaptations in the Twenty-First Century* (New York and Basingstoke: Palgrave Macmillan, 2013).

Cartelli, T. and K. Rowe, *New Wave Shakespeare on Screen* (Cambridge and Malden: Polity Press, 2007).

Collick, J., *Shakespeare, Cinema and Society* (Manchester and New York: Manchester University Press, 1989).

Cook, H. M., 'Two *Lears* for Television: an Exploration of Televisual Strategies', *Literature/Film Quarterly* 14 (1986): 179–86.

Coursen, H. R., *Watching Shakespeare on Television* (Rutherford: Fairleigh Dickinson University Press, 1993).

Shakespeare in Space: Recent Shakespeare Productions on Screen (New York: Peter Lang, 2002).

Contemporary Shakespeare Production (New York: Peter Lang, 2010).

Davies, A., *Filming Shakespeare's Plays: the Adaptations of Laurence Olivier, Orson Welles, Peter Brook and Akira Kurosawa* (Cambridge: Cambridge University Press, 1988).

'King Lear on Film', in J. Ogden and A. H. Scouten (eds.), *'Lear' from Study to Stage: Essays in Criticism* (Madison: Fairleigh Dickinson University Press, 1997), 247–66.

'Revisiting the Olivier *King Lear* on Television', in S. Hatchuel and N. Vienne-Guerrin (eds.), *Shakespeare on Screen: Television Shakespeare: Essays in Honour of Michèle Willems* (Mont-Saint-Aignan: Publications des Universités de Rouen et du Havre, 2008), 79–90.

Deleuze, G. and F. Guattari, *A Thousand Plateaus: Capitalism and Schizophrenia* (Minneapolis: University of Minnesota Press, 1987).

Donaldson, P. S., *Shakespearean Films/Shakespearean Directors* (Boston and London: Unwin Hyman, 1990).

Fazel, V. M. and L. Geddes (eds.), *The Shakespeare User: Critical and Creative Appropriations in a Networked Culture* (New York: Palgrave, 2017).

Fedderson, K. and J. M. Richardson, '*Slings & Arrows*: an Intermediated Shakespearean Adaptation', in D. Fischlin (ed.), *OuterSpeares: Shakespeare, Intermedia, and the Limits of Adaptation* (Toronto: University of Toronto Press, 2014), 205–29.

Fenwick, H., 'The Production', in P. Alexander et al. (eds.), *'King Lear': the BBC TV Shakespeare* (London: British Broadcasting Corporation, 1983), 19–34.

Földváry, K., 'Postcolonial Hybridity: the Making of a Bollywood *Lear* in London', *Shakespeare* (British Shakespeare Association) 9 (2013), 304–12.

García-Periago, R. M., 'English Shakespeares in Indian Cinema: *36 Chowringhee Lane* and *The Last Lear*', *Borrowers and Lenders: the Journal of Shakespeare and Appropriation* 9.2 (Fall/Winter 2015): www.borrowers.uga.edu/1634/show.

Griggs, Y., *Shakespeare's 'King Lear': the Relationship between Text and Film* (London: Methuen Drama, 2009).

Halio, J. L. (ed.), *The Tragedy of King Lear* (Cambridge: Cambridge University Press, 1992).

The First Quarto of King Lear (Cambridge: Cambridge University Press, 1994).

Hapgood, R., 'Kurosawa's Shakespeare Films: *Throne of Blood, The Bad Sleep Well, and Ran*', in A. Davies and S. Wells (eds.), *Shakespeare and the Moving Image: the Plays on Film and Television* (Cambridge: Cambridge University Press, 1994), 234–49.

Hatchuel, S. and N. Vienne-Guerrin (eds.), *Shakespeare on Screen: Television Shakespeare: Essays in Honour of Michèle Willems* (Mont-Saint-Aignan: Publications des Universités de Rouen et du Havre, 2008).

Holland, P., 'Two-Dimensional Shakespeare: *King Lear* on Film', in A. Davies and S. Wells (eds.), *Shakespeare and the Moving Image: the Plays on Film and Television* (Cambridge: Cambridge University Press, 1994), 50–68.

'Peter Brook', in P. Holland (ed.), *Brook, Hall, Ninagawa, Lepage*, vol. XVIII of *Great Shakespeareans* (London and New York: Bloomsbury, 2013), 7–46.

Ibraheem, N. M., ''Abd al-Raḥīm Kamāl's *Dahsha*: an Upper Egyptian *Lear*', *Critical Survey* 28.3 (Winter 2016): 67–85.

Jackson, M. P., 'Screening the Tragedies: *King Lear*', in M. Neill and D. Schalkwyk (eds.), *The Oxford Handbook of Shakespearean Tragedy* (Oxford: Oxford University Press, 2016), 607–23.

Kimbrough, R. A., 'Olivier's *Lear* and the Limits of Video', in J. C. Bulman and H. R. Coursen (eds.), *Shakespeare on Television: an Anthology of Essays and Reviews* (Hanover and London: University Press of New England, 1988), 115–22.

Kott, J., *The Bottom Translation: Marlowe and Shakespeare and the Carnival Tradition*, trans. D. Miedzyrzecka and L. Vallee (Evanston: Northwestern University Press, 1987).

Kozintsev, G., *'King Lear': the Space of Tragedy*, trans. M. Mackintosh (Berkeley: University of California Press, 1977).

Lanier, D. M., 'Shakespeare/Not Shakespeare: Afterword', in C. Desmet, N. Loper and J. Casey (eds.), *Shakespeare/Not Shakespeare* (Cham: Palgrave Macmillan, 2017), 293–306.

'Shakespeare Rhizomatics: Adaptation, Ethics, Value', in A. Huang and E. Rivlin (eds.), *Shakespeare and the Ethics of Appropriation* (New York: Palgrave Macmillan, 2014), 21–40.

Leggatt, A., *King Lear*, 2nd edition (Manchester and New York: Manchester University Press, 2004).

Lehmann, C., 'A Thousand Shakespeares: from Cinematic Saga to Feminist Geography or, The Escape from Iceland', in B. Hodgdon and W. B. Worthen (eds.), *A Companion to Shakespeare and Performance* (Malden and Oxford: Blackwell, 2005), 588–609.

'Grigori Kozintsev', in M. T. Burnett, C. Lehmann, M. H. Rippy and R. Wray, *Welles, Kurosawa, Kozintsev, Zeffirelli*, vol. XVII of *Great Shakespeareans* (London and New York: Bloomsbury, 2013), 92–140.

Marino, A., 'Cut'n'mix *King Lear*: Second Generation and Asian-British Identities', in C. Dente and S. Soncini (eds.), *Shakespeare and Conflict: a European Perspective* (Basingstoke and New York: Palgrave Macmillan, 2013), 170–83.

McDonald, K., *Japanese Classical Theater in Films* (Rutherford: Fairleigh Dickinson University Press, 1994).

Nannicelli, T., *Appreciating the Art of Television: a Philosophical Perspective* (London: Taylor & Francis, 2016).

Nordin, K. D., 'Buddhist Symbolism in Akira Kurosawa's *Ran*: a Counterpoint to Human Chaos', *Asian Cinema* 16.2 (2005): 242–54.

Osborne, L. E., 'Serial Shakespeare: Intermedial Performance and the Outrageous Fortunes of *Slings & Arrows*', *Borrowers and Lenders: the Journal of Shakespeare and Appropriation* 6.2 (Fall/Winter 2011): www.borrowers.uga.edu/783090/show.

Oya, R., 'Filming "The Weight of This Sad Time": Yasujiro Ozu's Rereading of *King Lear* in *Tokyo Story* (1953)', *Shakespeare Survey* 66 (2013): 55–66.

Prince, S., *The Warrior's Camera: the Cinema of Akira Kurosawa*, revised and expanded edition (Princeton: Princeton University Press, 1999).

Richie, D., *The Films of Akira Kurosawa*, 3rd expanded edition (Berkeley and Los Angeles: University of California Press, 1996).

Rippy, M. H., 'Orson Welles', in M. T. Burnett, C. Lehmann, M. H. Rippy and R. Wray, *Welles, Kurosawa, Kozintsev, Zeffirelli*, vol. XVII of *Great Shakespeareans* (London and New York: Bloomsbury, 2013), 7–53.

Rothwell, K. S., *A History of Shakespeare on Screen: a Century of Film and Television*, 2nd edition (Cambridge: Cambridge University Press, 2004).

Rowe, K., 'Medium-Specificity and Other Critical Scripts for Screen Shakespeare', in D. E. Henderson (ed.), *Alternative Shakespeares 3* (London and New York: Routledge, 2008), 34–53.

Schlueter, J., *Dramatic Closure: Reading the End* (Madison: Fairleigh Dickinson University Press, 1995).

Wadsworth, F. W., '"Sound and Fury"– *King Lear* on Television', *Quarterly of Film, Radio, and Television* 8 (1954): 254–68.

Walworth, A., 'Cinema *Hysterica Passio*: Voice and Gaze in Jean-Luc Godard's *King Lear*', in L. S. Starks and C. Lehmann (eds.), *The Reel Shakespeare: Alternative Cinema and Theory* (Madison and Teaneck: Fairleigh Dickinson University Press, 2002), 59–94.

Wells, S., 'Television Shakespeare', *Shakespeare Quarterly* 33.3 (1982): 261–77.

Worthen, W. B., 'The Player's Eye: Shakespeare on Television', *Comparative Drama* 18 (1984): 193–202.

PART I

Surviving Lear*: Revisiting the Canon*

Lear's Fool on Film: Peter Brook, Grigori Kozintsev, Akira Kurosawa

Samuel Crowl

Shakespeare's unlicensed clowns and his 'all-licens'd' fools challenge film-makers to radically reimagine them in cinematic idioms and conventions. Shakespeare's unlicensed clowns – fools by nature rather than profession – are typically discovered in everyday settings which embody and empower their uncensored vernacular truths: rural Warwickshire, the London tavern, the urban constabulary, the graveyard. These clowns step out of worlds we recognize and so quite often step comfortably back into established film conventions: Keystone cop, day-dreaming dandy, Vaudeville comedian.

But what of Shakespeare's 'all-licens'd' fools? What license can the filmmaker and actor bring to the cinematic creation of Touchstone, Feste and most significantly Lear's Fool? His dramatic imagination was drawn to the way in which the fool could be realized not just as a voice of irony or misrule in the comedies but as a vehicle for speaking truth to power in a hierarchical social system in which such truth-telling invited tragic consequences. With two important exceptions, the role of the jester disappears in Shakespeare's tragedies: Hamlet proves to be Yorick's heir as he plays a bitter fool to Claudius and a brazen one to Gertrude and Lear's wry Fool leads his master into searing self-consciousness and eventual madness. Shakespeare plucks a device from Henry VIII's Tudor court, where Will Somers was the king's beloved fool and companion, and ties it directly to the ways in which tragic drama itself in the Elizabethan and Jacobean age became the voice that spoke truth to power through its focus on creating narratives of personal guilt and political corruption. The dramatic event, the play itself, eventually replaced the fool as the centre of court entertainment, just as two of Shakespeare's greatest tragic heroes, Hamlet and Lear, incorporated the function of the fool by absorbing and ventriloquizing his style and substance.

We have three remarkable films of *King Lear* created in England, Russia and Japan by three directors of international stature: Peter Brook, Grigori Kozintsev and Akira Kurosawa. All three were made between the mid-sixties and mid-eighties in the last century when *Lear* rivalled *Hamlet* as the Shakespearean tragedy that best represented the nuclear age of existential angst and apocalyptic anxiety. The films are all set in the past: Brook's in something suggesting the early middle ages with tribal huts passing for great palaces; Kozintsev's in a correspondingly barren landscape roughly equivalent with the early fifteenth century; and Kurosawa in his familiar Sengoku period of Japan's sixteenth-century civil wars, featuring the samurai warrior and his strict, violent code of behaviour. Because the Fool's role is so central to the substance and structure of Shakespeare's play, looking at how these three directors cinematically reimagined the Fool to speak out from inside their own cultures to a modern audience will provide insight not only into their powers as film directors but also into the ways they reinvent Shakespeare's bleakest tragedy for the screen. Each director uses his conception of the Fool as a means of anchoring Lear's story within a cinematic narrative.

Peter Brook's *King Lear* (1971)

Not surprisingly, Peter Brook came to his film of *Lear* through the stage. He was one of Peter Hall's key partners in the founding of the Royal Shakespeare Company in 1960. Both men were committed to moving Stratford away from the festival model of a limited season of plays largely starring leading actors from the West End and the Old Vic. Hall and Brook wanted to create a company of actors who would sign extended contracts of eighteen months or more and who would develop leaders from within the company rather than importing 'stars' from London or Broadway.[1]

The new company's first production to mark a radical shift in presenting Shakespeare on stage was Brook's 1962 *King Lear*. Brook's production fused ideas circulating at Stratford inspired by the work of Antonin Artaud, Bertolt Brecht and Jan Kott. Brook had his cast commit themselves to a careful re-examination of the text so as not to repeat old patterns of interpretation and performance and to insist on stripping the play down to its essence by scraping away unexamined performance details accreted over the first half of the century. As an example of textual re-examination, Brook and the actresses playing Goneril (Irene Worth) and Regan (Patience Collier) became convinced that their opening speeches could be expressed as genuine statements of affection rather than empty flattery and thus revise our thinking about their father and his treatment by them when he (and his hundred knights) are rude and wild in their stay with Goneril. Such a move allows Lear to be seen immediately as a patriarchal terror not an aged victim, and Goneril and Regan as daughters perhaps more sinned against than sinning.

In a similar re-examination of performance tradition, Brook swept away outworn practices by creating a minimalist set, stucco and timber walls decorated principally by iron thunder sheets hanging from the flies and black and brown leather costumes (within a decade to become an RSC cliché but daringly new at the time). Brook's production did have a star, Paul Scofield, but he refused a star's turn by creating a tough, bitter Lear repressing his anger and monumental rhetorical power. The production announced the arrival of the Royal Shakespeare Company as a new vibrant source in reimagining Shakespeare on stage.

When Brook came to translate the production from stage to screen five years later (the film was shot in Jutland in the winter of 1968 but not released until 1971), Brook's ideas about the play had only deepened and darkened as the modern world was spinning out of control prompted by America's involvement in Vietnam and the subsequent student revolution which swept through college campuses in the United States and the streets of Chicago, Paris and Prague in 1968. Brook went to work to sharpen the production. He tightened the screenplay to remove even more of the play's poetry, he chose the barren snow-covered landscape of Jutland for location shooting, he jettisoned most of the original cast, keeping only Paul Scofield (Lear), Irene Worth (Goneril), Tom Fleming (Kent) and Alan Webb (Gloucester), and he linked influence by Brecht and Artaud with the radical film style inspired by the French New Wave cinema of the 1960s. But most significantly Brook cast Jack MacGowran, a veteran Beckett actor, as the Fool, firmly associating the production with the minimalist world of Samuel Beckett.

Brook's film of *Lear* is hard work for the viewer not only because of the screenplay's insistence on the play's inherent cruelty but also because of its atypical cinematic means of representation. We get few establishing shots to situate the action. The camera is most often in close-up or tight two-shot so the focus is relentlessly on faces. The film seeks to alienate the viewer. The puzzling opening sequence is tantalizingly slow as the camera pans back and forth across a host of silent faces waiting, but waiting for what or for whom? Then the film cuts to the back of a large phallic object in the middle of a circular room which might well be a burial vault (or nuclear bunker). We hear a door shut and cut to the front side where we discover the seated Scofield and realize that the phallic object is his totemic throne. After a long pause, Scofield utters a single word and pauses again as we scramble to understand what he has said. Is it 'No' or 'Know'? Negativity or knowledge? Brook's journey through *Lear* proceeds between those two poles, as does Scofield's in a performance that is perfectly matched with Brook's film style.

Scofield's Lear is presented to us, as Kenneth Rothwell observes, as a 'talking head', his face unmoving and expressionless.[2] His right lip droops into a curl, suggesting to Peter Holland that this Lear has had a stroke, with his voice reduced to a repressed growl.[3] Scofield's Lear is terrifying before he utters a single curse. The camera then captures Goneril and Regan, each shot in medium and then full close-up, delivering their expressions of devotion directly to the camera without gesture or vocal inflection. What's going on here?

Moments of entropy, like this beginning sequence, are followed by explosions of activity spurred by Lear's temper. When Lear disrupts his world, Brook throws the cinematic Brechtian book at us: title cards, blackouts, dark interiors, bleak snow-covered exteriors where the sun never shines, hand-held camera shots, zoom shots, jump cuts and the frame repeatedly disrupted by presenting old faces at odd angles. A face may appear on the right, then on the left. At a crucial moment at the end of the film, Lear's head slowly sinks from the top of the frame and disappears out of the bottom, leaving only a white void. Brook refuses to give us anything to mitigate his bleak apocalyptic reading of the play except in his presentation of the Fool and the Fool's relationship with Lear. MacGowran's Fool grounds the film: in a world swirling with sound and fury, his voice remains calm, sane and witty. MacGowran is melancholy but never mad; perplexed but never perturbed; moved but never maudlin.

The Fool makes the only music in the film. Brook's *Lear* is the only major Shakespeare film that completely dispenses with a musical soundtrack. Music is an essential element in film's rhetoric and its absence indicates how far Brook was willing to go to challenge his audience. Because Brook and Scofield intentionally squash the powerful poetry of Lear's outbursts and curses, the poetry that remains is contained in the rapid fire one-liners that dart back and forth between the Fool and his master. The tone of Beckett's banter is substituted for Shakespeare's and MacGowran and Scofield are masters of its delivery.

In their first encounter, Lear enters the frame from the right, sits by the fire and calls for the Fool. The camera quickly pans to the left and finds MacGowran, then quickly pans back to the king, then zips back to the

Fool – the quick back and forth movement suggesting the verbal exchange which will follow. The Fool gets Lear's attention by his query 'Can you make no use of nothing, nuncle?' (1.4.115). And Scofield's response is brilliantly conceived as he discovers half way through his quick reply 'Why, no, boy; nothing can be made of nothing' (1.4.116) the echo of his use of the thought and the words in his earlier exchange with Cordelia, here revealed as Scofield pauses after 'be' and quietly chokes up on the last three words.

MacGowran moves to sit next to Scofield in front of the fire and in Brook's deeply revised and rearranged text, turns to him with an egg in his hand and delivers the parable of the two crowns given away by the king, leaving him with only a witless bald one in the exchange. A quick cut reveals the Fool and Lear eating together as the Fool continues his lesson in royal economics and then a jump cut has the Fool sitting on the floor leaning back against the table where Lear continues to digest more than he eats. The Fool rises and sings his revelations about wise men, fops and apes as he moves among Lear's men, who have been silent witnesses to this play between wit and power. The camera catches his song and movement in long shot, giving the Fool's remarks a larger audience and wider context. That context is shattered when the frame is suddenly filled with a close-up of Irene Worth's face. The new voice of authority (Goneril) has come to chastise both father and Fool.

Worth's calm, polite delivery of the lines about Lear's 'all-licens'd fool' and 'other insolent retinue' (1.4.160–1) makes her appear to be the very soul of rationality and reasonableness. The lines, however, have the opposite effect (so often true in family quarrels) and lead to Lear's savage explosion and the overturning of the dinner tables as his men trash the dining room before storming out into the snow, and the Fool reminds us 'So, out went the candle, and we were left darkling' (1.4.177). And Brook's film plunges us into that darkness until it reaches Dover Beach. Emotional sterility is matched by barren landscape as Goneril and Regan reject and reduce their once monumental father, as Lear dredges up from the inner deep his appalling curses and as Cornwall (Patrick Magee, another Beckett import) becomes a one-man theatre of cruelty. Lear's anger is translated into the film's restlessness and, as he rumbles away to his other daughter, we get his second great scene with the Fool.

They sit side by side on the front seat of the giant cart Lear drives. Lear and the Fool face the camera in a medium two-shot and the Fool goes back to work on the interrelated ideas of daughters, inheritance and power expressed in little riddles about crabs and apples and oysters and snails until Lear answers a riddle correctly and wins the title 'Fool'. 'Let me not be mad' (1.5.37), he insists, as the cart trundles along its rutted path. Brook's camera and editing hold steady throughout this last sequence of stability to underline its importance. As Brook comments, 'The gradual self-discovery of [Lear's] vast ignorance is the motor of the action. It is the richness of this discovery that gradually seeps and then floods through the gaps.'[4] Lear's self-discovery is prompted by his relationship with the Fool, and Brook makes these two moments central to his film. Once Lear and the film arrive at Gloucester's, the descent into cinematic and narrative chaos is complete and does not end until Scofield's face sinks slowly out of the blank frame as Lear expires at the 'promised end' (5.3.237).

For Brook, the Fool defines Lear and once Lear's mind splits and crumbles and Poor Tom usurps the Fool's role as his prime companion, the film goes dark and wild. Brook takes his inspiration for the storm scene from Lear's taunt 'Crack nature's moulds, all germens spill at once' (3.2.8). The storm and the hovel scenes are filled with an excess of cinematic devices: jump cuts, zooms and reverse zooms, and unstable hand-held camera shots. The screen goes black, then is briefly illuminated by a lightning blast, then goes black again; faces appear on one side of the frame and then are transposed to the other, fantasy images of Goneril, Regan and Cordelia appear and disappear, and a storm unfolds which rivals Noah's flood with the frame filled with drowned rodents. The last exchange between Lear and his Fool is a silent one. The two have been rescued from the hovel and are being driven towards Dover in one of the wagons. At one point Lear raises the rear flap and slips out of the back and places his finger on his lips as a signal of silence to the Fool who gazes after him and then quietly lowers the flap and disappears back into the wagon.

As earlier Poor Tom replaced the Fool as Lear's 'yoke-fellow of equity' (3.6.31 Q1), now it is Tom's blind father who performs a similar function, as the King and the Duke are reunited on Dover Beach. But the closing beats of Brook's film remain as emotionally radical as its beginning. Suffering does not bring redemption. The reunion of father and daughter does not release Lear from the wheel of fire. Edgar's victory over Edmund is not heroic but simply – in one fatal blow of his huge axe – a further savage extension of the brutal iron age the film creates as a context for this Lear. The end is apocalyptic as Scofield's head, floating on a horizontal line in the middle of the frame, slowly sinks out of sight. 'This is a world', one critic posits, 'that exists only in the film'.[5] Except, I would suggest, for the world of the Fool, whose melancholy humanity draws us to him rather than drives us away; he tethers Brook's radical vision to Shakespeare's text and to our world.

Grigori Kozintsev's *King Lear* (1970)

For obvious reasons, the Brook and Kozintsev films of *King Lear* have been linked since their release within a year of each other in 1970–1971. Both were made by leading stage and screen directors in their respective countries; both were made at the same historical moment; both were shot in black and white; both sought out remote landscapes for location shooting: Jutland for Brook, the Crimea, Ukraine and Estonia for Kozintsev; and both men were professional admirers who corresponded as they were developing their screenplays. Yet the films they made are remarkably different. Critical readings of that difference have remained consistent over time by Shakespeare on film critics ranging from Jack Jorgens (1977) and Alexander Leggatt (1991) to Yvonne Griggs (2009) and Courtney Lehmann (2013).

All four of these critics, separated by age, nationality and gender, see the Brook film as a bleak, uncompromising, radical version of Shakespeare's text in screenplay, shooting script and editing, while Kozintsev presents us with a more familiar film narrative and more humanistic approach to capturing the arc of Lear's journey as traced in Shakespeare's play. As Alexander Leggatt writes, 'Brook's version takes a grimmer view of humanity than Kozintsev's ... In Kozintsev the old social values of courtesy and simple decency are just starting to flake away ... Brook's world is more pervasively, endemically brutal. It is perhaps for this reason that the violence [in Brook's film] is swift and simple, not protracted; it comes naturally.'[6] Lehmann expresses the bold distinction between the two films with a cinematic metaphor: 'The directors managed to create their respective versions of *Lear* as photo negatives of each other's work.'[7]

With one or two arguable exceptions, the religious references in Shakespeare's play are to 'the gods'. The atmosphere seems now pagan, now pre-Christian. The spiritual landscape of Brook's film seems godless and empty, while Kozintsev laces his film with Christian images. Kozintsev uses Shakespeare's play to introduce spiritual and religious ideas unwelcome in a materialist dispensation. There are primitive Celtic signs carved in the rocks the peasants pass in the opening moments of the film as they make an arduous journey to Lear's castle to hear his decree. France and Cordelia are married on the shore in front of a wooden crucifix before they embark for France. On the heath, Edgar lifts clothes from a scarecrow who, when stripped, appears as an image of the naked Christ. The shirt Edgar takes is a piece of 'looped and windowed raggedness' (3.4.31) that he will later remove from his shoulders to help tie together the two twigs of a cross that he plants to mark his father's grave. The film privileges this piece of loosely woven cloth by having the opening and closing credits projected on it. In almost every narrative facet, Kozintsev's film is less brutal and more spiritual than Brook's – except in its treatment of the Fool.

The actor who plays the Fool, Oleg Dahl, seems trapped between boy and man. He is all skin and bones with deep sunken eyes, a shaved head, a wide mouth and huge ears. As Kozintsev comments, 'He is the boy from Auschwitz whom they forced to play the violin in an orchestra of dead men; and beat him so that he should play merrier tunes. He has childlike tormented eyes.'[8] The film associates the Fool with two sounds – the bells on his ankles and the plaintive wail of the clarinet. The film is framed by those sounds. The clarinet's melancholy wail is the first sound we hear as the film cuts from the credits to the laborious progression of Lear's subjects making their way to his castle. Then before we meet Lear or glimpse the Fool we hear the sound of bells and then laughter from behind a closed door. When the door opens we see Lear and the Fool playing with a lady's mask fashioned out of a mop, suggesting a social world of artifice and hypocrisy soon to be exploded by Cordelia's stubborn refusal to follow flattery with flattery. Moments later, when Lear sits before a roaring fire in the throne room, we see his robes move and the Fool's head pop up from under them. The bond between them seems strong and genuine. Yet after the violent family quarrel that ends with Lear's bolting off to Goneril's, Kozintsev's camera pans the long line of Lear's hundred knights, his caged falcons and his hunting dogs straining on their leads and we discover the Fool, his hands bound, being led by a rope around his neck, included with this retinue. On the journey itself the camera twice provides us with the sad image of the Fool being treated as a dog, a verbal image Kozintsev lifts from the text to remind us, at least at the beginning, that however much Lear enjoys the Fool's company, he regards him with the same indifference he does his hunting dogs and his hundred knights.

Kozintsev had to find his Fool in his own culture, not Shakespeare's. Books about fools and fooling were not of help, as Kozintsev discovered:

> One must take away from the role of the Fool everything that is associated with clownery. There should be no grimaces, funny faces, no chequered costume, no coxcomb cap. And a little rattle is also unnecessary. There should be no eccentricities, not the slightest kind of virtuosity in the singing

and dancing. The most amazing situation then appears: he is laughed at not because he is a Fool but because he speaks the truth. He is a village idiot – or rather they think he is an idiot.[9]

Kozintsev finds his Fool in Dostoyevsky. He's the village idiot; he's the holy fool. He's laughed at for being poor and debased and powerless and for speaking the truth. And as Lear's Fool knows, to speak the truth to power is dangerous: 'Truth's a dog must to kennel. He must be whipped out, when Lady Brach may stand by th'fire and stink' (1.4.97–8). Here is the image that resonated with Kozintsev as he came to understand the Fool in relationship to the powerful: 'They think nothing is funnier than the truth. They laugh at the truth, kick truth with their spurs for amusement and relegate truth to the doghouse in order to make it a laughing stock. The fool is like a dog. He snaps like a dog.'[10] And there is Kozintsev's Fool being marched along, rope about his neck, with the dogs.

Following Shakespeare's text, the Fool disappears after the hovel scene when he has vowed 'to go to bed at noon' (3.6.41). But Kozintsev brings him back twice, most tellingly in the last powerful image of his film. After Cordelia is hanged and Lear dies, they are placed on a straw litter and are carried back across the castle courtyard where the ravages of the battle are still evident: dead bodies are scattered everywhere, fires still blaze, black smoke swirls through the air, and we hear the jingle of the fool's bells and the sound of his crying. He sits, dressed in rags, along the path the bearers of Lear and Cordelia are following and as they pass him, one of the soldiers raises his boot and kicks him in the back and the Fool topples over. This is one of the few Kott-inspired moments in the film and a brilliant image of the Grand Mechanism at work, wheeling from one destructive cycle to the next.[11] But Kozintsev is not Kott, for in his film the Fool does not remain in the gutter but rights himself and begins to play on his pipe and we hear the same melancholy notes from the clarinet that we heard at the very beginning of the film. And in the rear of the frame we see some people beginning to clear up the ravages of war and a man raise a fallen timber from the ground as the rebuilding begins. For Kozintsev, man can be defeated but not silenced. Man the maker begins to rebuild his world as man the artist puts his pipe to his lips and plays.

Shostakovich's music for Kozintsev's *Lear* is best known for its powerful expression of scenic and thematic extremes in the film: contrasts between power and dispossession, interior and exterior settings, binaries of plot and character. The composer's use of orchestral colours, vivid solo and ensemble effects, striking dynamic and rhythmic contrasts are inseparable from action and image on screen. Less well recognized is the way in which Shostakovich's music for the Fool mirrors the way in which Kozintsev's conception of the character reflects and shapes the film. The Fool's music not only tracks the character but enlarges his role, especially *after* he disappears from Shakespeare's text. The Fool's clarinet speaks as an aural frame for the beginning and ending of the film, and in between undergoes a transformation in mood and medium (from instrumental to choral) after the Fool's textual disappearance. In the film the Fool returns first as silent witness to the reunion of Lear and Cordelia before their capture by Edmund's army, then again at the end, voiced by his rustic pipe (as before a clarinet on the soundtrack) after the Fool's textual disappearance.

At this point the Fool has become the collective voice of the film and his final image carries also a more specific historical reference to the film's collective makers: director, composer, script writer. As the Fool picks up his pipe and plays after being kicked aside by the funeral cortege, we witness the resurgent energies of Kozintsev, Shostakovich and Pasternak kicking back, whether against new or old dispensations.

Kozintsev understands that Lear's world is not redeemed by his heroic descent into madness and subsequent recognition of his own complicity in the world's injustice, nor by his eventual reunion with Cordelia where he longs for his daughter to 'forget/ And forgive' (4.6.81–2) him for his unjust behaviour. The boot in the Fool's back is the film's bitter reminder that not only has Lear's life been destroyed but his spirit has been trampled upon as well. There is no music at the end of Brook's *Lear* – just an empty frame. By contrast, the Fool's music at the end of Kozintsev's film is the acknowledgement of suffering and loss but it surely signals something more than a silent empty space and suggests at least the possibility of tragic recognition and catharsis.

Akira Kurosawa's *Ran* (1985)

Both Brook and Kozintsev resist the epic impulse in their *Lear* films; Kurosawa embraces it. His Japanese version of the Lear story is painted on a vast 70 mm canvas in vital primary colours: reds, blues, yellows and greens dominate. Brook and Kozintsev favour the close-up, but Kurosawa's *Ran* is filled with long shots where outline and image trump body and face. He turns Lear's three daughters into sons to heighten masculine aggression and the struggle for military power, though he follows Shakespeare in making the third son (Saburô) the Cordelia figure in his ultimate loyalty to his father and his initial refusal to become caught up in the power struggle between his older brothers.

While the existence of the fool and court jester is an established historical reality in the East (especially in China and India), Japanese culture,
according to Beatrice Otto's exhaustive study of the fool figure, has not
yielded a similar historical tradition.[12] Not finding the fool in the *jidai-geki*
genre or in the feudal *Sengoku Jidai* period allows Kurosawa to make a bold
cultural and artistic move. A few central characters in *Ran* are imagined as
figures from Noh drama with their faces contorted into static Noh masks.
Hidetora (the Lear figure) is one of them. But Kurosawa provides him with
a fool created from modern rather than classical elements. Kurosawa
refashions Shakespeare's Fool into an androgynous entertainer who min-
gles song and dance and parable. He gives the character a name, Kyoami,
rather than calling him by his function. That name is roughly translated as
'everyday friend', which speaks to Kyoami's quotidian desire to please and
entertain rather than to mirror or mock the samurai warrior code.[13]

Kyoami is further humanized by being played by the transvestite actor
and pop star Shinnosuke Ikehata (known to his fans as 'Peter' for his Pan-
like qualities). Kyoami moves with a lively grace and his countenance is as
mild as Hidetora's is harsh; his face and skin are as smooth and clear as
a baby's; his hair is pulled up in a ponytail while his master's face is lined by
age – a condition that radically accelerates as the film progresses: his unruly
white hair stands straight up and his movements become progressively
awkward and disjointed. In a film conceived as a riot of colour, Kyoami's
costumes stand out. Unlike the sixteenth-century robes and military
armour worn by the other men in the film, Kyoami's clothes might well
find themselves on a modern 'style' runway in Paris or New York. In the
opening scene, Kyoami is wearing a red, yellow and blue (the colours of the
Ichimonji clan) striped top and red balloon pants. Later he wears a red and
green plaid top tucked into white pants with red socks and finally he is
dressed in a modified white kimono robe decorated with red, yellow and
blue butterflies.

Kurosawa's cinematic adaptation of *Lear* is transformative in multiple
and radical ways, and the figure of Kyoami embodies and dramatizes our
perspective on these transformations. Music is a cue to the way we share the
Fool's perspective. In the opening boar hunting scene that prefigures
Hidetora's abdication, Kyoami performs an antic comic fable about
a rabbit. The fable is preceded by a very brief musical prelude: a cuckoo
call, then a passage of high-pitched blurry woodwind notes which is
intercut by bell-like sounds played by tiny cymbals. While this music
plays (and it captures everyone's attention as though Nature herself were
speaking), those plaintive sounds seem to emanate from the mountains

themselves and provide an overture and transcendent perspective for the rabbit fable. Having captured and directed his listeners' attention, Kyoami performs his fable as a forecast of the power struggle which is to explode from Hidetora's decision to divide up his kingdom.

In contrast to the Eastern folk-like quality of the fable music, an extended uninterrupted orchestral score accompanies the war scenes. Here an expanded orchestra employing Mahlerian effects of instrumental colour – especially horns and woodwinds – and with Mahlerian narrative intensity, accompanies the battle for Azuzu Castle. In the midst of the battle, the score suddenly vanishes from the soundtrack and we hear again the Fool's music of the mountains as Hidetora emerges from the burning castle and moves out into the desert. Thus the rabbit's fable is confirmed musically as a comic or ironic forecast of the civil war and catastrophe that follow. Kyoami's dumb show, its music and his character embody and enact the proposition posed by this Japanese adaptation of *Lear*: trade places, East for West, male for female, folk instruments for full orchestra, Kurosawa for Shakespeare, and which is the justice, which the thief? Radical reversals raised by *Ran* are epitomized in the composite figure and function of the transvestite Fool and his music.

He weeps for his lord when the old king is in his rage and then again in the penultimate beat of the film where Saburô is shot in the back after he has rescued Hidetora and they are riding together towards Saburô's victorious troops. Saburô falls from his horse; Hidetora quickly dismounts and covers his son's body with his own and Kyoami mirrors his action as he cries out: 'Is there no God or Buddha in this world? Damnation! God and Buddha are nothing but mischievous urchins! Are they so bored in heaven that they enjoy watching men die like worms? Damn God! Is it so amusing to see and hear human beings cry and scream.'[14] Here Kurosawa and Kyoami evoke and modify Gloucester's famous utterance of cynical despair: 'As flies to wanton boys are we to th'gods;/They kill us for their sport' (4.1.36–7). Kyoami refuses to be matter-of-fact about cruelty and injustice. If it is human to suffer then it is also human to cry and complain. Kurosawa makes the figure of the Fool the most fully human in the world of *Ran*; Kyoami remains a vivid colourful and gentle force for life surrounded by a barren landscape of death and destruction. He cares amid chaos and is, until the bitter end, a bright spark of life against the dark.

The long and bending cultural arc which emerges from Kurosawa's gender-bending Fool is all the more striking for the absence of prototypes in Japanese culture. In Kyoami, Kurosawa created a figure that helps the film to bridge the medieval with the modern, East with West, passion with compassion, male with female and the quotidian with the epic. Kyoami is the crucial link between Hidetora's patriarchal power and his paternal vulnerability. Who else can weep for the irascible old man?

Each of these films creates a fool who becomes a talisman for the approach each filmmaker takes to Shakespeare's text. Jack MacGowran provides us with a deadpan Irish imp with Beckett's stoic impassivity and brings suggestions of our wasteland to Shakespeare's; working from the other side of the curtain (so to speak), Grigori Kozintsev gives us a holy fool who pipes his way to survival and potential renewal in the apocalypse which ends the film; and Kurosawa reimagines the Fool as a transvestite entertainer placed at the centre of an epic tale of slaughter and destruction – the only figure to survive this apocalypse with his humanity fully exhibited and expressed. None of these fools is fashioned after a Will Somers or even a Feste. Each director finds the suggestion for the Fool in his own age and then transforms that suggestion into each film's signature vision of *Lear's* universe.

Notes

1. See S. Beauman, *The Royal Shakespeare Company: a History of Ten Decades* (Oxford: Oxford University Press, 1982), 238–65.
2. K. S. Rothwell, *A History of Shakespeare on Screen: a Century of Film and Television* (Cambridge: Cambridge University Press, 1999), 151.
3. P. Holland, 'Peter Brook' in P. Holland (ed.), *Brook, Hall, Ninagawa, Lepage*, vol. XVIII of *Great Shakespeareans* (London and New York: Bloomsbury, 2013), 7–46.
4. P. Brook, *The Quality of Mercy* (New York: Theatre Communications Group, 2014), 55.
5. A. Leggatt, *Shakespeare in Performance: 'King Lear'* (Manchester: Manchester University Press, 1991), 96.
6. Leggatt, *King Lear*, 100–1.
7. C. Lehmann, 'Grigori Kozintsev', in M. T. Burnett, C. Lehmann, M. Rippy and R. Wray, *Welles, Kurosawa, Kozintsev, Zeffirelli*, vol. XVII of *Great Shakespeareans* (London and New York: Bloomsbury, 2013), 136.
8. G. Kozintsev, *'King Lear': the Space of Tragedy*, trans. M. Mackintosh (Berkeley: University of California Press, 1977), 72.
9. *Ibid.*
10. *Ibid.*
11. J. Kott, *Shakespeare Our Contemporary* (New York: Anchor Books, 1966), 6–7.
12. B. Otto, *Fools Are Everywhere: the Court Jester around the World* (Chicago: University of Chicago Press, 2010), 239.
13. I want to thank our son Sam, who spent several years working in Japan after college, for this translation.
14. A. Kurosawa, *Ran* (Boston and London: Shambhala, 1986), 99.

WORKS CITED

Beauman, S., *The Royal Shakespeare Company: a History of Ten Decades* (Oxford: Oxford University Press, 1982).

Brook, P., *The Quality of Mercy* (New York: Theatre Communications Group, 2014).

Griggs, Y., *Shakespeare's 'King Lear': the Relationship between Text and Film* (London: Methuen, 2009).

Holland, P., 'Peter Brook' in P. Holland (ed.), *Brook, Hall, Ninagawa, Lepage,* vol. XVIII of *Great Shakespeareans* (London and New York: Bloomsbury, 2013), 7–46.

Jorgens, J., *Shakespeare on Film* (Bloomington: Indiana University Press, 1977).

Kott, J., *Shakespeare Our Contemporary*, trans. B. Taborski (New York: Anchor Books, 1966).

Kozintsev, G., *'King Lear': the Space of Tragedy*, trans. M. Mackintosh (Berkeley: University of California Press, 1977).

Kurosawa. A., *Ran* (Boston and London: Shambhala, 1986).

Leggatt, A., *Shakespeare in Performance: 'King Lear'* (Manchester: Manchester University Press, 1991).

Lehmann, C., 'Grigori Kozintsev', in M. T. Burnett, C. Lehmann, M. Rippy and R. Wray, *Welles, Kurosawa, Kozintsev, Zeffirelli,* vol. XVII of *Great Shakespeareans* (London and New York: Bloomsbury, 2013), 92–140.

Otto, B., *Fools Are Everywhere: the Court Jester around the World* (Chicago: University of Chicago Press, 2010).

Rothwell, K. S., *A History of Shakespeare on Screen: a Century of Film and Television* (Cambridge: Cambridge University Press, 1999).

CHAPTER 3

Wicked Humans and Weeping Buddhas: (Post)humanism and Hell in Kurosawa's Ran

Melissa Croteau

In September 1923, shortly after the Great Kantō Earthquake, Heigo Kurosawa took his 13-year-old younger brother, Akira, to see the devastation around Tokyo. The powerful earthquake, and subsequent fires that ravaged Tokyo, resulted in over 150,000 deaths.[1] Furthermore, Koreans in Japan were bizarrely blamed for the disaster, resulting in 6,000 of them being rounded up and massacred over the following days.[2] Kurosawa remembers thinking, 'This must be the end of the world', and describes a 'burned landscape', punctuated by 'every kind of corpse imaginable'.[3] He thought that 'the lake of blood they say exists in Buddhist hell couldn't possibly be as bad as this'. In this annihilated nightmare-scape, Kurosawa felt they were 'standing at the gates of hell'.[4] Surprisingly, Akira slept soundly that night and his older brother Heigo explained, 'If you shut your eyes to a frightening sight, you end up being frightened. If you look at everything straight on, there is nothing to be afraid of'; Akira then understood, 'It had been an expedition to conquer fear'.[5]

Kurosawa made films that attempt to look at life and its complexity 'straight on', and much of his work can be read as 'expeditions to conquer fear'. However, none of his films forces us to stare into the potential for humans to create hell on earth quite as formidably as *Ran* (1985). Kurosawa's film work has often been praised for its humanism, its affirmation that the human will can make a positive difference in the world when individuals choose to serve others and take responsibility for their communities. While Kurosawa often uses Buddhist symbols to refer to or express this enlightenment, it is a *secular* ethical message of selflessness and sacrifice he is communicating. The superb *Ikiru* (1952) and *Red Beard* (1965) portray two of the most nuanced and poignant humanistic narratives ever to be filmed. However, one does not have to go deeply into his canon to discover the darkness and pessimism that also pervade many of his films. This combination of a grim pessimism punctuated with glimmers of

hope has been labelled a 'unique brand of skeptical humanism',[6] with
Kurosawa even described as a 'posthumanist', one who 'show[s] "care" for
the human, humanness, humanity but also embrace[s] the new plurality
and the new questions that are put to humanism, anti-humanism, posthumanism, even transhumanism alike: questions of human survival in late
modern, global, techno-scientific hypercapitalist societies'.[7] 'Above all',
argues Stefan Herbrechter, posthumanism 'wants to confront humanism
with its "specters" – the inhuman, the superhuman, and the nonhuman in
all its invented, constructed or actual forms'.[8] This posthumanist perspective – which challenges ideals of ethical and existential humanism as well as
religious ideologies – provides insight into the films of Kurosawa that offer
unblinking views of a world corrupted by human violence and greed,
leaving no escape for the good, enlightened or pure. It is, perhaps, no
accident that three of the darkest Kurosawa films are his adaptations of
Shakespeare tragedies: *Throne of Blood* (1957), *The Bad Sleep Well* (1960)
and *Ran* (1985), adaptations of *Macbeth*, *Hamlet* and *King Lear*, respectively. Adapting a canonical Western text potentially supplies the filmmaker and his audiences with more distance from the diegetic horror, an
effect Kurosawa also achieves by employing formal Japanese Noh theatre
elements in *Throne of Blood* and *Ran*. In Shakespeare, Kurosawa found an
unflinching gaze that refuses to look away, particularly in *Lear*, which he
saw as Shakespeare's most 'cosmic' play.[9] Andy Mousley avers that the play
evokes 'a *caring* posthumanist scepticism, a scepticism which not only
questions our investments in the human but also generates concern, to
the point of angst, about the human condition'.[10] The brutality and beauty
of *Ran* majestically depicts this trepidation about humanity and its (im)
possible future. In *Ran*, as in *Lear*, there is no '"humanist" celebration' of
personal 'freedom' or 'agency' in the absence of supernatural coherence or
purpose;[11] there is only the revelation of man as a 'poor, bare, forked
animal' (3.4.96). Kurosawa saw *Ran* as his 'best' work; and it was through
Ran that he intended to communicate his final statement about the
cosmos.[12]

His work is famously didactic, though he believed that the messages in
his films are not 'very obvious'.[13] Yet Kurosawa's oeuvre reveals that it is
imbued with philosophical, even moral, lessons about the nature and
responsibilities of humanity. Kurosawa kept silent about any personal
religious beliefs, but encouraged others to seek him out in his films:
'There is nothing that says more about its creator than the work itself',
further declaring, 'The root of any film project for me is this inner need to
express something'.[14] As an auteur who co-wrote and edited nearly every

film he made, as well as being intimately involved with the production design and music, Kurosawa integrated all aspects of his productions such that every detail of his cinema serves to illuminate the essence of his worldview, which was richly complex and dynamic over the fifty years of his career. However, salient patterns can be traced, as James Mark Shields observes: 'Taken as a whole, Kurosawa's films display a deep and abiding humanism, yet one that refuses to get lost in lofty ideals or otherworldly realms. It is a humanism that pushes on in spite of the facts, including, most importantly, the blurred lines that exist between right and wrong, good and evil, friend and foe, heaven and hell'.[15] Evident here is the posthumanist interrogation of more mainstream humanistic views, such as faith in human rationality or goodness. Stephen Teo also recognizes that Kurosawa's moral messaging only 'superficially conforms' to the expression of humanistic ideals, and asserts that there is an essential dialectic between didacticism and violence in Kurosawa's work: most of his films use violence (of various kinds) as a counterpoint to human compassion.[16] This provides evidence that, despite the blurring of distinctions between good and evil in Kurosawa's work, there is no Buddhist denial of dualism, which posits that there are no essential differences. Although this doctrine pervades the medieval Japanese Noh drama the director so loved and emulated, Kurosawa clearly believes there *is* a difference between virtue and wickedness. However, he is not interested in notions of an auspicious rebirth or an afterlife in a heavenly realm, such as the paradise sought by Pure Land Buddhists who worship the Amida (Amitabha) Buddha of Infinite Light, a prominent symbolic presence in *Ran*. Stephen Prince reminds us that Kurosawa 'both affirms and rejects the principles of Zen': he shares the Buddhist view that existence in this world is defined by 'universal suffering' in an 'eternal cycle of pain' (see Buddhism's First Noble Truth); however, Kurosawa does *not* believe the Buddhist idea that human will or desire is the cause of that suffering and, therefore, should be replaced by serene non-attachment and emptiness (see the Second and Third Noble Truths).[17] Instead, Kurosawa's work bespeaks the compelling need for the individual to transcend the unending cycles of violence that plague *this* world by taking an active role. The path to this sort of enlightenment is always depicted as fraught with thorny obstacles, beset by malignant forces both internal and external; the rewards for virtue are often uncertain or, in his most pessimistic films, denied entirely. Kurosawa communicates this message through narratives of compassionate engagement with individuals or communities, which display hope, qualified and flawed as it may be; however, he also made films, both *jidai-geki* (period films) and *gendai-geki* (contemporary films), that present a hellish world where there is no escape from the horror of human violence – such as *Ran*.

Kurosawa worked on the script for nearly a decade before obtaining funding from a French financer. The Japanese title *Ran* can be translated several ways: chaos, confusion, rebellion, disintegration and desolation, both macrocosmic – in the body politic and the 'great globe itself' – and microcosmic – in the family and the human soul, themes central to *Lear*.[18] Yet Kurosawa was first inspired by an episode in medieval Japanese history, the 'legend of Motonari Mori [1497–1571], whose three sons are admired in Japan as the ideal of family loyalty'.[19] James Goodwin notes that this story inspired the first scene, in which the Great Lord Hidetora tries to teach his three sons an object lesson about strength in unity by giving each one an arrow and telling him to break it, which each does easily. Hidetora then hands each a bundle of three arrows and asks them to break the three together, which cannot be done in the legend; nor can it be done by Hidetora's two eldest sons, but the youngest, Saburô, splits them apart with his knee. This demonstrates the irony of Motonari Mori's well-known 'political maxim that a leader should not trust anyone, particularly not family members'.[20] Goodwin thus notes that '[t]hough plot elements, important incidents, and central metaphors are drawn from Shakespeare's tragedy, the textual treatment of adapted material is governed by Kurosawa's original conception of an inversion to Japanese ideals of family and political loyalty'.[21] *Ran* is a pageant replete with symbols and abstractions ironically designating unity, balance and Buddhist non-attachment in a world collapsing under the weight of human ambition; here, icons have lost their power to cohere and now serve only to deconstruct or mock the ideals they represent. In *Ran*, Kurosawa illustrates that the inverted history is the most honest about human existence; it is the truth that must be faced.

Kurosawa set *Ran* in sixteenth-century Japan, during the Age of the Civil Wars (*Sengoku Jidai*), an era of battling warlords, internecine struggles, murder and treachery.[22] The lack of a central political government caused a descent into chaos. Kurosawa set four of his films during this period, including *Throne of Blood* (1957), clearly sensing a connection between his own historical moment and this vicious century of upheaval. In keeping with this era's culture and with his Motonari Mori source, Kurosawa transforms Lear's three daughters into sons. *Ran* opens with a poetically filmed scene of a boar hunt in the grassy mountains surrounding Mt. Fuji. After the hunt, the brutal Great Lord of the region, Hidetora Ichimonji, announces to his sons and two local warlords, Fujimaki and Ayabe, that he is handing over his power to his eldest son, Taro. He instructs his younger sons, Jiro and Saburô, to support their brother's rule and thereby defend the honour and dominance of the Ichimonji family. When the youngest son voices his disapproval of his father's decision, Saburô is banished, along with Tango (an analogue for *Lear*'s Kent), a loyal lord who defends Saburô. As in *Lear*, when Hidetora goes to live with his eldest son in the First Castle, his son and daughter-in-law – the wicked, vengeful Lady Kaede – show him and his entourage profound disrespect, so he moves on to Jiro's Second Castle, where his devoutly Buddhist daughter-in-law Sué receives him with honour, but his son's contempt leads him to depart in anger. After some confused meandering, realizing his desperate straits, he decides to stay in the Third Castle, which is empty due to Saburô's banishment. Taro's and Jiro's soldiers surround his retinue there and wage a bloody battle against Hidetora, slaughtering everyone with him, warriors and concubines alike, in a gory, infernal spectacle. In the midst of this, Jiro's advisor murders Taro so Jiro can take the role of Great Lord. Hidetora survives this savagery, his attempts at *seppuku* (ritual suicide) having failed, but it pushes him into madness; he emerges from the Third Castle to wander like a ghost on the stormy volcanic plains. His fool, Kyoami, and Tango find him there, and they retreat from the storm into a small, poor hut, which they discover is inhabited by Lady Sué's brother, Tsurumaru, whose parents Hidetora had killed and whose eyes he had gouged out in exchange for allowing him to live. When Hidetora discovers the identity of their humble host, he flees in terror, thinking his sins are haunting him. Wandering again in the open, Hidetora's madness increases as Kyoami tries to care for him while they take shelter in the ruins of Azusa Castle, the seat of Sué and Tsurumaru's family, which Hidetora had destroyed. The wreckage he created now engulfs him, representing the ruination of his life. Meanwhile, the widowed Lady Kaede, whose family also was annihilated by Hidetora, seduces Jiro and manipulates him in her quest to exterminate the entire Ichimonji clan. Saburô, who has taken refuge with Fujimaki, hears of his father's fate and madness, returns, and tries to save Hidetora, inadvertently sparking a battle between Fujimaki's and Jiro's troops, which allows Ayabe to launch a surprise attack on the First Castle. The implacable violence spirals into utter chaos. When Saburô finally finds Hidetora on the dark plains, they enjoy a poignant reunion, very like that between Lear and Cordelia, in which Hidetora's wits are restored. However, the happiness is short-lived, as Saburô is shot when he and Hidetora are riding away from the devastated Ichimonji-owned region. Hidetora dies of heartbreak, hunched woefully over Saburô's body. Lady Sué is assassinated by Jiro's henchmen set on by Lady Kaede.

In the final images of the film, we see the small, solitary figure of blind Tsurumaru on the ruined ramparts of Azusa Castle, inching towards a precipice, a symbol of doomed humanity.

Ran is told visually and aurally through symbol and metaphor, much like the Noh theatre that inspired it, and, as in Noh theatre, Kurosawa purposely departs from realism in order to confront viewers with a truth about humanity. The director stated that he allowed this film to 'ripen' in his mind for years, until it had become 'simpler' and 'clearer',[23] distilled into a 'morality play' in which a distantiated audience is 'looking down upon the folly of men' as it views human events from the position of impotent heavenly deities.[24] In keeping with Kurosawa's inversion of the Motonari Mori legend and his transformation of Lear into a bloody tyrant, the director takes the ritualistic, extremely formal Noh theatre, created to entertain, comfort and indoctrinate the samurai class, and subverts it by breaking apart its structures on several levels in order to undermine Noh's feudalistic and religious worldview and reveal the calamitous consequences of its philosophies. Violence wrought by feudal warriors leads only to disintegration, suffering and annihilation in a world where no hope can be placed in a posthumous paradise or karmic reincarnation. While Noh plays preach *individual* karma and tell tales of warriors and others redeemed from hellish torment, *Ran* shows that even the innocent, such as Saburô and Sué, suffer for the nation's irrepressible bellicosity. The karmic cause-and-effect logic does not work for these characters in a world of uncontained chaos. Indeed, *Ran* does not present us with the closed, *mandala*-like structure of *Throne of Blood*, which contains its 'bloody deeds' by framing them within a Buddhist chorus that chants the film's moral message. In *Ran*, as Stephen Prince asserts, 'the frame is burst. Hell is everywhere'.[25] Donald Richie notes the prevalence of circular or spiral forms in Kurosawa's work and observes that *Ran* deviates from this pattern: its 'compositions ... consist largely of *broken* circles and *unstable* triangles'.[26] The formal structures of Noh are broken apart.

Noh stage design mirrors the space roped off for the earlier theophanic field rituals (*dengaku*), reflecting its historical origins; the stage is a sacred space representing a microcosm, or centre, of the world. In *Ran*, this centre no longer holds; all is chaos. Kurosawa explodes Noh's formal boundaries in the opening scene, in which Hidetora and his party share a feast while sitting ceremonially inside a rectangular enclosure on top of an open hill, where Hidetora plans to stage his abdication.[27] This enclosure is formed by walls of tall bunting displaying the Ichimonji family crest – a golden insignia of a full sun above a crescent moon, a common Buddhist symbol of unity (clearly used ironically throughout the film). Instead of proceeding with the ceremony, Hidetora invites his fool, Kyoami, to sing a song from kyōgen, the comical interludes performed between Noh plays, and then falls asleep. As Sam Crowl elaborates in the present volume, it is significant that Kyoami is played by Peter, a cross-dressing celebrity in Japan, expressing a transgression of gender boundaries. Kyoami is interrupted by Saburô, who sees the song as a crude allegory of Hidetora's predatory nature. The kyōgen is out of place here, as it disrupts the ritual flow and tone of the Noh dramatic line and potentially erodes the puissant, dignified façade of the warrior (Hidetora) at the centre of this story. This deviant insertion of kyōgen elements in this epic tragedy via Kyoami persists through the rest of the film, reminding us of the absurdity of the violent samurai code. Hidetora's embarrassed sons and guests leave the enclosure and, later, the Great Lord erupts through its borders, terrified by a dream he has had of an open, empty wilderness. Kathy Howlett suggests that, in breaking out of this 'sacred space', Hidetora 'literally bursts outside the frame of the samurai enclosure', rupturing the confines of the Noh performance space as well as the figurative ones of the samurai codes (121).[28]

Later, when Hidetora has entered the blind Tsurumaru's hut to take shelter from the storm, the mad old man breaks through one of the hut's flimsy walls to escape from the guilt his victim represents to him, once again bursting out of an enclosure, but this time rushing out onto a barren plain resembling his earlier nightmare. What Hidetora does not understand is that hell has no boundaries in our chaotic world, as evidenced by the many shots of monumental castle gates in the film, the opening and closing of which samurai warriors desperately demand but to no avail. Salvation and protection are impossible; infernality lies both within and without the physical structures as well as human souls.

Tsurumaru's character is adapted from two blind young men in Noh tradition, Shuntoku-maru in *Yoroboshi* (meaning lowly blind beggar) and Semimaru in the play named after him. Interestingly, in the five groups of Noh plays – those centring on gods, warriors, women, frenzy/madness and demons (performed strictly in this order) – *Yoroboshi* and *Semimaru* are both fourth-group Noh (frenzy) plays that fall into the subcategory of *kyōran-mono: kyō* meaning 'mad' and *ran* meaning 'disorder', as in the film's title.[29] The complex connection between blindness and madness that can be seen in *Yoroboshi, Semimaru* and *Lear* is skilfully woven into *Ran*, in which tragedy and trauma can cause madness and blindness, both literal and figurative. Although madness might be perceived as an appropriate response to the horrors of this world, John Collick asserts, 'Hidetora's madness and Tsurumaru's sightless retreat from the world (both of which are traditionally associated with spiritual transcendence and reconciliation) are wholly inappropriate weapons against the tragic violence of feudal Japan'.[30] In both *Yoroboshi* and *Semimaru*, the young men have been exiled by their fathers but, in keeping with the rule that *kyōran-mono* end happily, Shuntoku-maru ends up joyfully reunited with his penitent father.[31] Semimaru, on the other hand, is briefly reunited with his mad sister Sakagami, as Tsurumaru is with his sister Sué, and then they part in great sorrow, a denouement unique in the *kyōran-mono* group. The only comfort for Semimaru is his strong Buddhist faith. Donald Keene calls *Semimaru* 'perhaps the most tragic play' of the entire Noh repertory,[32] rendering it an apropos intertext for *Ran* and highlighting the film's rejection of the formal logic of the *kyōran-mono* by refusing to take solace in human reunion. It ends with the stark extreme long shot of the helpless, solitary figure of blind Tsurumaru in the ruins of his family as the preternatural (almost nuclear) orange sunset fades behind him.

The first three groups of Noh plays – god, warrior and woman plays – are the most formal and prescribed, while the *zatsu*, or miscellaneous, Noh of the fourth group has the greatest diversity in regard to content in that it includes both 'visional/supernatural' and 'realistic' plays and various types of protagonists (*shite*). Unsurprisingly, Kurosawa's inspiration in *Ran* comes primarily from the less structured fourth group, which, along with the fifth group, carries the *zatsu* label with its connotation of being 'unpurified of worldly things'.[33] Though Kurosawa has been inspired by the least 'contained' type of Noh in form and content, he subverts even that. While most fourth Noh are realistic (*genzai*) pieces, including *Yoroboshi* and *Semimaru*, Kurosawa portrays a bleak, non-realistic world populated by a phantasmal, postapocalyptic Hidetora and a spectral, gender-liminal Tsurumaru, who rejects belief in Amida Buddha despite his despair. The director turns Noh 'realism' into a ghost world, more *mugen* (phantasmal) than *genzai*. In addition, the five-play Noh sequence, when performed in traditional order, presents a metanarrative of human redemption, 'delineat[ing] man in innocence, fall, repentance, redemption, and final glory', but Kurosawa leaves us in the typical fourth Noh realization that 'hell exists in our own world' without resolving this crisis with the fifth Noh ritual defeat of a supernatural evil.[34] There is no *deus ex machina* that can help us; humans are responsible for the evil that rules the world. Tango, after the Great Lord dies, thus chides the fool Kyoami for railing against the deities, who 'kill us for their sport' (*Lear* 4.1.37):

Stop it! Do not curse the gods. It is they who weep. In every age they've watched us tread the path of evil, unable to live without killing each other. They can't save us from ourselves. Stop crying! This is the way of the world! Men live not for joy but for sorrow, not for peace but for suffering.

Kurosawa directly states *Ran*'s bleak theology here. Prince argues that, whereas Kurosawa's earlier films directly critique social and cultural problems, '[w]hat was once a materialist program of reform has become instead a transcendental lament'.[35] Prince, among others, connects this shift in worldview to changes in Kurosawa's cinematic style in *Ran*, particularly a pulling back of the camera, distancing the viewer from the hostile human world. This 'strategy of withdrawal' results in a plethora of long shots and long takes, along with far fewer close-ups.[36] Critics have noted Kurosawa's desire to present this cinematic narrative from the perspective of the 'gods'.[37] Kurosawa declared, '[S]ome of the essential scenes of this film are based on my wondering how God and Buddha, if they actually exist, perceive this human life, this mankind stuck in the same behavior patterns'.[38] This distancing of the camera operates in conjunction with the cinematically incongruous Noh elements, which display powerful signifiers ripped from their signifieds, to achieve a distantiation of the viewer. For example, the stunning long shots of clouds throughout the film remind us that we are watching from above, mournful but impotent to stop the madness. This point of view aligns with the concept of posthumanism, the term itself indicating a distancing and defamiliarization of the human and a critique of humanism.[39] The most poignant example of this is the gruesome battle scene at the Third Castle, the cinematography and editing of which puts us in the position of the gods gazing down in horror and sorrow. In the screenplay, Kurosawa, who is usually sparing in his descriptions in scripts, describes the monstrous scene in vivid, metaphorically and religiously loaded language:

> A terrible scroll of Hell is shown depicting the fall of the castle. There are no real sounds as the scroll unfolds like a daytime nightmare. It is a scene of human evildoing, the way of the demonic Asura, *as seen by the Buddha in tears*. The music superimposed on these pictures is, like the Buddha's heart, measured in beats of profound anguish, the chanting of a melody full of sorrow that begins like sobbing and rises gradually as it is repeated, like karmic cycles, then finally sounds like *the wailing of countless Buddhas*.[40]

During several minutes of this battle scene, all diegetic sound disappears and is replaced by a tempestuous, discordant symphonic score that Kurosawa commissioned Toru Takemitsu to write, dictating that it should resemble and 'go beyond' Gustav Mahler's bittersweet composition *The Song of the Earth*, which shares many dark themes with *Ran*; Kurosawa told him that, like the cinematographic point of view, 'The music, too, must come from the sky!'[41] Musicologist Kendra Leonard connects the disturbing undulations of this score to the harrowing scene it accompanies, expressing both the weeping of the celestial onlookers (the audience) and Hidetora's state of mind: 'Represented by a never resolving seventh-scale degree, Hidetora's search for suicide, meaning, or stability is futile; quite literally, he cannot reach the "final"'.[42] Thus, Takemitsu's score gives us another broken circle that is not redeemed by a resolution. The grief of these spectatorial Buddhas reflects Kurosawa's pain, hearkening back to his traumatic exposure to cataclysm as a child and his many close encounters with destruction during the Second World War. He reflected, 'Maybe it is my vivid memory and unblinking gaze that makes me frightened of it [violence]. Or maybe it's my fear that compels me to stare straight on'.[43]

Scholars have debated the humanist and transcendent content of *Ran*. Many assert that its salient sacred elements ironically underscore the hopelessness of a world where cycles of human violence proceed endlessly, while a few argue that these same elements convey the potential for redemption in a bleak world. Collick, for instance, contends that in the last shots – featuring Tsurumaru dropping a scroll of Amida Buddha to the rocks below as he wavers on the precipice of doom – we see Kurosawa optimistically 'suggesting that engagement with reality is preferable to spiritual escapism', offering a Nietzschean reading,[44] despite the fact that Kurosawa's final word in the screenplay is 'Wretchedness!'[45] Kenneth Nordin analyses the Buddhist symbolism, concluding that these symbols together 'point to the Buddhist path of enlightenment' and 'stand as powerful counterpoints to the chaos and destruction upon which the movie is built'.[46] Kurosawa's own reflections on the film have been used to support both these positions. Kurosawa commented that Hidetora is on a journey towards transcendence: 'Forced ultimately to confront the consequences of his misdeeds, [Hidetora] is driven mad. But only by confronting his evil head-on can he transcend it and begin to struggle toward virtue'.[47] Shortly after releasing *Ran*, Kurosawa explained that when he was younger he believed his films could make a genuine impact on larger social issues but, older and wiser now, he had changed his mind:

> I believe that the world would not change even if I made a direct statement . . . Moreover, the world will not change unless we steadily change human nature itself and our very way of thinking. We have to exorcise the

essential evil in human nature, rather than presenting concrete solutions to problems or directly depicting social problems. Therefore, my films might have become more philosophical.[48]

Andrew Spitznas has argued that Kurosawa's work from 1965 on – when he began to make fewer films and to struggle to find financing – bears the marks of Kurosawa's traumatic experiences, particularly in their fluctuation between utter dejection and faith in humanity:

> survivors of trauma often lose their ability to trust in other people or in one's ability to effect meaningful change in one's own life or surroundings ... Recovery from trauma often involves a lifelong battle between a sense of effective agency and the death grip of powerlessness. [In] Kurosawa's late films, this type of oscillation between hope and despair in his work, so common in the life of trauma survivors, ... become[s] evident.[49]

This explains the divergence of Kurosawa's own views about *Ran*, which he believed to be 'less pessimistic' and 'less tragic' than *Lear* because 'Hidetora reflects on his past and regrets it'.[50] (One certainly could argue that Lear does, too, though he is not depicted as the bloodthirsty tyrant Hidetora is.) Kurosawa intimates, here, that there is hope for humanity, or at least for an individual human, who can look honestly at the past, take responsibility for it and move forward. This resonates with existential and ethical humanism; however, in *Ran*, survival is not the focus and humans are not fundamentally good; nor is human evil the fault of a corrupt system. Instead, humans make choices, but the freedom to choose is not an unadulterated good either. There is truth in Spitznas's assertion that '[t]he theology of *Ran* wavers, as it does for many trauma survivors, between an angry atheism and a belief in a weeping God who is largely powerless to change humanity's course';[51] however, this combination of rage and despondence does not erase the potential for transcendence that one sees in the characters of Saburô, Tango, Sué and Kyoami, who all look directly at the truth – albeit through very different lenses – yet choose to ignore the rules of the ruthless world, acting sacrificially instead to protect and preserve the life and dignity of others. Even the wicked Hidetora, Kurosawa contends, transcends evil by confronting his own viciousness head-on. There is no upward or downward transcendence, no movement towards a supernatural heaven or hell. Hell – evoked so often in the screenplay and in the imagery of the film – is here. Thornton has argued that in Japanese historical epics, 'Buddhism ... lends meaning and significance to the battlefield itself: it is a picture of hell; it is meant to horrify people and turn them to religion',[52] but Kurosawa employs visions of the

Buddhist netherworld for a different purpose. Richie affirms that *Ran*'s 'didactic message' is that life, indeed, is a hopeless 'tragedy'; however, understanding this 'is enough. We do not need to be freed from this truth'.[53] *Ran*, in all its beauty and horror, tells us that we have the power *not* to turn away from suffering. We can choose to face the inevitable hells on earth and look at them straight on, but this courage will not 'save' us, nor will it make us heroes. However, it has the potential to inspire us to be more human(e). The various modes of distantiation and abstraction help us comprehend the significance of this tragic pageant and, perhaps, lead us to recognize that 'we are "not yet" completely and irreversibly "post"-human'.[54] If there is any hope attached to this film, it is most likely to be located in the viewer rather than the thing itself. Watching from a distance, we may gain the courage to refuse to feed the fires of violence and human degradation. The potential to conquer fear in this life lies in that brave gaze.

Notes

1. C. Goto-Jones, *Modern Japan: a Very Short Introduction* (Oxford: Oxford University Press, 2009), 76.
2. A. Spitznas, 'The Flayed Hare: Trauma and Hope in the Late Films of Kurosawa', in K. R. Morefield (ed.), *Faith and Spirituality in the Masters of World Cinema* (Newcastle-upon-Tyne: Cambridge Scholars Publishing, 2011), 12.
3. A. Kurosawa, *Something like an Autobiography*, trans. A. E. Bock (New York: Random House, 1983), 50, 52–3.
4. *Ibid.*, 53.
5. *Ibid.*, 54.
6. J. M. Shields, 'Kurosawa, Akira (1910–1998)', in E. M. Mazur (ed.), *Encyclopedia of Religion and Film* (Santa Barbara: ABC-CLIO, 2011), 279.
7. S. Herbrechter, 'Introduction: Shakespeare ever after', in S. Herbrechter and I. Callus (eds.), *Posthumanist Shakespeares* (New York: Palgrave Macmillan, 2012), 4–5.
8. *Ibid.*, 5.
9. M. Tessier, 'Interview with Toru Takemitsu', in *DVD Booklet, Ran (1985)*, dir. Akira Kurosawa (Criterion, 2005), 20.
10. A. Mousley, 'Care, Scepticism and Speaking in the Plural: Posthumanisms and Humanisms in *King Lear*', in S. Herbrechter and I. Callus (eds.), *Posthumanist Shakespeares* (New York: Palgrave Macmillan, 2012), 108.
11. *Ibid.*
12. D. Richie, *The Films of Akira Kurosawa*, 3rd edition, expanded and updated (Berkeley and Los Angeles: University of California Press, 1996), 214.
13. Interview in B. Cardullo, *World Directors in Dialogue: Conversations on Cinema* (Blue Ridge Summit: Scarecrow Press, 2011), 57.

14. Kurosawa, *Something like an Autobiography*, 189, 192.

15. Shields, 'Kurosawa', 283.

16. S. Teo, *The Asian Cinema Experience: Styles, Spaces, Theory* (New York: Routledge, 2013), 17–20.

17. S. Prince, 'Zen and Selfhood: Patterns of Eastern Thought in Kurosawa's Films', in J. Goodwin (ed.), *Perspectives on Akira Kurosawa* (New York: G. K. Hall, 1994), 226–7.

18. Several scholars have examined the connections between the narratives of *Ran* and *King Lear*, such as E. Dodson-Robinson, 'Karma, Revenge, Apocalypse: *Ran*'s Violent Victim-Agent through Japanese and Western Contexts', *Shakespeare Bulletin* 31.2 (2013): 233–55; and J. Goodwin, *Akira Kurosawa and Intertextual Cinema* (Baltimore: Johns Hopkins University Press, 1994), 191–216.

19. Goodwin, *Kurosawa and Intertextual Cinema*, 196.

20. *Ibid.*, 196.

21. *Ibid.*, 197.

22. S. Prince, *The Warrior's Camera: the Cinema of Akira Kurosawa*, revised and expanded edition (Princeton: Princeton University Press, 1999), 204.

23. K. Watanabe, 'Interview with Akira Kurosawa on *Ran*', in *DVD Booklet, Ran (1985)*, dir. Akira Kurosawa (Criterion, 2005), 14.

24. Richie, *Films of Akira Kurosawa*, 219.

25. Prince, *Warrior's Camera*, 289.

26. Richie, *Films of Akira Kurosawa*, 232; my emphasis.

27. On Noh elements in *Throne of Blood* and *Ran*, see Richie, *Films of Akira Kurosawa*, Prince, *Warrior's Camera*, J. Collick, *Shakespeare, Cinema and Society* (Manchester: Manchester University Press, 1989) and, especially, K. McDonald, *Japanese Classical Theater in Films* (Rutherford: Fairleigh Dickinson University Press, 1994).

28. K. M. Howlett, *Framing Shakespeare on Film* (Athens: Ohio University Press, 2000), 121.

29. C. Shimazaki, *Restless Spirits from Japanese Noh Plays of the Fourth Group* (Ithaca: Cornell University Press, 1995), 40.

30. Collick, *Shakespeare, Cinema and Society*, 186.

31. Shimazaki, *Restless Spirits*, 47.

32. D. Keene (ed.), *Twenty Plays of the Nō Theater* (New York: Columbia University Press, 1970), 23.

33. C. Shimazaki, *Troubled Souls from Japanese Noh Plays of the Fourth Group* (Ithaca: Cornell University Press, 1998), 2.

34. M. Ueda, *The Old Pine Tree and Other Noh Plays*, trans. M. Ueda (Lincoln, NE: University of Nebraska Press, 1962), xx–xxi.

35. Prince, *Warrior's Camera*, 289.

36. *Ibid.*

37. Richie, *Films of Akira Kurosawa*, 214; and K. Geist, 'Late Kurosawa: *Kagemusha* and *Ran*', *Post Script: Essays in Film and the Humanities* 12.1 (Fall 1992): 29.

38. Quoted in Prince, *Warrior's Camera*, 284–5.
39. Herbrechter, 'Introduction', 4.
40. A. Kurosawa, H. Oguni and I. Masato, *Ran* [screenplay] (Boston: Shambala, 1986), 46; my emphasis.
41. See Tessier, 'Interview with Toru Takemitsu', 20.
42. K. Leonard, *Shakespeare, Madness, and Music: Scoring Insanity in Cinematic Adaptations* (Lanham: Scarecrow Press, 2009), 110.
43. 'A. K.', dir. Chris Marker, documentary on Disc 2 of *Ran (1985)* (Criterion, 2005).
44. Collick, *Shakespeare, Cinema and Society*, 186.
45. Kurosawa et al., *Ran* [screenplay], 106.
46. K. D. Nordin, 'Buddhist Symbolism in Akira Kurosawa's *Ran*: a Counterpoint to Human Chaos', *Asian Cinema* 16.2 (2005): 242–54; 242.
47. Interview in P. Grilli, 'Kurosawa Directs a Cinematic *Lear*', in J. Goodwin (ed.), *Perspectives on Akira Kurosawa* (New York: G. K. Hall, 1994), 60.
48. Interview in K. Hirano, 'Making Films for All the People', in J. Goodwin (ed.), *Perspectives on Akira Kurosawa* (New York: G. K. Hall, 1994), 57.
49. Spitznas, 'Flayed Hare', 14.
50. Quoted in Goodwin, *Akira Kurosawa*, 212.
51. Spitznas, 'Flayed Hare', 24.
52. S. A. Thornton, *The Japanese Period Film: a Critical Analysis* (Jefferson: McFarland, 2007), 155.
53. Richie, *The Films of Akira Kurosawa*, 219.
54. Mousley, 'Care, Scepticism and Speaking', 108.

WORKS CITED

Cardullo, B., *World Directors in Dialogue: Conversations on Cinema* (Blue Ridge Summit: Scarecrow Press, 2011).

Collick, J., *Shakespeare, Cinema and Society* (Manchester: Manchester University Press, 1989).

Dodson-Robinson, E., 'Karma, Revenge, Apocalypse: *Ran*'s Violent Victim-Agent through Japanese and Western Contexts', *Shakespeare Bulletin* 31.2 (2013): 233–55.

Geist, K., 'Late Kurosawa: *Kagemusha* and *Ran*', *Post Script: Essays in Film and the Humanities* 12.1 (Fall 1992): 26–36.

Goodwin, J., *Akira Kurosawa and Intertextual Cinema* (Baltimore: Johns Hopkins University Press, 1994).

Goto-Jones, C., *Modern Japan: a Very Short Introduction* (Oxford: Oxford University Press, 2009).

Grilli, P., 'Kurosawa Directs a Cinematic *Lear*', in J. Goodwin (ed.), *Perspectives on Akira Kurosawa* (New York: G. K. Hall, 1994), 60.

Herbrechter, S., 'Introduction: Shakespeare ever after', in S. Herbrechter and I. Callus (eds.), *Posthumanist Shakespeares* (New York: Palgrave Macmillan, 2012), 1–19.

Hirano, K., 'Making Films for All the People' in J. Goodwin (ed.), *Perspectives on Akira Kurosawa* (New York: G. K. Hall, 1994), 57–8.

Howlett, K. M., *Framing Shakespeare on Film* (Athens: Ohio University Press, 2000).

Keene, D. (ed.), *Twenty Plays of the Nō Theater* (New York: Columbia University Press, 1970).

Kurosawa, A., *Something like an Autobiography*, trans. A. E. Bock (New York: Random House, 1983).

H. Oguni and I. Masato, *Ran* [screenplay] (Boston: Shambala, 1986).

Leonard, K. P., *Shakespeare, Madness, and Music: Scoring Insanity in Cinematic Adaptations* (Lanham: Scarecrow Press, 2009).

Marker, C. (dir.), 'A. K.', documentary on Disc 2 of *Ran (1985)*, dir. Akira Kurosawa (Criterion, 2005).

McDonald, K., *Japanese Classical Theater in Films* (Rutherford: Fairleigh Dickinson University Press, 1994).

Mousley, A., 'Care, Scepticism and Speaking in the Plural: Posthumanisms and Humanisms in *King Lear*', in S. Herbrechter and I. Callus (eds.), *Posthumanist Shakespeares* (New York: Palgrave Macmillan, 2012), 97–113.

Nordin, K. D., 'Buddhist Symbolism in Akira Kurosawa's *Ran*: a Counterpoint to Human Chaos', *Asian Cinema* 16.2 (2005): 242–54.

Prince, S., *The Warrior's Camera: the Cinema of Akira Kurosawa*, revised and expanded edition (Princeton: Princeton University Press, 1999).

'Zen and Selfhood: Patterns of Eastern Thought in Kurosawa's Films', in J. Goodwin (ed.), *Perspectives on Akira Kurosawa* (New York: G. K. Hall, 1994), 225–35.

Richie, D., *The Films of Akira Kurosawa*, 3rd edition, expanded and updated (Berkeley and Los Angeles: University of California Press, 1996).

Shields, J. M., 'Kurosawa, Akira (1910–1998)', in E. M. Mazur (ed.), *Encyclopedia of Religion and Film* (Santa Barbara: ABC-CLIO, 2011), 279–83.

Shimazaki, C., *Restless Spirits from Japanese Noh Plays of the Fourth Group* (Ithaca: Cornell University Press, 1995).

Troubled Souls from Japanese Noh Plays of the Fourth Group (Ithaca: Cornell University Press, 1998).

Spitznas, A., 'The Flayed Hare: Trauma and Hope in the Late Films of Kurosawa', in K. R. Morefield (ed.), *Faith and Spirituality in the Masters of World Cinema* (Newcastle-upon-Tyne: Cambridge Scholars Publishing, 2011), 11–41.

Teo, S., *The Asian Cinema Experience: Styles, Spaces, Theory* (New York: Routledge, 2013).

Tessier, M., 'Interview with Toru Takemitsu', in *DVD Booklet, Ran (1985)*, dir. Akira Kurosawa (Criterion, 2005), 19–22.

Thornton, S. A., *The Japanese Period Film: a Critical Analysis* (Jefferson: McFarland, 2007).

Ueda, M., *The Old Pine Tree and Other Noh Plays*, trans. M. Ueda (Lincoln, NE: University of Nebraska Press, 1962).

Watanabe, K., 'Interview with Akira Kurosawa on *Ran*', in *DVD Booklet, Ran (1985)*, dir. Akira Kurosawa (Criterion, 2005), 10–17.

Lear *en Abyme: Metatheatre and the Screen*

CHAPTER 4

Filming Metatheatre: the 'Dover Cliff' Scene on Screen

Sarah Hatchuel

In Act 4, scene 5, Edgar, disguised as Poor Tom, guides his blind father Gloucester towards Dover. Gloucester has asked to be conducted to the top of a cliff so that he can end his days. But the cliff is only an illusion created verbally by Edgar, who wants to protect his father's life. Stanley Cavell has summed up the situation, which plays with our (and Gloucester's) expectations, as: 'up no hill to no cliff to no suicide'.[1] A three-minute amateur animated film entitled 'The Cliff Scene from King Lear', posted on YouTube on 12 December 2010, highlights how nonsensical this whole dramatic situation actually is.[2] The video shows the two men standing still in a modern kitchen. Edgar is young and dressed casually; Gloucester is bald with dark glasses. The computer graphics were generated using Xtranormal Movie Maker, do-it-yourself animation software: the images are, therefore, minimalist, while the two synthetic voices remain very unemotional and matter-of-fact throughout the sequence. Shakespeare's playtext has been modernized, simplified and slightly parodied to a point where the original scene's irrationality and cruelty are emphasized:

EDGAR:	Can't you tell we are walking a steep cliff?
GLOUCESTER:	It doesn't feel like it.
EDGAR:	That's because you're blind. . . .
GLOUCESTER:	But are you sure we are almost there?
EDGAR:	Yes. Can't you smell the ocean breeze?
GLOUCESTER:	No.
EDGAR:	Can't you hear the seagulls?
GLOUCESTER:	No.
EDGAR:	That's because you're blind. If you had eyes, you would be able to smell the ocean and hear the seagulls.
GLOUCESTER:	That makes no sense.
EDGAR:	Yes it does.
GLOUCESTER:	OK, I trust you, a person I know nothing about and have never met before today...

Through the stern repetition of 'That's because you're blind', even when sight is not the sense that would be useful to Gloucester to smell the sea and hear the birds, the short animated film offers a tongue-in-cheek commentary on the suspension of disbelief that the Shakespeare scene asks of its audience and on the dark humour it is based upon. At the moment of the fall, the blind man continues to remain absolutely still. He is convinced he has taken the plunge only through Edgar's words. But the audience is never tricked and never encouraged to question the situation: we are only invited to laugh at the silliness of the script.

While the Shakespearean scene can be turned into dark comedy rather easily, it is much more difficult to address its aesthetic ambiguity and tragic tone. This scene, in fact, mobilizes and problematizes the conventions of the Elizabethan stage to become a moment of pure theatre, calling for a bare stage to retain all its fluidity and ambiguity – since the signified elements are conjured only through words. While Jan Kott thought that the transposition of this scene to the screen was impossible, 'unless one were to film a stage performance',[3] the aim of this chapter will be to qualify this assertion by showing how cinema and television can sometimes maintain, and even facilitate, the scene's paradoxes of a *non-space* and reflect on the film medium itself. After outlining the aesthetic complexity of this very peculiar moment, the chapter will interrogate the possibilities offered by the screen to reflect the scene's dramatic and metadramatic tensions by exploring several film productions of *King Lear* that use Shakespeare's playtext. These screen productions, emerging from different media and production contexts, all present different strategies to represent the 'cliff' scene: they can share Edgar's point of view from the start, thus verging towards comic relief, or try to retain some spatial ambiguity and uncomfortable suspense. They can also go as far as making us believe in the reality of the abyss even after Gloucester has jumped, turning the scene into a very emotional and cathartic moment. From Richard Eyre's 1998 film of the National Theatre stage production, to films made for television and video release (Tony Davenall's for Thames Television in 1974; Jonathan Miller's for the BBC in 1982; Brian Blessed's in 1999; Eyre's for the BBC in 2018), to feature films (Peter Brook's in 1971) – they all attempt, through textual cuts, framing and/or editing, to circumvent the problem posed by a scene that seems to encapsulate the very essence of the bare Elizabethan stage.

When Edgar reaches the top of the 'cliff', he draws from the techniques of linear perspective used in visual art to describe what he 'sees': 'How fearful/ And dizzy 'tis to cast one's eyes so low./ The crows and choughs that wing the midway air/ Show scarce so gross as beetles. Half-way down/ Hangs one that gathers samphire, dreadful trade!/ Methinks he seems no bigger than his head' (4.5.11–16). The speech offers a *verbal* three-dimensional perspective: the viewer, who remains still, sees an image organized around a vanishing point in which the elements seem to shrink the farther they are from the observing eye, until they disappear ('I'll look no more', 4.5.22).[4] As Jonathan Goldberg remarks, the illusion of a continuous space depends on the fact that we can no longer see when the vanishing point is reached. Paradoxically, vision depends on the absence of vision.[5] This paradox is reflected in the fact that Gloucester, now a blind man, finds himself in the position of the observer of a picture ('Come on, sir, here's the place. Stand still', says Edgar to his father, 4.5.11), as if blindness could only lead to sight, awareness and discovery.

Below, birds look like insects; even lower down, a man is as small as his head; at the lowest, men are just mice and things become only parts of themselves in an infinite regression that reproduces Gloucester's and Lear's journeys from prosperity to animality.[6] The decrease in scale reaches the confines of vision ('almost too small for sight', 4.5.20) within a construct where the rule of appearance reigns ('show', 'seems', 'appear'). In the speech, words create sounds of nature through assonance and alliteration ('The murmuring surge,/ That on th'unnumbered idle pebble chafes', 21) but immediately come to deny their very own existence ('cannot be heard so high', 22): sounds and images, be they real or not within the fiction, remain illusory and verbal creations.

This hyperrealism conjured by the extremely detailed description is ironically denied by the very absence of the cliff, not only from the bare Elizabethan stage (since no cliff was represented visually) but also within the story world (since the cliff is nothing more than a fiction created by Edgar). When Edgar describes the perspective, the spectators find themselves in an ambivalent position regarding what they hear. On the one hand, we know that, on the Elizabethan stage, a scene really taking place near a cliff would only show a bare and flat platform anyway: be it genuine or imaginary, a location will always be created verbally. On the other hand, we also know that Gloucester is now blind and cannot confirm Edgar's description. Hence, spectators must make their own decision whether the cliff is real or not in a scene that keeps encouraging uncertainty and doubt. Edgar may be describing something that actually exists in the story world – just as Shakespeare, in other scenes and plays, engenders castles, battlefields or Roman forums through the mere power of words.[7] The Elizabethan stage puts the sighted spectators in the same position as the blind character.

The speech thus highlights both the power of words to conjure mental images in the spectators' minds and the limits of this power. As Goldberg asserts, 'In *Lear*, nothing comes of nothing, and the very language which would seem (to us) solidly to locate the world slides into an abyss, an uncreating, annihilative nothingness'.[8] In the end, words may never materialize what they refer to; they only perpetuate illusion.

R. A. Foakes is convinced that spectators attending a stage performance of *King Lear* never believe at any point in the existence of the cliff: 'I think that from the opening lines onwards the scene makes the audience aware that Edgar is hoaxing his father with conscious deception'.[9] Like other critics such as Michael Mooney[10] or Derek Peat,[11] I am more inclined to think that the scene is meant to play with the spectators' beliefs, all the more so since the ambiguity is made possible by the very nature of the Elizabethan stage.

At first, as we listen to Edgar, we are invited to believe that the cliff is real indeed. Like blind Gloucester, we create the location in our minds: just as Edgar fools his father, Shakespeare tricks his audience. The very realistic high-angle depiction has had, in fact, tangible consequences on England's artistic memory and geographical representation. One of the cliffs at Dover actually bears the name 'Shakespeare Cliff'. With its impressive height (120 metres) and its pointy shape, it stands in the British imagination as the last stronghold against the continent. Jeremy Price suggests that 'Shakespeare Cliff has become an iconic site of memory, a beacon of Britishness'.[12] In the nineteenth century, the cliff was represented in paintings and engravings on a regular basis. Shakespeare's cliff scene thus prefigures implicitly the pictorial productions that came to replace, from the Restoration onwards, the performances on the bare stage, but it also reveals how both pictorialism and verbalism can hide the truth: the cliff described verbally in such a realistic way remains a mere fancy. The whole representation relies on *invisibility*, i.e. on the fact that neither Gloucester nor the spectator can be a witness to what Edgar is describing. In such a context, Gloucester stands as a spectator who is content with words to build the fiction and falls into the *trompe-l'oeil* abyss of the story.

The speech is so potent in its ability to create a 'real' location that some actors playing Edgar feel sometimes obliged to wink at the audience to warn them of the deception. This was, for instance, the case in a production at the Globe Theatre in London in 2001.[13] But if there is no clue given by the actor, at which stage are we supposed to understand that all this is a trick devised by Edgar? Simon Ryle believes that spectators encountering the play for the first time become aware of

Edgar's hoax during his aside 'Why I do trifle thus with his despair/ Is done to cure it' (4.5.33–4).[14] However, according to Harry Levin, the aside simply reveals that Edgar has thought of a stratagem to prevent his father from committing suicide: it does not imply necessarily that the cliff's existence is a fake.[15] Peat argues that the aside may actually point to other forms of craftiness and cunning: 'Does he intend to prevent Gloucester from jumping, or does he hope his father will change his mind if given enough time? An unfamiliar spectator may well think Edgar means to cast off his disguise at the last moment'.[16] The illusion of the cliff's existence can thus persist until Gloucester's fall – and even afterwards, when Edgar wonders if his father may have died from believing that he fell: 'And yet I know not how conceit may rob/ The treasury of life when life itself/ Yields to the theft' (4.5.42–4).

Not a single character in the play actually succeeds in reaching the cliffs of Dover, which remain a site of unfulfilled desire. In Grigori Kozintsev's reading, Dover is where England – and civilization – stops.[17] It is, therefore, unsurprising that Dover embodies the very frontier of representation. Edgar's realistic description points to the 'failure' of the Elizabethan stage to make the signified tangible, while underlining its considerable power of conviction. When Gloucester takes the plunge into what he believes is a void, the moment of the fall places the spectators in intellectual and emotional limbo, between the presence and absence of an abyss that pushes the possibilities offered by the Elizabethan stage to its limits. As Jan Kott states, in this moment, 'Shakespeare shows the paradox of pure theatre'.[18]

What becomes of this dizziness when the conditions of performance change – when, for instance, the theatre mobilizes realistic settings? According to Jan Kott[19] or Marvin Rosenberg,[20] the cliff scene should always be played on even ground to preserve spatial ambiguity as long as possible, before revealing the scheme suddenly. However, when Gloucester takes a leap from his mere height and touches the stage floor almost immediately, this may elicit some smiles and sneers in the audience. It is therefore no wonder that Kott should have read the scene as verging on the grotesque and the absurd – hereby recalling George Wilson Knight's famous interpretation of Gloucester's fall:

> The old man falls from his kneeling posture a few inches, flat, face foremost. Instead of the dizzy circling to crash and spill his life on the rocks below – just this. The grotesque merged into the ridiculous reaches a consummation in this bathos of tragedy.[21]

To avoid such an unfortunate effect, Winfried Schleiner advises that the actor playing Gloucester should fall from a certain height – even a symbolic one.[22] A slight extra height would preserve the ambiguity of the location while allowing the performance to be more credible and tragic.

In Peter Brook's 1962 stage production for the Royal Shakespeare Company, Gloucester (played by Alan Webb) walked with a heavy stick; at the moment of his fall, he seemed to decide otherwise at the last second and caught hold of his cane, his feet hanging in the air. Before letting go, Gloucester engendered a literal cliffhanger during which the emotional and intellectual vertigo could take place. In 1993, Adrian Noble's RSC production showed Gloucester (David Bradley) and Edgar (Simon Russell Beale) sitting at the very edge of the stage. The idea of a dangerous height was thus created by using the elevation between the stage and the auditorium, turning the abyss into the metatheatrical gap separating actors from spectators. On a stage using realistic scenery, spatial ambiguity becomes impossible to uphold: either Gloucester is on top of a cliff or he is not. This is why, on the nineteenth-century stage, the Dover cliff scene was very often cut, or turned into a moment when, in front of a painted set showing the actual presence of cliffs, Gloucester fainted and fell down right in Edgar's arms, thus avoiding any injury. Sometimes, the setting signalled that the scene did not take place up a cliff but on the beach.[23] In these cases, the Dover cliff is no longer a non-space: through the choice of a particular setting, *either* the cliff does exist and we share Gloucester's point of view, fearing the fall to come; *or* the cliff does not exist and we share Edgar's point of view, following his scheme knowingly.

On screen, the scene becomes even more challenging. The idea of the non-space is all the more frustrating for a film director since the medium makes it possible to show the place in a visually realistic and credible way, but can only do so by sacrificing the dramatic effects and the tensions in the story. This dilemma may explain why Peter Brook, who adapted the play for a 1953 CBS broadcast with Orson Welles as Lear, chose not to include the passage. Kozintsev also decided to cut the scene in his 1970 *King Lear* (*Korol Lir*). We can only find a silent scene in which, lost in a desert of stones, father (Karl Sebris) and son (Leonhard Merzin) become pathetic figures, made even more vulnerable by the camera's high-angle shot. A close-up shows Edgar's face, which Gloucester's hands slowly touch and progressively recognize. The old man's emotion is too intense, and, in another high-angle shot, Gloucester collapses and dies, thus anticipating the end of the play.

Yet critics have been too inclined to suppose that the absence of the Dover cliff scene in Kozintsev's *Lear* is evidence of the limits of cinema as a medium. Richard Ashby argues that the cliff scene is not in Kozintsev's film because it would be redundant. Whereas Edgar's speech goes beyond the confines of theatrical space to offer a view of the ordinary lives of fishermen, sailors and samphire gatherers, Kozintsev makes use of the realist space of film to literally show working men who continue to lead precarious and difficult lives outside of the main narrative events of the play. Through its crowd scenes from beginning to end, the film gives us a glimpse of the 'unnumbered' (4.6.21) and usually unrepresented plebeians who try to survive away from the noble characters and the cataclysmic events they have triggered. The Dover cliff is therefore 'at once absent from, and yet paradoxically dispersed throughout, the film'.[24] However, if the social themes present in Edgar's description are still present through this visual diffraction, the reflexive questioning of the medium disappears.

In the 1974 production directed by Tony Davenall for Thames Television, the scene is not cut but is adapted using realistic scenery, reproducing the countryside inside the television studio. As Gloucester (Ronald Radd) and Edgar (Robert Coleby) walk on grassy ground, the camera tracks back and reveals that there is no cliff in sight. When Edgar asks his father if he can hear the sea, we ironically hear chirping birds on the soundtrack: the characters are definitely not near the sea. Edgar's scheme is disclosed straight away, and TV spectators are invited to share his point of view entirely. The film does not preserve spatial ambiguity and tends to turn the scene into a comic one. Any tragic suspense disappears since we are sure that Gloucester does not risk anything if he 'falls' over.

In Richard Eyre's 1998 version, which remediates for television a production staged at the National Theatre in 1997, a long shot reveals Gloucester (Timothy West) and Edgar (Paul Rhys) in a misty environment. The oblique framing adds to the disorientation. Sounds of waves and seagulls are evocative of the seaside. When Gloucester takes the jump, he is lost in the white fog that hovers over the boards of the stage, casting doubt, for a while, over the outcome of his fall. Losing the character in the mist could have been a very effective idea to preserve the ambiguity of the scene but, as the touch of realism brought by the white haze is not supported by the impression that there *could be* some kind of dangerous vacuum somewhere, the suspense cannot be sustained long. Eyre recently came back to the play in 2018, this time directing a high-budget production designed specifically for high-definition television with a 16:9 image ratio.[25] Dizzying shots of a real cliff at Dover spectacularly open the scene, and Edgar (Andrew Scott) positions his father (Jim Broadbent) a few metres away from the abyss. The *mise-en-scène* thus recalls the nineteenth-century stage productions in which the cliff was undoubtedly there but its danger was contained. Although Eyre's new take on the scene does not rely on, or create, spatial ambiguity, it nevertheless succeeds in generating fearful uncertainty: by bringing his father so close to the edge, Edgar is certainly taking a risk, and viewers may ask themselves if the distance is safe enough for Gloucester not to fall, even if inadvertently.

The production directed by Jonathan Miller in 1982 for the BBC aims to both sustain and discredit Edgar's account for viewers. At the start of the sequence, on a flat and barren ground, Edgar (Anton Lesser) carries Gloucester (Norman Rodway) on his back. Since Gloucester's feet do not touch the floor, the director offers a credible explanation for the fact that Gloucester cannot check if there is indeed a slope or not. The camera soon gets very close to the two characters. By hiding the environment, creating a mysterious 'off-field' and avoiding any long shots that could reveal the absence of a cliff, the BBC version thus creates an ambiguous non-space. When Gloucester falls over, he disappears from the camera field and, for a few seconds, produces doubt as to his fate. However, Edgar's acting prevents the moment from becoming truly suspenseful. By describing the perspective with his eyes closed, Edgar puts himself in the position of Gloucester picturing the abyss in his mind, but he also makes us quickly understand that the cliff is just the product of his imagination. Moreover, Edgar remains calm and facetious in his farewell to his father, never expressing any fear or attempting to prevent the old man from taking the plunge. The ambiguity generated by the medium is thus eventually denied by the actor's performance.

Michael Elliott's 1983 TV production benefits even more from the possibilities offered by the screen. Gloucester (Leo McKern) and Edgar (David Threlfall) are walking on ground that remains unknown because they are framed down to their knees only. A few blades of grass and a grey sky are the only details we are allowed to see. The camera then frames the two faces in close-up, preserving the uncertainty of the location. Suspense is intensified through empathetic, extra-diegetic music with tragic overtones, which makes us feel that Gloucester's life will definitely be under threat if he takes the leap. When he falls, the music suddenly stops, signalling the change in mood and viewpoint: the camera shows Gloucester in low-angle shot from a distance, revealing that the old man has fainted face down in the sand. The tragedy turns into absurd and grotesque comedy. Only Edgar, who performs his goodbye as he pretends to go, gives away a clue about the scheme just a few seconds before the 'plunge'.

If both TV versions directed by Jonathan Miller and by Michael Elliott take advantage of the tight framing offered by the camera, other productions use another filmic technique to create a misleading environment – editing. In his 1971 film, Peter Brook makes us move between different spaces through cinematic cuts and montage. The scene starts by losing both characters and viewers in an uncertain location through a blurry shot of the two men walking, a blinding shot of the sun and a close-up of feet on an indistinct ground. The camera moves back to eventually reveal a space that seems infinitely flat, a stony desert very similar to Kozintsev's sequence. However, in the background, the sea is visible – not a cliff but a beach. In Brook's version, Edgar (Robert Lloyd) is honest when he asks his father (Alan Webb) whether he hears the sounds of the sea, but the location is now disclosed and is far from threatening. However, an abrupt cut engenders indecision once more. Time seems to have elapsed and we cannot be sure any longer where the scene is now taking place. Edgar carries his father on his back, taking him on spins and turns to fool Gloucester's perceptions – as well as ours. From this moment on, action is only shown in close-ups, denying any sight of the geographical surroundings. The two men's faces and hands fill the screen, Gloucester's gouged-out eyes becoming the very symbol of human suffering, but also of the vision that is now impeded for the spectators. Are the characters still on the safe beach, or have they now reached the summit of an impressive cliff? Edgar's performance contributes, this time, to the suspense: the fear of heights may be perceived on his face while he tries to hold back his father. As in the other versions, Gloucester's leap takes him out of the camera field. A high-angle shot then reveals the irony of the fall: the old man is lying still in the desert, having only fallen from his own height. By offering the opportunity to create a space that oscillates between certainty and uncertainty, editing has allowed Brook to disorientate the viewers and create ambiguity as to what they are watching.

Brian Blessed's 1999 film fully realizes our belief in the existence of the cliff through both framing and editing. The scene, shot on location, is extremely realistic since what we see is a real cliff at Dover as in Eyre's 2018 production – but the similarities between the two versions end here. Blessed's camera moves to a series of close-ups of faces, obliterating the space around the characters. However, because the previous shot has shown us a cliff, we are invited to think that the precipice is still there and we fully identify with Gloucester. To insist on the presence of a gulf, the camera films the faces in low-angle shots as if we were viewing Edgar (Mark Burgess) and Gloucester (Robert Whelan) from the bottom of the abyss. Edgar's face is filled with terror as he holds his father back and, when he turns his head away to say farewell, we wonder if he is trying to pretend he is leaving or avoiding the sight of the impending suicide. The camera follows Gloucester through his fall, only to reach immediately the sand of the beach. Between the shot of the cliff and the shot of the sand, film editing constructed an ellipsis – a hidden moment in which Edgar eventually brought his father to the safe space of the beach. The viewers are thus led to question the construction of their expectations, to realize how the processes of editing and framing encouraged us to believe that Gloucester would find a void beneath his feet. By understanding the way we were deluded by the cinematic medium, we are invited to interrogate our perceptions in front of a screen and to analyse the other sequences in the film – and in other films. This most enlightening reflection on the medium may prompt us to be more vigilant concerning the aesthetic and ideological construction of visual discourse.

The sequence in Blessed's film is particularly adapted, it seems, to viewers who are already familiar with the play – since, even though we know the outcome of the scene, we are surprised to find ourselves still believing in the presence of the abyss. The meaning and expectation created by both editing and framing directly contradict what we know is Edgar's scheme. That we should think there could be a different ending testifies to the strength of image manipulation, while reflecting Edgar's trickery itself: viewers who are generally the witnesses of Gloucester being fooled are themselves fooled.

The bare stage of a theatre is the only environment where the Dover cliff scene can preserve its spatial uncertainty to play with the spectators' vacillating faith in what they see, casting doubt on both Edgar's account and Gloucester's perception, and forming the cliff in the viewers' minds before revealing it as a verbal and illusory creation. Through this highly metatheatrical scene, the bare stage discloses its very workings while asserting its power of suggestion. However, cinema has tools specific to its art that can remediate the scene in rich and ambiguous ways. Films such as Peter Brook's and Brian Blessed's certainly embrace the spatial complexity and fluid emotions raised by this 'dramedic' moment. By foregrounding explicitly the fact that filmic space is constructed through framing and editing, they disclose the power of images and remind us, just as Shakespeare does, that the vertigo of fiction is always there, around us. It is up to us to deconstruct visual discourse to avoid falling into its abyss of illusion.

Notes

1. S. Cavell, *Disowning Knowledge in Seven Plays of Shakespeare* (Cambridge: Cambridge University Press, 2003 [1987]), 55.
2. The video can be seen at www.youtube.com/watch?v=ZoFNwLljBkA (accessed 15 December 2017).
3. J. Kott, *Shakespeare Our Contemporary*, trans. B. Taborski (London: Methuen, 1964), 117.
4. See M. McLuhan, *The Gutenberg Galaxy: the Making of Typographic Man* (Toronto: University of Toronto Press, 1962), 15–17.
5. J. Goldberg, 'Dover Cliff and the Conditions of Representations: *King Lear* 4:6 in Perspective', *Poetics Today* 5.3 (1984), 542.
6. See A. B. Kernan, 'Formalism and Realism in Elizabethan Drama: the Miracles in *King Lear*', *Renaissance Drama* ns 9 (1966), 63.
7. See R. Meek, *Narrating the Visual in Shakespeare* (New York: Routledge, 2016 [2009]).
8. Goldberg, 'Dover Cliff and the Conditions of Representations', 544.
9. R. A. Foakes (ed.), *King Lear*, The Arden Shakespeare, 3rd edition (London: Thomas Nelson & Sons, 1997), 329.
10. M. Mooney, *Shakespeare's Dramatic Transactions* (Durham, NC: Duke University Press, 1990), 142.
11. D. Peat, '"And That's True Too": *King Lear* and the Tension of Uncertainty', *Shakespeare Survey* 33 (1980), 47: 'it strikes me that the working of the scene depends on our remaining confused about the existence of cliff and sea'.
12. My translation of 'Shakespeare Cliff est devenu un lieu de mémoire icône, phare de la britannité'. J. Price, 'Shakespeare Cliff, Rempart Symbolique aux Portes du Royaume', *Les Cahiers du MIMMOC* 1 (2006), http://mimmoc.revues.org/101 (accessed 7 October 2017).
13. Actor Paul Brennen, who played Edgar at the Globe in 2001, reported: 'Often the people at the side of the theatre can feel a bit isolated from the action, and so at one point of the play I share a moment with them so they feel a part of what is going on. It is when Gloucester is about to jump off the cliff, and I wink to the audience as I am "helping" do this!'. GlobeLink – globe Education's Online Resource Centre, www.globelink.org/resourcecentre/kinglear2001/edgar (accessed 10 January 2018).
14. S. J. Ryle, 'Filming Non-Space: the Vanishing Point and the Face in Brook's *King Lear*', *Literature/Film Quarterly* 35.2 (2007): 140–7.
15. H. Levin, 'The Heights and the Depths: a Scene from *King Lear*', in J. Garrett (ed.), *More Talking of Shakespeare* (London: Longmans, 1959), 98.
16. Peat, '*King Lear* and the Tension of Uncertainty', 48.
17. G. Kozintsev, *'King Lear': the Space of Tragedy*, trans. M. Mackintosh (London: Heinemann, 1977), 130.
18. Kott, *Shakespeare Our Contemporary*, 117.
19. *Ibid.*, 114.
20. M. Rosenberg, *The Masks of King Lear* (Berkeley, Los Angeles and London: University of California Press, 1972), 264.

21. G. W. Knight, *The Wheel of Fire* (London: Methuen, 1949 [1930]), 171.
22. W. Schleiner, 'Justifying the Unjustifiable: the Dover Cliff Scene in *King Lear*', *Shakespeare Quarterly* 36.3 (1985): 337–43. In the playtext, the stage direction 'He falls' appears in the Quarto but not in the Folio. This is the only difference in this scene between Q and F.
23. W. F. McNeir, 'The Staging of the Dover Cliff Scene in *King Lear*', in W. F. McNeir (ed.), *Studies in English Renaissance Literature* (Baton Rouge: Louisiana State University Press, 1962), 91; Levin, 'The Heights and the Depths', 98.
24. R. Ashby, 'Crowding out Dover "Cliff" in *Korol Lir*', *Adaptation* 10.2 (2017), 210–29, https://academic.oup.com/adaptation/article/10/2/210/3782658/Crowding-out-Dover-Cliff-in-Korol-Lir?rss=1 (accessed 9 October 2017).
25. For more on Eyre's 2018 film, see Peter J. Smith's review in the volume's online resources

WORKS CITED

Ashby, R., 'Crowding out Dover "Cliff" in *Korol Lir*', *Adaptation* 10.2 (2017): 210–29.
Cavell, S., *Disowning Knowledge in Seven Plays of Shakespeare* (Cambridge: Cambridge University Press, 2003 [1987]).
Foakes, R. A. (ed.), *King Lear*, The Arden Shakespeare, 3rd edition (London: Thomas Nelson & Sons, 1997).
Goldberg, J., 'Dover Cliff and the Conditions of Representations: *King Lear* 4:6 in Perspective', *Poetics Today* 5.3 (1984): 537–47.
Kernan, A. B., 'Formalism and Realism in Elizabethan Drama: the Miracles in *King Lear*', *Renaissance Drama* ns 9 (1966): 59–66.
Knight, G. W., *The Wheel of Fire* (London: Methuen, 1949 [1930]).
Kott, J., *Shakespeare Our Contemporary*, trans. B. Taborski (London: Methuen, 1964).
Kozintsev, G., *'King Lear': the Space of Tragedy*, trans. M. Mackintosh (London: Heinemann, 1977).
Levin, H., 'The Heights and the Depths: a Scene from *King Lear*', in J. Garrett (ed.), *More Talking of Shakespeare* (London: Longmans, 1959), 87–103.
McLuhan, M., *The Gutenberg Galaxy: the Making of Typographic Man* (Toronto: University of Toronto Press, 1962).
McNeir, W. F., 'The Staging of the Dover Cliff Scene in *King Lear*', in W. F. McNeir (ed.), *Studies in English Renaissance Literature* (Baton Rouge: Louisiana State University Press, 1962), 87–104.
Meek, R., *Narrating the Visual in Shakespeare* (New York: Routledge, 2016 [2009]).
Mooney, M. E., *Shakespeare's Dramatic Transactions* (Durham, NC: Duke University Press, 1990).
Peat, D., '"And that's true too": *King Lear* and the Tension of Uncertainty', *Shakespeare Survey* 33 (1980): 43–53.

Price, J., 'Shakespeare Cliff, Rempart Symbolique aux Portes du Royaume', *Les Cahiers du MIMMOC* 1 (2006): http://mimmoc.revues.org/101 (accessed 7 October 2017).

Rosenberg, M., *The Masks of King Lear* (Berkeley, Los Angeles and London: University of California Press, 1972).

Ryle, S. J., 'Filming Non-Space: the Vanishing Point and the Face in Brook's *King Lear*', *Literature/Film Quarterly* 35.2 (2007): 140–7.

Schleiner, W., 'Justifying the Unjustifiable: the Dover Cliff Scene in *King Lear*', *Shakespeare Quarterly* 36.3 (Autumn 1985): 337–43.

CHAPTER 5

New Ways of Looking at Lear: Changing Relationships between Theatre, Screen and Audience in Live Broadcasts of King Lear (2011–2016)

Rachael Nicholas

On 3 February 2011, National Theatre Live, then a relatively new initiative, broadcast the Donmar Warehouse production of *King Lear,* with Derek Jacobi in the title role, live to cinema screens across the UK and around the world.[1] Tasked with broadcasting stage productions to a wider audience, this was NT Live's seventh broadcast, and only its second attempt at broadcasting outside the National's complex on the South Bank. There were technical problems. As reviewers of the broadcast recalled, shortly after an emotional Dover cliff scene between Paul Jesson as Gloucester and Gwilym Lee as Edgar, screens went blank and the stage manager intervened to stop the performance.[2] Ironically, the fault was caused by a storm, with high winds knocking an uplink satellite dish out of place, and the work of two engineers '5 floors up and in a howling gale' was required to restore the feed.[3] Despite the issues faced by this first live broadcast of *King Lear,* the play has subsequently appeared more frequently on screen through broadcast than any other Shakespeare play, with seven full-length stage productions digitally distributed between 2011 and the end of 2016.[4] All of these screen *Lear*s were captured digitally and in front of live audience members, but models of distribution have varied. Three of them – the 2011 NT Live, another NT Live in 2014 and a 2016 Royal Shakespeare Company production – were edited in real time and broadcast live to cinema screens. Also distributed via cinema, a 2014 Stratford Ontario Festival production was recorded live, but edited in postproduction and broadcast in February 2015. The three remaining productions were all distributed online: in 2012 Belarus Free Theatre streamed their *King Lear* live as part of Shakespeare's Globe's 'Globe to Globe' festival, reviving and re-streaming it in 2015; Derby-based 1623 Theatre Company livestreamed

their double-bill adaptation, *Lear/Cordelia*, in 2016; and Talawa Theatre
Company recorded their production of the same year over two performances, making the edit available to watch for a limited period of time via
two BBC websites.

In this chapter, I explore the contribution these broadcasts make to
a discussion of *King Lear* on screen, arguing that these new models of
distribution have worked to change relationships between stage productions of the play, screen adaptations and their audiences. Focusing on three
of the four broadcasts filmed for cinematic release – all of which were
directed for screen by multi-camera director Robin Lough – I begin by
addressing how the mechanism of filming these stage productions of *King
Lear* shaped and created meaning for screen audiences. In particular,
I examine how Lough's approach to filming moments of extreme violence
across the three productions illuminates the challenges and complexities of
capturing the play, and a stage director's vision of it, for broadcast. In these
cinema broadcasts, increasing access to stage productions of *King Lear* was
an aim in and of itself. The second part of this chapter explores how online
streams of the play fulfilled functions beyond accessibility through shaping
audience experience. I argue that online streaming provided opportunities
for these productions to engage with their audiences in new ways, enabling
them to increase awareness of the social and political issues that they
explore through their productions of *King Lear*. In the case of 1623
Theatre's production, livestreaming also became an intrinsic part of the
production process, suggesting that the line between stage and screen is
becoming less distinct in an age of digital distribution. Indeed, by changing
the dynamics between the stage and the screen, both cinema and online
theatre broadcasting have had an important, and lasting, impact on the
ways that audiences encounter *King Lear* on screen in the second decade of
the twenty-first century.

Robin Lough's *Lears*

Writing in 2009, on the cusp of the expansion of live theatre broadcasting,
Yvonne Griggs excludes the 2008 television broadcast of Trevor Nunn's
King Lear from her discussion of screen adaptations of the play on the
grounds that she felt there was 'little attempt to relocate' the RSC stage
production, which was filmed in a studio, 'into the very different medium
of television'. Griggs laments the inability of the production to 'transcend
its stage origins', concluding that because of this, it 'brings nothing fresh to
our reading of Shakespeare's play'.[5] A different medium to the television

broadcast, the NT Live cinema broadcasts of the play in 2011 and 2014, and the RSC's cinema broadcast in 2016, also made no attempt to hide their stage origins. On the contrary, they sought to minimize their status as cinema, selling themselves on replicating the theatre experience as closely as possible. Rather than meaning that these productions have nothing new to tell us about *King Lear*, their relationship to the stage illuminates the challenges the play poses to screen presentation, as well as raising questions about the differences between spectatorships of the play in the theatre and in the cinema.

John Wyver has drawn attention to the significant amount of labour and creative craftsmanship required to realize the translation from stage to screen, arguing that theatre broadcasts to cinema constitute 'distinct creative achievements'.[6] The main creative responsible for this translation is the director for screen. Between 2009 and 2016, multi-camera director Robin Lough translated a total of twenty-eight Shakespeare productions from stage to screen for Shakespeare's Globe, NT Live, the RSC and the Almeida theatre, including three cinema broadcasts of *King Lear*. Lough's process involves creating an extensive camera script from a single-view recording of the performance, which then undergoes changes after two camera rehearsals and a consultation with the stage director.[7] John Wyver describes this process as one of 'translation', reflecting the 'strong degree of fidelity to the pre-existing original as well as a recognition of inevitable and intentional creative mediation'.[8] Also acknowledging his own creative agency in the process, Lough himself describes his job as one of 'story-telling', stating that his aim is to find the narrative of the stage production, breaking it down 'in terms of five or six cameras' in order to articulate it on screen.[9]

In *King Lear*, the focus on seeing and not seeing, and the play's scenes of extreme violence, mean that the weight attached to what, and who, the screen audience gets to see, is heightened. Thinking through how modern spectators in the theatre might approach Shakespeare's plays, Pascale Aebischer has argued that performance 'offers the attentive spectator alternative narratives, viewpoints and protagonists' by which they can navigate elements that they find problematic.[10] In guiding the gaze, filming a performance inevitably risks limiting the capacity of the audience to find these alternatives: the screen director must necessarily reject the validity of some readings, while reinforcing the authority of others. This closing off of alternative narratives was clear in Lough's first *Lear* broadcast – the 2011 NT Live production – in which tight framing worked with the intimate space of the Donmar Warehouse to strongly convey Michael Grandage's directorial focus on Lear's personal struggle. In the opening scene, the camera closed in on Jacobi's Lear after wide shots that established a sense of the confined space and pictured the family together. As the scene progressed, close-ups reinforced the growing sense of emotional distance between Lear and his daughters, a distance which was emphasized as Lear drew towards Cordelia, played by Pippa Bennett-Warner, to receive her reply to the love test. As Lear lunged in anger towards Cordelia, she recoiled backwards out of the frame, as the camera remained on Jacobi. This was a pivotal moment in the broadcast – from this moment on, the camera direction placed Lear at the centre of the story, often denying the audience access to reaction shots of other characters. Lough's tight camerawork helped to communicate the personal and emotional focus of the stage production, but shut down the potential for alternative narratives that audiences might have constructed for themselves had they been watching in the theatre.

In his review of the broadcast, Peter Kirwan notes that the 'audience freedom to see whatever isn't in the camera's frame' was sacrificed in exchange for the increased access provided by NT Live.[11] While audience freedom was a casualty of access, it was also curbed by the desire to portray the stage director's vision of the play on film. Speaking about the influence of the stage director on his decision-making, Lough has stated that he tries 'to get in my terms what he would want if he was directing the cameras'.[12] Lough's privileging of directorial intention meant that frustration of the audience's gaze was characteristic of this broadcast and this was acutely felt during the blinding of Gloucester in Act 3, scene 7. As Cornwall went to remove Gloucester's second eye, the camera closely followed Justine Mitchell's Regan as she threatened an off-screen servant with a sword, blocking the main action from the view of the screen audience. The focus on Regan foregrounded her involvement in the act of violence, reflecting the focus of the production on the breakdown of family and Lear's mistreatment at the hands of his daughters. However, screening the scene in this way had wider implications for the cinema audience. Aebischer argues that, on stage, the blinding represents a crucial moment of identification for the audience in which they are 'made to feel complicit in the violence perpetrated' by the act of witnessing it. She suggests that the scene 'performs its own violence on the audience' as they are torn between empathy and aesthetic appreciation.[13] Lough's filming prevents the screen audience from participating in this aesthetic appreciation, and, because they are physically distant from the stage with no hope of intervening, it detracts from their complicity in the act. Instead, the violence performed on the audience is one of a lack of control – at the exact moment in the play where the metaphorical dangers of seeing and not seeing are made manifest, the audience were made aware of their own incapacity to choose where to look.

While restricting the audience's view of the scene may have metaphorically subjected the audience to Lear's emotional tyranny by carefully manipulating and frustrating their gaze, on a more practical level, the decision to avoid showing the gouging itself may also have been determined by the difficulties inherent in filming stage violence. The challenge of capturing staged violence without exposing its theatricality, and thus undermining its impact, is demonstrated by a moment in Lough's second broadcast of *King Lear*. In this 2014 production, stage director Sam Mendes added an extra-textual ending to the mock-trial scene in which Lear, mistaking the Fool's performance as Regan for the real thing, batters him to death in a bathtub. The archived production bible contains a 'blood plot', detailing how any scene involving stage blood was managed. It describes how the illusion of this attack was created by Simon Russell Beale's Lear beating the Fool with a rubber pipe before subtly exchanging it for a metal equivalent clipped to the inside of the bath. This was then thrown to the ground, creating a convincing clang.[14] While audiences in the Olivier Theatre were far enough away for this to seem realistic, as the camera tightened in on Russell Beale in the broadcast, the rubber pipe with which he was beating the Fool was visibly bendy, making the scene uncomfortably funny. In a reversal of the filming of the Donmar's blinding scene, the camera got too close to the stage violence, rendering it ridiculous. Lough's choice to film the scene in this way seems all the more confusing considering that wide shots of the vast Olivier stage were possible, and were often utilized during the broadcast. Again, Lough's decisions here can be seen as guided by the stage director's vision. In contrast to Grandage's period design, Mendes's production focused on the epic and the political, and was set in a vaguely dystopian contemporary world over which Lear was dictator. The close-up of Russell Beale's face portrayed the unpredictable brutality of this Lear, but prioritized the director's reading over translating the theatre audience's experience onto screen.

The sheer scale of this production, in both size and theme, seems to have posed other problems for Lough's translation to broadcast. From interviews with Mendes, Jonathan Croall reports that the size of the Olivier stage was the key driving factor in all production decisions, resulting in what Peter Kirwan describes as 'an enormous, spectacular reading' with 'a flair for the gory, melodramatic and noisy'.[15] Conversely, as Janice Wardle argues, Lough's camera angles 'seemed to favour a narrative about family politics rather than Mendes's desired expanded focus on the wider political significance of the play'. Wardle attributes this to a predominance of tracking shots and close-ups that obscured the production's wider political resonances, working instead to tell the story of Lear's deteriorating mental state, which was figured throughout as the result of dementia.[16] With the broadcast perhaps magnifying a conflict between Mendes's political reading of the play and Russell Beale's medical diagnosis of Lear, Wardle notes that throughout the first half of the play, close-ups of Russell Beale's 'hand tremors, repeated scratching ... and a stooped shuffling walk' presented the symptoms of dementia clearly to the cinema audience.[17] The pre-recorded interviews with cast members shown in the interval of the broadcast also contributed to the portrayal of this narrative by focusing heavily on Russell Beale's research into the disease and his application of this research to his characterization of Lear. As Wardle argues, this 'ratcheted up' audience sympathy for Lear, and in the second half of the play, the use of more obvious, and problematic, signposting of mental illness, including a straitjacket and sedative injection, felt jarring on screen. As the filming of this production demonstrates, the multiple possible readings of *King Lear* complicate the broadcast process. Although Lough states that translating the director's vision is primary, in practice, this purpose can be derailed by a number of factors, including (as here) the influence of the star actor playing Lear. If a number of readings are present, or competing, in a production, the screen director must either choose which narrative to tell or to reflect the contradictions inherent in the production. While the second option might, arguably, faithfully represent the experience of the theatre audience, the decision is complicated by the impulse to create a coherent narrative for the cinema audience, and by the practical production conditions, under which the screen director is employed by the theatre company to create a favourable screen version of the stage production that must be commercially acceptable.

The narratives that screen directors are able to tell are also heavily shaped by the size and space of the theatres in which they are filming. In capturing Gregory Doran's RSC 2016 production of *King Lear* for cinema, Lough was able to use the depth of the Royal Shakespeare Theatre's thrust stage to provide the cinema audience with access to multiple focal points within the same shot, visually setting up relationships between characters. In the opening scene, Lough was aided in this by Niki Turner's set design, which sat Antony Sher's Lear on top of a glass box above the rest of the

ensemble. The addition of height enabled the use of a single long shot from
the front of the stage to capture the entrance of the court. As the camera
panned slowly down, it framed Cordelia, played by Natalie Simpson,
centrally, blocking Lear from view. This shot and others in the opening
scene, including a shot of Cordelia and Nia Gwynne's Goneril greeting
each other warmly beneath Lear's glass case, foregrounded the female
characters and suggested the existence of a story beyond Lear's narrative.
In stark contrast to the filming of the same scene in the 2011 NT Live
broadcast, when Lear denounced Cordelia, the camera remained on her,
capturing her reaction to her father's anger.

While this difference in filming shows a potential progression in how
mainstream UK stages have chosen to deal with the misogyny in the play,
these moments only hinted at possible alternative narratives, and the
production fell back on a relatively traditional interpretation, focused on
Lear. Andrew Cowie argues that there was a 'glimpse of something stranger
and more interesting beneath [this] traditional period presentation' but
that the production ultimately failed to 'challenge accusations of a creeping
conservatism' at the RSC under Greg Doran's artistic directorship.[18]
Lough's shot choice picked up on, and often amplified, these 'glimpses',
but the measured shot compositions and slow editing pace that allowed
Lough to highlight alternative relationships could also have contributed to
a sense of conservatism, by creating a distanced, and emotionally detached,
mode of spectatorship. This was evident in the filming of the blinding
scene, which occurred inside of another transparent box in the middle of
the stage. Although the blinding itself was shot in full view, it was filmed
through the glass, distancing the cinema audience from the immediacy of
the act. The glass box served to stage the blinding as a spectacle, shifting the
focus from the act itself to the witnessing of it. The focus on the violence of
witnessing was further heightened in the broadcast by the thrust stage of
the RST, which meant that the theatre audience seated on either side of the
stage were occasionally visible in shot. Twice removed from the action,
firstly by the glass box and then the camera lens, and constantly reminded
of the artifice of the act by the presence of the audience, the cinema
audience were distanced from the scene's emotional energy.

In all of Lough's productions of *King Lear*, translating moments of
violence from the stage to the screen was a stumbling block. Designed to
have an effect on physically present audience members in the theatre, the
impact of the stage violence was necessarily altered when translated to
screen for audiences who were physically distant from the action. Close-
ups, framing and the sequence of shots also contributed to altering the

cinema audience's relationship to the play. In theory, these decisions attempted to create a narrative that enhanced 'the viewer's perception of the original production's impact by continuously guiding the viewer into a position to apprehend the stage director's vision'.[19] But in practice, the versions of the play the cinema audience experienced were influenced by multiple factors and possible interpretations of the play. These included not just those of the director or the actors but also the audience's own expectations, formed by previous encounters with the play. In shaping meaning for the audience, and creating less scope for alternative viewpoints, these cinema broadcasts set up new negotiations between stage productions of *King Lear* and screen audiences, in which frustration of expectations, as well as tensions between creatives, was a key aspect of both production and reception.

Lear Livestreamed

While camera direction in Lough's cinema broadcasts altered meaning for screen audiences, the physical conditions of cinema reception closely replicated those of the theatre: audiences watched the broadcasts, complete with an interval, at a prescribed time, in a darkened auditorium, along with other audience members.[20] However, during the same period, more radical ways of encountering the play in performance were also being established through online streaming. Free at the point of access, audiences could watch these productions anywhere with a reliable internet connection and they could start, stop or catch up later as they liked. They could also connect with other audience members online through social media, or give feedback to the theatre company as they watched. Due to the development of streaming functions in free-to-use platforms such as Facebook and YouTube, online streaming is simpler and less expensive than cinema distribution, making it available to companies with smaller budgets. As the streams do not necessarily have to be commercially profitable, it is possible to stream work that takes greater risks, or even work that is incomplete. As well as affecting reception, this form of distribution has altered what kinds of *King Lear* audiences can access on screen, and has challenged traditional models of production.

Unlike cinema broadcast production, which begins when the stage production is '"locked" at press night', online streaming was an integral part of the different agendas of these productions.[21] Providing greater, and more convenient, access to (partially publically funded) mainstream productions of the play was the main purpose of the cinema broadcasts, and the process of broadcasting had little to no influence on, or relationship with, the stage production processes. While access was a driving factor in the online streams of *King Lear*, all three used the play to explore contemporary social and political issues, and utilized streaming as a way of raising awareness. Related to a broader use of the Internet for campaigning and activism, online streaming provided a way of increasing the visibility of the socially focused agendas of the productions. For example, in Talawa Theatre Company's *King Lear: the Film* – directed for stage by Michael Buffong and for screen by Bridget Caldwell – Lear's family is cast as black, serving to remind audiences 'that the presence and influence of black people is potentially un-documented in our ancient history', while also addressing 'the debate about the lack of availability of roles for black actors in the UK'.[22] The production was made available to watch for free online via the BBC's 'Shakespeare Lives' website in 2016, increasing the visibility of the issues at play, as well as of the actors themselves.

Similarly, Belarus Free Theatre's livestream of *King Lear*, directed for stage by Vladimir Shcherban and performed in Belarusian, had political activism at its heart. Exiled from their own country, the company's performance was part of their 'Staging a Revolution' festival, which sought to raise awareness of censorship in Belarus, as well as aiming to 'invigorate and inspire UK audiences to see themselves as positive change-makers'. The festival performances, all of which were livestreamed, were followed by panel discussions with experts, artists, campaigners and activists, based around a theme linked to the performance. Their production of *King Lear* explored their own experiences of tyranny and exile, 'drawing parallels between Lear's spiraling court and Belarusian society' and was followed by a panel called 'Let's Act: Mortality', a discussion around the future of old age, featuring biologists, neuroscientists and philosophers.[23] As the only way that audiences in Belarus could watch the performance, livestreaming was not only a way of gaining visibility but also a political and revolutionary tool.

The inclusion of panels alongside the production in the case of Belarus Free Theatre indicates the increasingly discursive mode of participation emerging alongside online broadcasts. I have argued elsewhere that, through social media and comment functions online, streams of Shakespeare productions enable a two-way interaction between the audience and the theatre company.[24] The sense that the online audience can be active participants in, and not just respondents to, a production was further explored by the livestream of 1623 Theatre Company's adaptation, *Lear/ Cordelia*. The back-to-back productions foregrounded the issues surrounding living with, and caring for, those with dementia, and were part of the company's ongoing research and development project exploring *King Lear* in the context of the disease. The first play, written and directed by Ben Spiller, resituated Lear into a modern-day care home. In fragmented episodes, Lear, played by David Henry, failed to recognize his only visitor, his daughter Cordelia (Gemma Paige North), and had recollections of a family birthday party in which distorted projections of Goneril and Regan, created by digital artist Darius Powell, played out behind him. The second play, newly written by Farrah Chaudhry and directed by Louie Ingram, focused on the relationship between Cordelia and Lear, and was driven by a desire to 'give this marginalised female character a strong voice to tell her untold story'.[25]

The filming of the production was undertaken by Pilot Theatre, a theatre company in their own right, who specialize in livestreaming performance. The stream was hosted on the 1623 Theatre website via YouTube's livestreaming function, along with a British Sign Language interpreted feed. Recordings of both performances, along with a Q&A discussion with the audience, to which they had invited experts and campaigners in the area of dementia research, remain available to watch on the 1623 website.[26] Unlike the other online and cinema broadcasts, which were of 'finished' productions, this livestream was of a pilot production. Rather than being a recording of a final piece, it was part of an active process of development, used partly to attract crowdfunding for a future tour, as well as to gather audience feedback.[27] The audience of the live-stream were not only able to respond and react to the performance through Twitter using the hashtag #LearCordelia, but this response had real impact in shaping the story that the company continue to tell of *King Lear* and dementia. As well as allowing more people to see the production (as of September 2017, the production had 1570 views including 311 views with British Sign Language interpretation), by extending access to audience members who might find the theatre or the cinema a stressful or impossible experience, this livestreamed adaptation of *King Lear* altered traditional one-way relationships between theatre broadcasts and the audience.[28]

These productions demonstrate how online streaming of the play can go beyond increasing accessibility, challenging ideas about what theatre broadcasting and screen versions of *King Lear* can be used for. Beyond access, they used *King Lear* as a way of widening conversations around pressing social issues, and the architecture of online streaming and social media allowed them to extend those conversations beyond the theatre auditorium. As Belarus Free Theatre argues on their website, 'the space for free exchange of ideas and open debate is as valuable as the space in which to see independent theatre'. Livestreaming opened up new spaces and channels for this exchange of ideas, stretching the conception of what was possible through digital distribution. Not only interested in access for its own sake or in bringing audiences into theatre auditoriums, through online streaming these productions prioritized marginalized narratives, characters and actors, using *King Lear* as a catalyst to provoke wider social and political action.

The Future of *King Lear* on Screen?

During this five-year period, audiences have had access to a relatively high number of new screen versions of *King Lear* through theatre broadcasting. There was not enough space in this chapter to discuss Stratford Festival HD's broadcast of the play to cinemas from Ontario, Canada, in 2015, and Shakespeare's Globe's broadcast of the play live to cinemas in September 2017 came too late to be included. Given both the frequency with which the play appears on stage, and the speed with which technology continues to develop, this corpus of *King Lear* broadcasts looks set both to grow, and to expand into new forms of screen performance. These productions characterize our contemporary moment of the play on screen, and will likely be a significant feature of *King Lear*'s future screen presentations. They also offer plenty of fresh ways of looking at the play. The extensive work by Robin Lough shows the effort that goes in to successfully 'relocating' theatrical presentations into cinema, demonstrating how camera direction is adapted to theatre spaces, production styles and stage directors' visions, all of which shape meaning for the audience.

Beyond camerawork, audience experience is also influenced by the mode of distribution itself. Online livestreams have created new ways of encountering *King Lear* in performance, reimagining traditional relationships between stage, screen and audience. In streams such as 1623's *Lear/Cordelia*, the screen becomes more than just a way of displaying the stage production. Instead, the online broadcast amplifies the social engagement the adaptation is designed to foster. These new ways of using online broadcasts create an increasingly porous boundary between stage and screen. Where previously screen audiences have been excluded from stage production processes, they can now talk back to them, influencing decision-making. These channels for conversation allow the political relevance of *King Lear* to provoke discussion and, potentially, action. The lower costs of online distribution and the usually free cost of access also mean that wider and more diverse audiences can participate in these discussions.[29]

The fluidity of the relationship between stage and screen in these broadcasts poses a challenge to the future study of Shakespeare on screen. Somewhere between the ephemerality of theatre and the permanency of film, they create screen versions that are often transient, with recordings or DVDs rarely made available. As broadcasts expand into new and emerging media forms and audience engagement becomes a more prominent feature of online broadcasts, capturing and understanding audience experience is of increased importance. In order to trace how Shakespeare's plays are received across screen media, future research will need to find ways of dealing with these challenges. Both the cinema and online broadcasts of *King Lear* are important developments in the performance history of the play. To date, online broadcasts of the play have been critically neglected, but they demonstrate sharply how screen versions of the play can be put to use in the twenty-first century. Their prioritization of action over access and the way they disrupt traditional interfaces between the stage, the screen and audiences make the future of this play on screen a particularly exciting prospect.

Notes

1. National Theatre Live was set up by the National Theatre in 2009 to broadcast their productions to cinemas. Productions are broadcast live in the UK, and 'as live', with a time delay, internationally. They were inspired by a similar programme organized by the Metropolitan Opera in New York, which has been running since 2006. Other Shakespeare institutions and theatres have since set up broadcasting schemes, including the RSC and Shakespeare's Globe. For a full list of digital screen broadcasts of Shakespeare productions, see R. Nicholas, 'Filmography', in P. Aebischer, S. Greenhalgh and L. E. Osborne (eds.), *Shakespeare and the 'Live' Theatre Broadcast Experience* (London: Bloomsbury, 2018), 227–42. 'National Theatre Live' will henceforth be referred to as 'NT Live'.

2. See P. Kirwan, 'King Lear (Donmar/NT Live) @Warwick Arts Centre Cinema' *The Bardathon*, 4 February 2011, http://blogs.nottingham.ac.uk/bardathon/2011/02/04/king-lear-donmarnt-live-warwick-arts-centre-cinema/ (accessed 15 December 2017). Also see D. Bowie-Sell, 'Donmar's King Lear at the Cinema has Technical Hiccups', *The Telegraph*, 4 February 2011, and S. Purcell, '*King Lear* Performed by the Donmar Warehouse (Review)', *Shakespeare Bulletin* 32.2 (2014): 264–6.

3. See https://satfacts.creativebroadcastsolutions.com/2011/02/04/nt-live-king-lear-3/ (accessed 14 December 2017).

4. A shortened adaptation of *King Lear* was also streamed as part of Forced Entertainment's *Complete Works: Table Top Shakespeare* in 2015.
5. Y. Griggs, *Shakespeare's 'King Lear': the Relationship between Text and Film* (London: Methuen Drama, 2009), 191–2.
6. J. Wyver, "'All the Trimmings?'": the Transfer of Theatre to Television in Adaptations of Shakespeare Stagings', *Adaptation* 7.2 (2014), 118. Wyver produces the RSC Live from Stratford-upon-Avon productions, henceforth referred to as 'RSC Live'.
7. For extensive details of the broadcast production process see J. Wyver, 'Screening the RSC Stage: the 2014 Live from Stratford-upon-Avon Cinema Broadcasts', *Shakespeare* (British Shakespeare Association) 11.3 (2015): 286–302. Also see A. Stone, 'Not Making a Movie: the Livecasting of Shakespeare Stage Productions by the Royal National Theatre and the Royal Shakespeare Company', *Shakespeare Bulletin* 34.4 (2016): 627–43.
8. Wyver, 'Screening', 290.
9. Quoted in Wyver, 'Screening', 296.
10. P. Aebischer, *Shakespeare's Violated Bodies: Stage and Screen Performance* (Cambridge: Cambridge UP, 2004), 5.
11. Kirwan, 'King Lear (Donmar/NT Live)'.
12. Quoted in Wyver, 'Screening', 293.
13. Aebischer, *Shakespeare's Violated Bodies*, 164.
14. Production bible for *King Lear* 2014, National Theatre Archive.
15. J. Croall, *Performing King Lear: Gielgud to Russell Beale* (London: Bloomsbury, 2015); P. Kirwan, 'King Lear (National Theatre/NT Live) @ The Broadway, Nottingham', *The Bardathon*, 2 May 2014, http://blogs.nottingham.ac.uk/barda thon/2014/05/02/king-lear-national-theatrent-live-the-broadway-nottingham/ (accessed 14 December 2017).
16. J. Wardle, '"Outside Broadcast": Looking Backwards and Forwards, Live Theatre in the Cinema – NT and RSC Live', *Adaptation* 7.2 (2014), 146.
17. Wardle, 'Outside Broadcast', 146.
18. A. Cowie, 'King Lear @ Royal Shakespeare Theatre', *Reviewing Shakespeare*, n.d.: http://bloggingshakespeare.com/reviewing-shakespeare/king-lear-rsc-royal-shake speare-theatre-stratford-upon-avon-england-2016/ (accessed 21 December 2017).
19. M. D. Friedman, 'The Shakespeare Cinemacast: *Coriolanus*', *Shakespeare Quarterly* 67.4 (2016), 470.
20. All three cinema broadcasts were transmitted live, with 'encore' screenings available. Only the RSC production was made available on DVD. The only legal way of watching recordings of the NT Live productions is at the NT Archives in London.
21. Wyver, 'Screening', 292.
22. 'King Lear Broadcast', *Talawa Theatre Company*, n.d., www.talawa.com/arti cles/king-lear-broadcast (accessed 12 October 2017). King Lear was played by Don Warrington. See J. Rogers, 'Talawa and Black Theatre Live: "Creating the Ira Aldridges that Are Remembered" – Live Theatre Broadcast and the Historical Record', in Aebischer, Greenhalgh and Osborne (eds.), *Shakespeare*

and the *'Live' Theatre Broadcast Experience* (2018), 147–59, for a detailed
discussion of the production.
23. 'Staging a Revolution', *Ministry of Counterculture*, 2 November 2015, https://
    moc.media/en/events/21 (accessed 21 December 2017).
24. R. Nicholas, 'Understanding "New" Encounters with Shakespeare: Hybrid
    Media and Emerging Audience Behaviours', in Aebischer, Greenhalgh and
    Osborne (eds.), *Shakespeare and the 'Live' Theatre Broadcast Experience*
    (London: Bloomsbury, 2018), 77–92.
25. 'Lear/dementia project update', *1623 Theatre Company*, 16 July 2014, www
    .1623theatre.co.uk/news/latest-news/291-leardementia-project-update
    (accessed 21 December 2017).
26. As of September 2017. *'Lear/Cordelia* livestream from Attenborough Arts
    Centre', *1623 Theatre Company*, n.d., www.1623theatre.co.uk/performance/l
    earcordelia (accessed 21 December 2017).
27. The crowdfunding page can be found at www.gofundme.com/LearCordeli
    a2018 (accessed 21 December 2017).
28. Thanks to Ben Spiller of 1623 Theatre for providing these figures.
29. A 2016 Arts Council England report into Live-to-digital theatre found that
    online audiences were younger and more diverse than cinema broadcast
    audiences. See B. K. Reidy, B. Schutt, D. Abramson and A. Durski, 'From
    Live-to-Digital: Understanding the Impact of Digital Developments in
    Theatre on Audiences, Production and Distribution', *Arts Council England*,
    11 October 2016: www.artscouncil.org.uk/publication/live-digital (accessed
    30 June 2017).

WORKS CITED

Aebischer, P., *Shakespeare's Violated Bodies: Stage and Screen Performance*
    (Cambridge: Cambridge University Press, 2004).
Cowie, A., 'King Lear @ Royal Shakespeare Theatre', *Reviewing Shakespeare*, n.d.:
    http://bloggingshakespeare.com/reviewing-shakespeare/king-lear-rsc-royal-sh
    akespeare-theatre-stratford-upon-avon-england-2016/ (accessed 21 December
    2017).
Croall, J., *Performing King Lear: Gielgud to Russell Beale* (London: Bloomsbury, 2015).
Friedman, M. D., 'The Shakespeare Cinemacast: *Coriolanus*', *Shakespeare
    Quarterly* 67.4 (2016): 457–80.
Griggs, Y., *Screen Adaptations: Shakespeare's 'King Lear': the Relationship between
    Text and Film* (London: Methuen Drama, 2009).
Kirwan, P., 'King Lear (Donmar/NT Live) @ Warwick Arts Centre Cinema' *The
    Bardathon*, 4 February 2011: http://blogs.nottingham.ac.uk/bardathon/2011/02/
    04/king-lear-donmarnt-live-warwick-arts-centre-cinema/ (accessed 21 December
    2017).
'King Lear (National Theatre/NT Live) @ The Broadway, Nottingham', *The
    Bardathon*, 2 May 2014: http://blogs.nottingham.ac.uk/bardathon/2014/05/

02/king-lear-national-theatrent-live-the-broadway-nottingham/ (accessed 21 December 2017).

Nicholas, R., 'Understanding "New" Encounters with Shakespeare: Hybrid Media and Emerging Audience Behaviours', in P. Aebischer, S. Greenhalgh and L. E. Osborne (eds.), *Shakespeare and the 'Live' Theatre Broadcast Experience* (London: Bloomsbury, 2018), 77–92.

'Filmography', in P. Aebischer, S. Greenhalgh and L. E. Osborne (eds.), *Shakespeare and the 'Live' Theatre Broadcast Experience* (London: Bloomsbury, 2018), 227–42.

Purcell, S., '*King Lear* Performed by the Donmar Warehouse (Review)', *Shakespeare Bulletin* 32.2 (2014): 264–6.

Reidy, B. K., B. Schutt, D. Abramson and A. Durski, 'From Live-to-Digital: Understanding the Impact of Digital Developments in Theatre on Audiences, Production and Distribution', *Arts Council England*, 11 October 2016: www.artscouncil.org.uk/publication/live-digital (accessed 30 June 2017).

Rogers, J., 'Talawa and Black Theatre Live: "Creating the Ira Aldridges That Are Remembered" – Live Theatre Broadcast and the Historical Record', in P. Aebischer, S. Greenhalgh and L. E. Osborne (eds.), *Shakespeare and the 'Live' Theatre Broadcast Experience* (London: Bloomsbury, 2018), 147–59.

Stone, A., 'Not Making a Movie: the Livecasting of Shakespeare Stage Productions by the Royal National Theatre and The Royal Shakespeare Company', *Shakespeare Bulletin* 34.4 (2016): 627–43.

Wardle, J., '"Outside Broadcast": Looking Backwards and Forwards, Live Theatre in the Cinema – NT and RSC Live', *Adaptation* 7.2 (2014): 134–53.

Wyver, J., '"All the Trimmings?": the Transfer of Theatre to Television in Adaptations of Shakespeare Stagings', *Adaptation* 7.2 (2014): 104–20.

'Screening the RSC Stage: the 2014 Live from Stratford-upon-Avon Cinema Broadcasts', *Shakespeare* 11.3 (2015): 286–302.

CHAPTER 6

Re-shaping Old Course in a Country New: Producing Nation, Culture and King Lear in Slings and Arrows

Lois Leveen

Only pseudo-intellectuals boast that they never watch television. If it ever comes around again, be sure to watch *Slings and Arrows*, a gentle Canadian TV satire series of six comic/dramatic episodes as actors struggle at the New Burbage Theatre. The problem with criticism of TV is that it consists mostly of telling people to watch or miss what they have already missed anyway. TV is ephemeral, but it actually has a greater impact on more people than almost all stage productions. Think of what BBC did to promote Shakespeare worldwide with its TV versions of all the plays. Think how many more people saw those productions than have seen the plays in theaters.[1]

I open with Leonard R. N. Ashley's appraisal of *Slings and Arrows* not because it is a useful assessment but because it is so flawed, in ways that underscore precisely why the series is worth scholarly consideration. Even as he lambastes pseudo-intellectuals for boasting that they never watch television, Ashley fails to recognize that intellectuals have tools for analysing television programmes, just as we do written texts. Moreover, while he lauds television for its ability to reach larger audiences than theatrical productions, he does not distinguish between the BBC TV Shakespeare or other productions that broadcast a single, fully staged play, and the more complicated show-within-a-show presentation of Shakespeare in the workplace dramedy *Slings and Arrows*.[2]

Ashley also falsely equates the ephemeral nature of a single broadcast with the medium itself. To state the obvious, the rebroadcasting of episodes, the home recording of shows by individual viewers and the release of entire series via VHS, DVD, Blu-Ray and digital streaming allow audiences to watch and re-watch television productions whenever they wish. These means of multiple viewings are essential for those who engage in the sort of television criticism Ashley fails to realize is possible. His superimposing the ephemeral nature of an unrecorded stage performance onto TV is particularly remarkable in light of the way that the television series *Slings and Arrows* makes the case for the supremacy of stage performance by using the full power of television as a medium. Moreover, Ashley, an American critic writing in English for a French-titled multilingual journal published in Switzerland, seems oblivious to the national and cultural tensions embodied in this 'gentle Canadian TV satire'. By contrast, in this essay I will focus on the overdetermined yet ambivalent relationship between television and stage production in *Slings and Arrows*, while also probing how assertions and assumptions about nation and culture shape the final season of the series, which focuses on the rehearsal and performance of *King Lear*.

Wooing in Festival Terms: Making *Lear* into Theatre's Love Story

Slings and Arrows originally aired on the Canadian cable channel The Movie Network from 2003 to 2006. Each of the series's three seasons corresponds to a performance season at the fictional New Burbage Festival in which the show is set. As the series begins, Geoffrey Tennant becomes artistic director of the festival following the sudden death of Oliver Welles, Geoffrey's one-time director – a mentor turned tormentor under whose egotistical guidance the festival has grown bloated and bereft of meaningfulness. Once dead, Welles appears as a ghost haunting and taunting Geoffrey as Geoffrey directs the festival cast and crew to prepare a mainstage production of that festival season's Shakespeare tragedy (*Hamlet*, *Macbeth* and *King Lear*, respectively), the themes of which infuse hilarious and heartbreaking backstage plots interweaving actors, directors, stage crew, business office staff and board members. *Slings and Arrows* thus provides an episodic, televisual adaptation akin to the Shakespeare films Kenneth Rothwell labels 'mirror movies'.[3] This thematic seepage highlights the idea that Shakespeare is indeed 'relatable', depicting emotional conflicts as relevant today as they were centuries ago.[4] Nevertheless, Shakespeare's supremacy demands defence: the main arc of the series involves the festival's struggle to stay culturally relevant and financially solvent. Throughout this paean to the power and importance of live theatre, plotlines mock the public's obsession with celebrity over talent, and deride actors drawn to the lucre and lustre of film and television over the artistic primacy of the stage (the fact that many of the actors in the series have performed at Canada's legendary Stratford Festival makes this japing all the more parodic).

But even as it knowingly winks at its own status as a television series, *Slings and Arrows* – which, in the years since it originally aired, has garnered far more viewers and far greater critical acclaim globally through rebroadcasts, DVD releases and streaming digital availability – embodies the tension between the ephemeral nature of live theatre and the lasting media of film and television. This tension comes to poignant fruition in the final season, in which Geoffrey discovers that Charles Kingman, the legendary actor he has cast as Lear, is dying of cancer: the impermanence of performance serves metonymically for the impermanence of life itself.[5] Yet the series finale reveals the possibility that television can mediate that impermanence, because a year after the final episode aired, William Hutt, who played Charles, died of leukaemia. Although Hutt was a mainstay of Canada's Stratford Festival for decades, his live performances as Lear were never recorded. Thus, this television production in which Hutt plays Charles playing Lear (depicted primarily in rehearsal scenes, emphasizing the process by which actors master roles) has become what survives of Hutt's theatrical artistry.

This preservation through television was an intentional outcome of *Slings and Arrows* – one that simultaneously reveals how the series invokes themes of national culture. Susan Coyne, who co-created and co-wrote the series (appearing in all eighteen episodes in the role of festival administrator Anna Conroy), notes that including the ageing and ailing Hutt was central to the decision to feature *Lear* in the final season:

> I had done a production of *Lear* with Bill Hutt at Stratford in the Young Company, and it always killed us, those of us who were there, that it didn't exist on film, his performance. So that was another reason we really wanted to do the *Lear* and get Bill. Because he'd done seven or eight productions of it by that point, and he is, sadly, gone, but he was, I think, one of the very best Shakespeare actors that North America has ever produced, and he was ours.[6]

Describing Hutt as 'one of the very best Shakespeare actors that North America has ever produced', then proudly proclaiming 'and he was ours', Coyne (perhaps inadvertently) calls out one of the show's central concerns: establishing the legitimacy of Canadian theatre, particularly as it is dominated on the one hand by its cultural debt to the English playwright and on the other by the cultural dominance of the United States. Hutt's greatness is measured by his talents as a Shakespearean among a competitive North American field, while his Canadianness is a source of (suitably humble) national pride.

But Hutt playing Charles playing Lear is not the same as Hutt performing Lear on stage for a live audience. *Slings and Arrows*'s recording of Hutt's performance involves a careful deploying of the technical aspects of television. In the series's penultimate episode, we see a rehearsal of Act 2, scene 4, which begins *in medias res* with the line 'I gave you all' (2.4.243). Here Charles delivers his Lear as amazing, unnerving and unhinged, a performance framed for television viewers by cross-cuts to the house of the theatre, where other cast members and the director watch in astonishment as Charles attacks New Burbage's mainstay leading lady Ellen Fanshaw, who portrays Regan. The unstable mental state of the speaker is underscored by the wandering gaze of the camera itself, which circles unsteadily on Charles and Ellen, and on the spectators within the theatre. At this point, Geoffrey is the only character who knows of Charles's illness. But the television audience is already aware of it and, as we watch, it is difficult to determine whether to attribute the raging performance (and its technical counterpart, the roving camera) to Charles's intentional acting as Lear, or whether what we are watching is partially or wholly the result of his illness, or of the multiple medications he is taking, or simply of his always bitter personality. Hutt's performance renders this one of the most emotionally wrenching scenes in the series, even as it distils a theme that runs through *Slings and Arrows* as a whole, and its *Lear* in particular: the blurred lines between acting and living, between what is merely a show and what is the world.

The scene exemplifies the characteristics of the series that have attracted scholarly attention. Elizabeth Klett argues that the series uses television techniques to teach the television audience how to appreciate Shakespeare: 'While we see a kind of "greatest hits" version of each play that foregrounds particular well-known lines and scenes, we also see numerous shots of audience members responding to what is happening onstage, and they are nearly always emotionally engaged.'[7] Osborne notes that 'While critiquing the relationship between television and theater, the series develops increasingly nuanced representations of how theater and recorded performances now collude to create twenty-first-century Shakespeare'. Referring to *Slings and Arrows*'s fictionalizing of the Stratford Festival as 'TV à clef', she categorizes it as a product of a particular national culture: 'Whereas televising Shakespeare in Britain and the US has most frequently taken the form of full performances or adaptations of individual plays, Canada's *Slings & Arrows* embraces the serial nature of television as a medium and deploys both sequencing and seasons to create a more extensive and sustained engagement with the problems of intermedial performance.'[8]

Other critics also focus on how Canadianness shapes the show's treatment of Shakespeare. Reading the series against the actual history of Canadian theatre in which 'promoting institutions like Stratford [served to] protect Canada from overwhelming American culture', Ormsby sees it as a 'comment more specifically on how postwar Canada has employed Shakespeare to assuage American cultural dominance'.[9] Identifying *Slings and Arrows*'s invocation of Shakespeare as an 'emotional realism' through which 'the series discredits directorial concepts, experimentation, and overly methodological approaches to Shakespeare as failing to honor Author and Text', Klett similarly identifies a particularly nationalized Bardolatry: 'As *Slings and Arrows* is a series about specifically Canadian approaches to Shakespeare, these views are perhaps unsurprising, as such a reverential approach to Shakespeare is particularly prevalent in Canada and other postcolonial cultures.'[10] Pittman problematizes this view, identifying at least some resistance in Canada's postcolonial status, as reflected in the fictitious name 'New Burbage', which is 'a mark of Canada's historical and cultural indebtedness' to England: 'As in all colonial relationships, the "new" suggests both derivation from an originary source and the liberating prospect of a fresh original untrammeled by the shackles of a homeland's traditions and dysfunctions.'[11]

I agree that, throughout the series, Geoffrey and his more dedicated actors must fend off the encroachment of film and television, of theme parks and musicals, of a crass commercialization associated in part with the United States, but also with the worst of Canadian corporatization, which infects the festival itself.[12] It is not difficult to read *Slings and Arrows* as an effort to assert the primacy not only of Shakespeare but of a particular kind of theatrical purity that eschews the production techniques that have come to be associated in the series with Oliver's directorship of the New Burbage Festival and with Stratford in real life. But I want to offer a more subversive reading of season three's treatment of how to produce *Lear*, and of the series finale overall, rooted in a broader examination of nationhood and the imbrication of culture with theatrical technique.

The Promised End? Escaping the Shakespeare Festival to Reclaim National and Cultural Identity

Slings and Arrows's show-within-a-show format repeatedly reveals aspects of theatrical technique while masking the corresponding aspects of television technique. For example, repeated audio motifs (a metronymic beat, harp arpeggios) cue the television audience's emotional response to specific Shakespeare performances.[13] These embedded elements – meant to be unexamined and perhaps even undetected by most viewers – contrast with the overdetermined focus in season three on theatrical sound effects. In the season's first episode, a sound designer excitedly demonstrates the Sierra System, an expensive, computer-driven technology which he wants to use for *Lear*. The television audience observes wind, rain, thunder and lightning sweeping across the empty mainstage, intercut with shots of Geoffrey, the stage manager and other crew members seated in the house, their faces alternately lit and darkened by the effects they are watching. Once the demonstration ends, the crew members applaud, while Geoffrey remains dubious. He notices Nahum, the festival's Nigerian-born security guard, making his way across the now quiet stage.

GEOFFREY: Nahum, what do you think?
NAHUM: Hard for me to say. In my theater in Nigeria, we would
             shake a large piece of tin. It worked quite well.

This seemingly noncommittal reply echoes a more revealing exchange Nahum has with Oliver in the first episode of the series, as the two watch the festival's premiere of *A Midsummer Night's Dream* (which turns out to be the last show Oliver directs before his death):

OLIVER: It's dreadful, isn't it?
NAHUM: The production values are very high.
OLIVER: Very diplomatic of you, Nahum. Oh God! There's not one
          moment of truth in this whole production.
NAHUM: Truth can be a very dangerous thing. Before I left Nigeria,
          I directed a production of Ken Saro-Wiwa's *The Wheel*,
          which was perhaps too openly critical of the Abacha regime.
OLIVER: How did it go over?
NAHUM: Oh, the soldiers came and burned our sets and beat the actors
          with sticks.
OLIVER: Thanks for the perspective.

While Nahum's response regarding the Sierra System might seem less overtly political, it actually sets up what is perhaps the most radical statement of the series, which plays out across the entire third season, through a combination of overt references to the theatrical sound effects used for the stage version of the storm and the covert use of televisual audio techniques. Although Nahum's 'It worked quite well' are the last words of dialogue spoken in the scene, the camera cuts back to Geoffrey for another five seconds, during which he is framed in close-up first against the crew members seated in the house and then against Nahum standing alone on stage, as folk music begins to play. The volume rises in an audio fade into the next scene, which begins with a visual shot of a Bolivian musical group performing the song we are hearing, underneath a banner proclaiming WORLD MUSIC FESTIVAL. The first lines of dialogue in this new scene are '*Canadian Business*', a seeming non sequitur uttered by Richard Smith-Jones, the New Burbage Festival's business manager, who is revealed sitting in the music festival audience beside Geoffrey. *Canadian Business* is the title of an actual magazine; within the fictional series, Richard and Geoffrey grace the cover of the current issue, a tribute to the festival's newfound financial success. As Los Perdidos perform their folk contribution on stage, Richard ignores them to gloat over this triumph, while Geoffrey ignores them to obsess over his vision for the upcoming *Lear*. So much for the power of live performance – an irony lost on all the characters.

Overt references to the Sierra System recur throughout the season, as it overwhelms the *Lear* rehearsals; these references continually contrast with the actual audio and visual effects used in the series itself. Several scenes in the season's third episode, 'That Way Madness Lies', show Geoffrey wandering the stormy streets of the town to find Charles, who, addled by medication, has gone missing; nothing within the series reminds the television audience of the apparatus by which this storm is produced. A scene in the final episode, 'The Promised End', begins with thunderous noise – which the viewer quickly realizes is not of a storm but of a bowling alley, also presented without any allusion to the mechanisms by which the audio effects are achieved, thereby naturalizing the televisual production. In this off-stage world, however, all attention turns back to the on-stage world of live theatre. Geoffrey and Charles are in the bowling alley because Richard, having learned of Charles's cancer, has cancelled the festival's production of *Lear* and fired Geoffrey, leaving director and actor nothing else to do. As Geoffrey attempts a difficult split, Charles begins to recite Lear's 'shake all cares and business from our age' speech (1.1.31ff.). This proves to be a crucial moment in both the festival and the television season, as the cancer-ridden actor realizes that neither Lear nor he really believe they are going to die; the televisual audio effects – the sound of the bowling alley fades, while a musical interlude comes up – heighten the dramatic effect of his epiphany. Bolstered by this new insight, Charles begs Geoffrey to let him try *Lear* again. Geoffrey grants this wish, commandeering a church social hall, imploring the other actors to participate in violation of their festival contracts, and even persuading the festival's stage manager to purloin the festival's costumes for the night. The Sierra System, alas, is left behind, but more subtle (and, we are meant to understand, appropriate) sound effects are offered by none other than Los Perdidos, who, cued by Nahum, shake rainsticks and play percussion on a metal sheet.

If the sound effects in this community-based *Lear* return us to the political and cultural honesty of Nahum's Nigerian theatre, it is only because Los Perdidos have been unable to return to their own homeland, due to a violent coup. Over the course of the season, Anna and Nahum have hidden the musicians backstage at the festival while the perpetually overworked, underappreciated Anna frantically tries to have their expired visas extended, and to determine what danger they might face were they to return to Bolivia. Los Perdidos show their gratitude with several impromptu musical performances in backstage areas of the theatre, during which Nahum translates for them – though not always accurately, as is revealed to the television audience through subtitles that indicate Nahum is speaking the unspoken and repressing what he thinks should go unsaid, as when Alvaro, the lead singer, serenades Anna with a song he describes as 'muy triste', but which Nahum sums up by assuring her: 'It has a happy ending.'[14]

Nahum's intentional mistranslation is astoundingly apt, given both the series finale and the Shakespearean in-joke hidden within the Nigerian refugee's name. Nahum Tate was an Irish writer who became England's poet laureate in 1692. In his 1681 adaptation of *Lear*, Tate gave the play a happy ending by marrying Cordelia to Edgar, a revision writ large in *Slings and Arrows*. In the depiction of the community performance of *Lear*, Charles masterfully delivers the 'And my poor fool is hang'd' speech (5.3.279ff.). But, moved though the audience (comprised of both the actors portraying the play's audience in the church and those of us watching the series) may be by the captivating performances delivered in the church social hall, the television show must go on. As Edgar's 'The weight of this sad time' speech concludes the play, Charles teasingly fools Geoffrey into thinking he has died on stage, then decamps to his makeshift dressing room only to discover Sophie and Paul, the young company actors who have played Cordelia and Edgar, making out – enacting a mirror story of Nahum Tate's happy ending. After the couple departs, Charles nods off as the ghost of Oliver watches, signalling to the audience that Charles, like the Lear he has just portrayed, now is gone indeed, a peaceful passing of the actor following the fulfilling of his last wish.

As for the other beloved refugees from New Burbage, their fates are less final. Sophie and Paul appear once more, making out again, this time in the bar where the cast members gather to celebrate Geoffrey and Ellen, who have at last cemented their own on-again-off-again romance by getting married before leaving for Montreal, where Geoffrey plans to resurrect his fly-by-night company, *Théâtre Sans Argent*. This news evokes the very first scenes of season one, in which Geoffrey, as director of a Toronto-based *Théâtre Sans Argent*, addresses his scrappy company by describing the storm that opens *The Tempest*. In that setting, Geoffrey proved able to transform the theatre with words alone: as he spoke (toilet plunger in hand – Geoffrey has just fixed the plumbing, a visceral reminder of all the shitty tasks involved in running a theatre), storm-raging special effects and dialogue-reciting actors in period costume appeared to take over the bare stage. It was all an illusion, of course, wrought through the magic of television: *Théâtre Sans Argent* lacked not only a Sierra System and costume budget but even money to pay utility bills or rent; when one of the theatrical lights blows, the theatre (and thus the entire screen) goes black, ending the opening scene as the season one theme music begins to play. This sequence anticipates much of what happens in the series as a whole, with televisual special effects deployed to show the television audience how mere words can transform the black box of the stage, creating a theatrical moment that we are meant to believe could be, like Nahum's Nigerian production or the church performance, the most visceral and true. By the series's end, it would be easy to presume that the remove to Montreal will mean a return to that kind of Shakespeare, stripped bare of all the financial resources, but also the financial pressures, of the New Burbage Festival.

But the series hints at an even more radical departure. Lear is dead, *Lear* is done, and Charles's passing is perhaps also Shakespeare's. In describing the upcoming move to Montreal, Geoffrey declares: 'I think it could work. It's bilingual for a start', suggesting broader theatrical fare than the Bardolatry that has dominated the series. Moreover, if Nahum has promised us a happy ending, it does not come entirely through either the double romances of Sophie/Paul and Geoffrey/Ellen or the revitalizing of artistic integrity in the resurrection of *Théâtre Sans Argent*. Instead, it takes a more radical form, in which cultural performance blends with political consciousness. The very last word of dialogue is 'Anna', called out by Ellen as she tosses her bouquet. We don't see Anna catch it – the scene goes black with the camera still on Ellen – but we know that Anna's migration will be even more dramatic than Ellen and Geoffrey's. In the same speech in which Geoffrey discusses the rebirth of *Théâtre Sans Argent*, he also reveals, 'Anna is finally taking a vacation. In Bolivia. Well, apparently there's some kind of counterrevolution going on, [and] . . . Anna has taken up with the leader of the revolutionaries.'

If Anna has found love among Los Perdidos, she has also found in their political struggle what the series ultimately hints has been lacking in all of the characters' artistic struggles. In the second episode of season one, Geoffrey, called upon to eulogize Oliver, quotes what Oliver had said to him years before: 'The theatre is an empty box, and it is our task to fill it with fury, and ecstasy, and with revolution.' From the vantage of season three, we are meant to understand that the Sierra System and its ilk might fill a theatre with sound but no real fury, and certainly no true revolution. In the eulogy, Geoffrey recalled how 'Oliver made us believe that what we did had meaning. He made us believe that . . . regimes could be toppled by the simple act of telling a story truthfully.' While the disaffected Geoffrey of season one dismisses this as 'a ridiculous ambition', Anna's newfound personal and political trajectory suggests that when the house lights come up and the applause ends, the most meaningful thing we can gain from Shakespeare is a determination to undertake the more complicated and truly dangerous acts of actual counterrevolution – ones that the series's postcolonial positionings of Nahum and Alvaro suggest might actually topple a regime.

I'll Teach You Differences: the Problem(atizing) with Criticism of TV

Although the conclusion of 'The Promised End', and thus of the series as a whole, suggests that a single great performance of Shakespeare can resolve all problems (even male erectile dysfunction!), as a cultural critic, I wish to problematize what we conclude about *Slings and Arrows*. Throughout this chapter, I have explored how overt references to the Sierra System naturalize the televisual effects the series deploys to promote purist, black box (or church social hall) productions of Shakespeare. Now I want to offer an analogous exploration contrasting how the series's deployment of '[a] Canadian programmatic multiculturalism which is meant to symbolise present-day Canada'[15] masks *Slings and Arrows*'s more complicated and troubling assumptions and assertions about culture.

Through the inclusion of Alvaro, Nahum and other characters of colour, *Slings and Arrows* seems to promote multiculturalism as it promotes the primacy of live theatre. But while theatrical craft always remains the central focus, people of colour are kept at the periphery. Meticulous in its (sometimes self-mocking) delineation and celebration of Canadian identity, the show is far less nuanced in its representation of foreign cultures. None of the members of Los Perdidos besides Alvaro is given a name or any dialogue, in English or in Spanish. We learn very little even about Alvaro and certainly nothing about the reasons for his decision to become leader of the counterrevolution; the Bolivian political struggle is reduced to Anna's naïve assessment that the general leading the coup is 'a bad man'. Moreover, technology like the Sierra System and Richard's BMW locate the events of season three in a particular early twenty-first-century historical moment, one in which there weren't any coups in Bolivia. Thus, 'Bolivia' and the band members stand in for a universalized notion of Third World Otherhood simultaneously marked by folk culture and political instability, both of which serve as primitivized contrasts to the series's conceptualization of advanced Canadianness. Richard's and Geoffrey's shared boredom during Los Perdidos's first appearance recurs throughout the season, as various Canadian audiences repeatedly grow restless while the band performs – a running gag about how 'we' all feel about folk music and a culturally supremacist inversion of how the series teaches viewers to appreciate Shakespeare. Folk music is so easily discounted that the 'muy triste' song with which Alvaro woos Anna is not actually a Bolivian folk song; it was written for the episode by Alvaro Oyarce, the Chilean-Canadian who plays Alvaro on the series. These blithely inaccurate details about *coups* and *canciones*, and the lack of individual character development afforded the members of Los Perdidos, suggest that when it comes to Latin America, and perhaps the entire Global South, all those people look and sound, alike – a presumption redoubled by the fact that Nigerian-born Nahum, the survivor of a similarly violent regime, is the only member of the New Burbage community who can converse fluently in Spanish with Los Perdidos.

The positioning of multiculturalism within the series's construction of Canadian theatre is just as troubling. In season three, Barbara Gorman, a black Canadian actor who has achieved enormous financial success working in (shlocky) American television, arrives in New Burbage to play Goneril. While this might seem a triumph for colourblind casting (one which Charles, at his orneriest, decries), it can as easily be seen as tokenism. Only once during the six episodes do we see Barbara playing Goneril; she delivers a single twenty-eight-word speech, far less than Ellen and Sophie, the white actors playing Regan and Cordelia. Only two other actors of colour are ever cast in New Burbage's Shakespeare productions, one per season: the first as Horatio and the second as Witch #3. They are not given any names or character arc in the backstage mirror plots and are rarely onscreen, even within rehearsal or performance scenes. And then there is Nahum. Drawing on his own experience as a director in Nigeria to offer insights first to Oliver and then to Geoffrey, Nahum reveals both his deep, passionate understanding of what constitutes effective theatre and his deft ability to manage egotistical and mentally unsteady white men who are his superiors, at least within the hierarchy of New Burbage. Race is inextricably part of that hierarchy: dark-skinned Nahum is a security guard relegated to menial tasks, as in the season two episode 'Fallow Time', when he must attend to a leaky urinal while Geoffrey obsesses about how to direct *Macbeth* – apparently, some of the excretory tasks of running a theatre can be relegated to (ethnic) others. By the end of season three, even Richard is able to grow into a creative role within New Burbage (albeit involving his preferred genre of musicals), while Nahum remains relegated to those thankless menial tasks that allow the festival to function.

Yet Nahum's role reveals what the series otherwise obscures. The entire arc of *Slings and Arrows* centres on Geoffrey's struggle to establish his identity as a director (and a man) both against and ultimately through his relationship with his own director Oliver, and, more comedically, in contrast to fellow director Darren Nichols. But how does Geoffrey-as-director define his identity in terms of Nahum-as-director? One could answer 'not at all', facilely supposing that Geoffrey need not define himself in relation to Nahum because within the series (and the geographical boundaries of Canada) Nahum is never actively directing. But Geoffrey, and by extension *Slings and Arrows* more broadly, exerts a particular cultural authority that depends on the simultaneous recognition and negation that a racial/cultural Other can be a legitimate theatrical director. This dynamic is integral to assertions about the primacy of Shakespeare, and of Canada as rightful inheritor/interpreter of a particular British imperialist legacy that crass America or primitive, violent Nigeria do not deserve.

I opened this essay using Ashley's simplistic understanding of TV criticism (telling people [what] to watch) as a foil to define a more informed and insightful cultural criticism, one explicating how national identity is constructed and promoted. Yet I confess: *Slings and Arrows* is my favourite television series, one I regularly recommend to friends inside and outside academia. I find the writing, acting and directing funny and moving, nearly flawless. But only if I accept the ideological imperatives about race and culture that undergird the series's exploration of Canadianness. If instead I draw on my training as a scholar of literature by and about African Americans, as well as my training in film and television studies, I find *Slings and Arrows* to be – like Lear and *Lear* and Shakespeare – rich *and* flawed, worth engaging with in a deeper way.

Notes

1. L. R. N. Ashley, 'Recent Publications on Elizabethan England and Related Fields', *Bibliothèque d'Humanisme et Renaissance* 68 (2006): 573–610.
2. I thank Jacek Fabiszak and Susan O'Malley for their thoughtful comments on this chapter.
3. K. S. Rothwell, *A History of Shakespeare on Screen: a Century of Film and Television* (Cambridge: Cambridge University Press, 1999), 209, 212–14.
4. Debates regarding the 'relatability' of *Lear* in the internet age raged when Ira Glass, host of the NPR programme *This American Life*, tweeted after attending a 2014 production: 'Shakespeare: not good. No stakes, not relatable. I think I'm realizing: Shakespeare sucks.' In response, Lois Beckett retold *King Lear* in a series of tweets composed in the style of a *This American Life* episode. Jesse Lansner preserved Beckett's tweets in an internet post entitled 'This American Lear', which might lead us to wonder if future Shakespeare on Screen series volumes will consider how Twitter, blogs and other text-based digital media reproduce Shakespeare across the screens of phones, computers and other as-yet unknown devices.
5. This elision between the fleeting nature of a particular performance and the fleeting nature of life is further extended to include the possibility that Shakespearean theatre itself cannot survive. Charles describes the effect cancer has on his body with the morbid observation: 'Like the theatre, I am boldly fighting a slow, undignified death.'
6. Quoted in T. VanDerWerff, 'The *Slings & Arrows* Creators Discuss their Writing Process and the Show's Future' *AV Club* 31 (May 2013): www.avclub.com/article/the-islings-arrowsi-creators-discuss-their-writing-98410 (accessed 9 September 2017).
7. E. Klett, 'Shakespearean Authority and Emotional Realism in *Slings and Arrows*', *Early Modern Studies Journal* 5 (2013): 4. www.uta.edu/english/emsjournal/articles/klett.html (accessed 9 September 2017).
8. L. E. Osborne, 'Serial Shakespeare: Intermedial Performance and the Outrageous Fortunes of *Slings & Arrows*', *Borrowers and Lenders* 6.2 (Fall/Winter 2011): www.borrowers.uga.edu/783090/show (accessed 9 September 2017).
9. R. Ormsby, '"This Famous Duke of Milan of Whom So Often I Have Heard Renown": William Hutt at the Stratford and New Burbage Festivals', *Canadian Theatre Review* 141 (2010): 10–15, 13.
10. Klett, 'Shakespearean Authority', 4.
11. L. M. Pittman, *Authorizing Shakespeare on Film and Television: Gender, Class, and Ethnicity in Adaptation* (New York: Peter Lang, 2011), 180. The name also functions within the TV-à-clef as allusion to Shakespeare's contemporaries, the Burbage family.

12. Even Ellen is tempted into a brief, disastrous foray into television during season three of *Slings and Arrows*, finding herself reciting an impassioned speech in futuristic costume before a green screen on the set of a science fiction series, before being assaulted by a series of clichés, from laser guns to cavemen. But what is most demoralizing for an actor, as she complains to Geoffrey, is that 'there's never time to talk about anything, not a scene, not even a line of dialogue', a stark contrast to the laborious time devoted to pre-performance discussions, explorations and rehearsals for the Shakespeare productions in the series. Indeed, through this very scene, like the Shakespeare rehearsal scenes, the television series inculcates its audience regarding the crafts of Shakespearean acting and directing.

13. Osborne, 'Serial Shakespeare'; Pittman, *Authorizing Shakespeare*, 187–8.

14. Here again the series deploys televisual techniques to promote the primacy of purist theatrical productions of Shakespeare. As Los Perdidos play, viewers see a montage in which the mainstage Lear set is dismantled and the actors clear out their dressing rooms, making way for the set and cast from the musical, a smash success that Richard has decided should take over the mainstage. There is little subtlety about the episode's suggestion that Richard is prostituting the artistic integrity of the Shakespeare festival: the musical is about the glorious rise of Lulu, a drug-addicted young sex worker. The only dialogue spoken over Los Perdidos's song involves Darren Nichols, director of the musical and Geoffrey's long-time nemesis, using the Sierra System to unleash a storm across the mainstage, yelling out, 'I love it!', to which Richard joyfully replies, 'It's yours!' If the Sierra system rightfully belongs with the meretricious musical, the audience is left to conclude that there is something more authentic about the folk sounds produced by Los Perdidos, both in the 'muy triste' song performed during this montage and, later, in the sound effects they provide during the storm scene in the church social hall production of *Lear*.

15. Jacek Fabiszak, personal correspondence with the author.

WORKS CITED

Ashley, L. R. N., 'Recent Publications on Elizabethan England and Related Fields', *Bibliothèque d'Humanisme et Renaissance* 68 (2006): 573–610.
Klett, E., 'Shakespearean Authority and Emotional Realism in *Slings and Arrows*', *Early Modern Studies Journal* 5 (2013): www.uta.edu/english/emsjournal/arti cles/klett.html (accessed 9 September 2017).
Ormsby, R., '"This Famous Duke of Milan of Whom So Often I Have Heard Renown": William Hutt at the Stratford and New Burbage Festivals', *Canadian Theatre Review* 141 (2010): 10–15.
Osborne, L. E., 'Serial Shakespeare: Intermedial Performance and the Outrageous Fortunes of *Slings & Arrows*', *Borrowers and Lenders* 6.2 (Fall/Winter 2011): www.borrowers.uga.edu/783090/show (accessed 9 September 2017).

Pittman, L. M., *Authorizing Shakespeare on Film and Television: Gender, Class, and Ethnicity in Adaptation* (New York: Peter Lang, 2011).

Rothwell, K. S., *A History of Shakespeare on Screen: a Century of Film and Television* (Cambridge: Cambridge University Press, 1999).

VanDerWerff, T., 'The *Slings & Arrows* Creators Discuss Their Writing Process and the Show's Future' *AV Club* 31 (May 2013): www.avclub.com/article/the-islings-arrowsi-creators-discuss-their-writing-98410 (accessed 9 September 2017).

PART III

The Genres of Lear

Negotiating Authorship, Genre and Race
in King of Texas *(2002)*

Pierre Kapitaniak

Surprisingly, one of the most ostensibly 'American' screen adaptations of *King Lear*, the TV movie *King of Texas* (2002), is the product of an international collaboration between British actor Patrick Stewart, German director Uli Edel, Hungarian-born producer Robert Halmi and American screenwriter and novelist Stephen Harrigan. This chapter outlines some of the film's production contexts and its complex intertextual dialogues with the Shakespearean hypotext, the setting of the early Republic of Texas (1836–1846) and the Western genre. I will explore several of the key issues that the film raises: the multi-authored nature of the hypertext; the question of genre and the radical transposition of the hypotext in terms of time and place; and the introduction of race, which displaces and re-orientates the play's critique of rank and legitimacy.

The Genesis of *King of Texas*: a Creative Cartel

The medium of film problematizes questions of authorship, as films are, by their very nature, polyvocal and multi-authored works. In 'Getting back to Shakespeare: Whose Film Is It Anyway?', Elsie Walker questions critics' excessive focus on 'the input of the director, often privileging *auteurs* (like Olivier, Welles, Kurosawa, Kozintsev, Branagh), who fulfil the "author-function" as, in Worthen's words, "stand-ins for Shakespeare"'.[1] Although it is common knowledge that a film is the product of a whole team of various specialists, it is still most often considered an artistic accomplishment of its director. Rather than looking for an authorial agency as an alternative to the director, I envisage authorship as a network, within which the interactions and negotiations among different agents of the creative process generate the final work. In the case of *King of Texas*, the question of 'authorship' is further complicated by contradictory statements from key figures in the project as to the initial idea of the Texas setting.

Considering the director as the key 'author' of the film would prove misleading here, particularly given that Uli Edel, the director, did not initiate the whole creative process and, prior to this film, had not ventured into the field of Shakespearean adaptation.

Born in 1947, Uli Edel established his career with *Christiane F. – We Children from Bahnhof Zoo* (1981), the story of a 13-year-old girl who is drawn into drugs and prostitution in the West Berlin of the 1970s. Continuing this theme, he made his debut in Hollywood with *Last Exit to Brooklyn* (1989), adapted from Hubert Selby's novel, following the ups and downs of a Brooklyn prostitute in the 1950s. He then directed *Body of Evidence* (1993), an erotic thriller starring Madonna and Willem Dafoe. During the following decade, Edel directed almost exclusively for television (participating in TV series like *Twin Peaks* (1990–1991) and *Oz* (1997–2003)). Until 2004, Edel continued to shoot films that were commissioned for different TV channels, and *King of Texas*, produced for Turner Network Television (part of Time Warner), was one of them, squeezed between an Arthurian miniseries *The Mists of Avalon* (2001) and a biopic on Julius Caesar (2002). In 2008, Edel returned to Germany and to his usual predilection for violence, directing the successful *Der Baader Meinhof Komplex* (2008). Edel's foray into Shakespearean adaptation thus appears as an exception to the rest of his oeuvre.

In an interview, Edel acknowledged that he was not part of the initial team for *King of Texas*, describing the project in the following terms: 'When Patrick Stewart approached me to do *King Lear* with him ....'[2] Just how little control Edel may have had over the whole creative process is evident in the fact that only two members of his crew had worked with him previously: the casting director and the editor.[3] Consequently, Edel cannot be considered as the leading (let alone the sole) authorial voice behind the film. The adaptation's genre as a Western may have led to the choice of Edel as director, since he had directed *Purgatory* (1999), a Western starring Sam Sheppard, and produced for the same Turner Network Television studio.

Patrick Stewart, in recalling the genesis of *King of Texas*, credited himself with the idea of adapting *King Lear* as a Western set in Texas. In an interview in 2010, he stated:

> Yes, I pitched it. I was having dinner with Robert Halmi,[4] a great man ... I said, 'Robert, I've had this idea about *King Lear* set in the American West, with Texas for Britain, just after the Mexican/Texas wars', and I told him a bit more and then asked him, 'What do you think?' And he said ... (*Adopts an uncannily accurate Robert Halmi impression*) 'Goddammit, we'll do it! It's

fucking brilliant!' (*Claps hands together again*) Done! And the next morning, I was getting contracts to sign.[5]

Journalist Christopher Rawson also credited Patrick Stewart with the original idea: 'Somewhere in the midst of other projects, Stewart's gnawing thoughts of Shakespeare suggested "King Lear" as a Texan. By himself, he worked out how the characters could be transposed to post-Alamo, pre-statehood Texas.'[6]

Stewart had spent twenty-seven years with the Royal Shakespeare Company so it is unsurprising that he should be behind adapting *King Lear*. Stewart's association with producer Robert Halmi was also a logical choice, since the latter had just produced Stewart's previous televisual appearances in a series on *Moby Dick* (1998), *A Christmas Carol* (1999) and *Animal Farm* (1999). Stewart co-produced *King of Texas* and, together with his wife Wendy Neuss-Stewart, was credited as executive producer. Stewart also brought in Colm Meaney, his friend from *Star Trek: The Next Generation* (Paramount, 1987–1994), to play Albany.

Stewart's recollections suggest that, by the time he struck a deal with Halmi, he had worked out most of the project and that subsequently the director and the screenwriter were hired to suit his choices. Writer Stephen Harrigan was chosen not for his expertise on Shakespeare (which he did not have), but for his knowledge of Texas and Mexico. Harrigan had received several awards for his widely acclaimed novel *The Gates of the Alamo* (2000),[7] had been working for TV studios as a screenwriter for nearly a decade and had signed several scripts for Westerns, the most recent being *Beyond the Prairie: the True Story of Laura Ingalls Wilder* (1999).

Interestingly, although Harrigan confirms Stewart's main involvement from the start, he offers an alternative perspective of the project's genesis:

> 'The idea of doing *King Lear* as a Western was something that Patrick Stewart and the producer, Robert Halmi Sr, cooked up', Harrigan tells *True West*. 'Halmi first mentioned it to me in London five or six years ago when we were working on a Cleopatra miniseries. At that time, the project was called *Boss Lear* and Gregory Peck was going to play the title role. A year or so later I had a meeting with Peck and Patrick Stewart at Peck's house in Los Angeles, in which I proposed setting the movie in Texas in the 1840s, a time and place that had a reasonable affinity to the England of Shakespeare's play.'[8]

His version still recognizes the initiating role played by Stewart and Halmi, but attributes the choice of setting and time to himself as screenwriter. If Harrigan is right, the project was initiated a few years before Harrigan wrote *The Gates of the Alamo* and became famous for it. Harrigan clearly claims to have been the one to suggest the period of post-Alamo Texas.

Thus, unlike the usual focus on director and screenwriter as the main sources of adapting choices, here the precise decision-making chain is uncertain and appears to stem from the lead actor (and co-producer). In summary, we may conceive the creative force behind the film as distributed among four co-adaptors: a British actor (Patrick Stewart), an American producer (Robert Halmi), an American screenwriter (Stephen Harrigan) and a German director (Uli Edel). On the one hand, these four people had been working in the USA for many years. Edel's career moved to the USA between 1989 and 2004. Patrick Stewart's social capital as an RSC actor was counterbalanced by his immense fame as an iconic figure of American popular culture, thanks to the roles of Captain Jean-Luc Picard in the *Star Trek* series and that of Professor Charles Xavier in the then-budding series of the *X-Men* franchise, with the first feature film shot in 2000. On the other hand, it might be expected that both Edel's and Stewart's European visions of the American West differed from a native one. To that extent, nineteenth-century American Texas is more likely to stand as an exotic displacement of Lear's story and background than as an appropriation of English cultural capital by American popular culture or, as Carolyn Jess-Cooke termed it, 'the "reterritorialization" of the past'.[9]

Historical Negotiations: from Legendary England to the Wild West

King of Texas's plot parallels *King Lear*'s in several respects. It is set in the independent Texas of the 1840s where John Lear, a cattle tycoon, decides to divide his empire among his three daughters, Susannah (Marcia Gay Harden), Rebecca (Lauren Holly) and Claudia (Julie Cox). After refusing to flatter her father, Claudia is evicted from the family and finds refuge in the hacienda of her Mexican fiancé Menchaca (Steven Bauer). While Tumlinson (Susannah's husband, played by Colm Meaney) is away, Susannah and Rebecca attack Menchaca's men. The lack of respect of the two daughters for Lear is explained by the fact that Lear had eyes only for a son who had been killed in the war. Soon Lear ends up homeless in the desert, accompanied only by his faithful black servant Rip (David Alan Grier). After a stormy night, Lear finds refuge at Menchaca's; it is during the attack on the hacienda by his two daughters' henchmen that Claudia is shot while running after her father, who tries to stop the fighting.

Transposing a seventeenth-century tragedy to a radically different time and place entails a series of negotiations, such as adapting the language and the plot to correlate in some respects with objective historical facts, if the adaptor seeks to recreate a coherent universe. In addition to the story itself, further negotiations and changes were needed to adapt *Lear* to the generic requirements and conventions of a Western. Courtney Lehmann argues that *King of Texas* constitutes one of the first post-9/11 Westerns.[10] While Lehmann's analysis of John Lear as a George W. Bush figure is convincing, the film itself was shot before 11 September, making Edel's film arguably one of the last pre-9/11 films. According to Stewart's interview with Christopher Rawson, the shooting of *King of Texas* began in April 2001 and lasted for two months: '[Stewart] began in January at Minneapolis' Guthrie Theatre, playing George in *Who's Afraid of Virginia Woolf?* Then came two months filming *King of Texas*. Next, he went back to England to perform *Shylock: Shakespeare's Alien*, a full-length solo show.'[11]

Who's Afraid of Virginia Woolf? ran from 23 February to 1 April, which meant that Stewart was not available in Mexico before early April. By the time filming started, the former Governor of Texas, George W. Bush, had been in presidential office for three months or so, which undoubtedly influenced the script's final vision of John Lear. Although the film was released on 2 June 2002 (with an earlier Turkish screening on 23 March),[12] it was probably in postproduction during the 9/11 attacks and it seems difficult to maintain that *King of Texas* 'adopts the only ethical stance available to post-9/11 culture'.[13] It was most likely the Texan George W. Bush turned president that inspired the film, rather than the one who was waging 'war on terror' when the film came out. Setting *King Lear* in Texas may have been all the more relevant in 2001 as official reports were piling up about the growing numbers of casualties on the US–Mexican border, especially since 1994.[14]

Speaking of his inspiration and engagement with the Western genre, Edel discussed the Germans' fondness for Westerns:

> I think it has to do with my origin as a German. In Germany, we grew up with Westerns. For some reason, the Germans have a strong affinity for Westerns. To dream about this endless sky and endless horizon, that's something I saw in a lot of Westerns and that's what drew me to them.[15]

Although Edel certainly grew up watching the *Winnetou* films in the 1960s,[16] his directing style betrays more affinities with the late 1960s Westerns by Sergio Leone. *King of Texas* opens with an extreme long shot of the desert, with a solitary dead tree on which two dead Mexicans are hanging, then alternates with extreme close-ups of the men's faces while waiting for Menchaca. The whole opening sequence is reminiscent of *Once upon a Time in the West* (1968), while at the same time providing the perfect context for *Lear*.

In the same interview, Edel refers to other famous Western directors who have evoked *King Lear*:

> When Patrick Stewart approached me to do *King Lear* with him, I started to think about Anthony Mann, the old Western director. He planned his whole life to do a *King Lear* version and never could get the money from the studios. Even Howard Hawks said that Shakespeare's *King Lear* could become a wonderful Western.[17]

Although Edel claims funding issues as the reason Mann had not been able to make *Lear* as a Western, in fact it was Mann's death that prevented him from directing a Western version of *King Lear* with John Wayne in the title role.[18] As for Hawks, he mentioned *King Lear* once in an interview about *Land of the Pharaohs* (1955), and the role of Shakespeare's play was even more anecdotal there, as Lear was one of the models for the Pharaoh's style of speech.[19]

Surprisingly, Edel does not mention Edward Dmytryk's earlier adaptation of *King Lear*, *Broken Lance* (1954), which was itself an adaptation of Joseph L. Mankiewicz's transposition of *King Lear* to the gangster genre, *House of Strangers* (1949), with Lear played by Edward G. Robinson. There are elements in Dmytryk's classical Western, such as rehabilitating the Native Americans and tackling the problems of mixed love stories, that resonate with *King of Texas*. In the opening sequence of *King of Texas*, both the main scene and some of the minor details echo *Broken Lance*. Menchaca's two hungry men hanged by Lear are reminiscent of a hanging that takes place during the trial that is central in *Broken Lance*, where we learn that the Lear figure Devereaux summarily hanged three men for stealing his cattle.[20] Another detail seems to deepen the echo: one of the men waiting for Menchaca plays with a lizard on a stick, the latter being shot in close-up. This recalls the moment in *Broken Lance* when Joe returns to his father's abandoned house and sees a lizard reclining on a bench in the garden. In both films, the lizards work as symbols of wild nature taking hold of man's property – an idiosyncratic choice in Dmytryk's case, and arguably a quotation in Edel's. More generally, despite different geographical and historical settings, Dmytryk's adaptation seems to have inspired the *King of Texas* team with the same transposition from royalty to cattle baron, and there are other parallels between the two versions.

In an interview with *True West*, Stewart comments on the natural affinities between *Lear* and the Western:

> 'Shakespeare and the Old West are a natural mix', the Emmy-nominated Stewart says. 'It's never been clear during which period Shakespeare's *King Lear* was set.' . . . 'There is a sense that it was probably set during a somewhat primitive period. A nation was being formed by ambitious, hungry people. The warring factions were very much in turmoil and could be dragged in any direction by the most powerful groups. I've learned that this was certainly the case with the Republic of Texas at this time.'[21]

Harrigan's association with the project from an early stage enabled the filmscript to benefit from his research for *The Gates of the Alamo*.[22] He explained the initial choice of the setting:

> My initial idea was to use the 1842 Mexican invasion of the infant Texas republic as a counterpoint to the French invasion in the play. The first few drafts had its climax at the Battle of the Salado, in which the Texans repelled the Mexican Army. But somewhere along the way budget realities decreed that we would have to bag the Mexican Army and the epic pitched battle, and so we ended up doing something simpler: a confrontation between Lear and his Texans and a dispossessed Mexican ranchero named Menchaca.[23]

This may be where Dmytryk's film became a useful intertext, providing a shift from warfare to cattle feud.

In the final version, it is unclear whether we are still in 1842 or a little earlier. The film starts with the celebration of Independence Day – i.e. 20 December 1835 – and when Henry Westover (the character of Gloucester played by Roy Scheider) offers Lear a black stallion, he alludes to the battle of San Jacinto, which took place on 21 April 1836.[24] A few minutes later, just before the scene of the division of the kingdom/ranch by Lear, Mr Tumlinson (the character of Albany) reads a proclamation through which Harrigan manages to provide small details that contribute to the adaptation's quality and historical accuracy:

TUMLINSON: John, President Houston asked me to deliver this.
LEAR: How is Sam? Has he ever sobered up?

Known for his drinking habits, Sam Houston was President of Texas twice: from October 1836 to December 1838, and then from December 1841 to December 1844, which makes both periods a possible moment for the fictional events that ensue, although specific references to the 1836 events suggest that the action was located in the earlier period. Harrigan adds that 'In an early draft, Sam Houston himself even made an appearance, but he succumbed to the inevitable streamlining.'[25]

The proclamation itself clearly refers to Independence Day: 'On this the anniversary of the birth of our young republic'. It then evokes an even more precise context of the 'darkest days of our struggle', namely the Battle of Alamo (6 March 1836) and the Goliad massacre (27 March 1836), at which Lear lost his only son. After these two introductory sentences, Lear interrupts Tumlinson to carry on with the division of his lands among his daughters. The background is thus set.

Despite the very precise and well-documented historical period chosen for the adaptation, most changes seem to have been dictated more by the Western genre than by the Republic of Texas setting, as with *Broken Lance*, set after 1886. *King of Texas*, like *Broken Lance*, departs from Shakespeare's language, although the paratexts of each film refer to the Shakespearean hypotext quite differently. The opening credits of *Broken Lance* advertise the film as 'Based on a story by Philip Yordan'. (Yordan wrote the screenplay for Mankiewicz's *House of Strangers*, adapted from Jerome Weidman's novel.) Shakespeare is not mentioned and the names of characters bear no resemblance to the original play. In contrast, *King of Texas* claims to be 'Based on the play *King Lear* by William Shakespeare' and, although many of the names of the characters have been changed to adapt to the historical period, the title character retains his surname – John Lear. For two of the daughters, Rebecca and Claudia, it follows the convention of retaining the first letters of the Shakespearean names, as in Jocelyn Moorhouse's *A Thousand Acres* (1997), although Susannah departs from Goneril. Harrigan explains that he 'had a good time generally substituting familiar Texas names from the period – Highsmith, Tumlinson, Warnell, Menchaca, et al. – for Shakespeare's characters'.[26]

In their interviews, Stewart and Harrigan both claim a deep incompatibility between Shakespeare's language and the Western genre, which freed them from the 'desire to reproduce the Shakespearean text'.[27] Yet, by acknowledging its debt to Shakespeare, *King of Texas* creates expectations in the audience, especially on famous passages that can sometimes be very close. For example Lear's exclamation that 'Nothing will come of nothing, speak again' (1.1.85), is retained nearly unchanged in the film: 'Nothing can come of nothing. You best think again' (0:14:26).

King of Texas, like *Broken Lance*, not only abandons Shakespeare's poetical language but also abandons all monologues and soliloquies, for which the Western genre seems to have no use. The only exception to this is Lear's mad scene in *King of Texas* where he addresses the sky and the gods, though he does so out loud in the presence of Rip, a convention that suggests madness rather than interior reflection. Presumably in transposing *Lear* to a Western genre, the film could not retain the original language and the soliloquies.

A second change necessitated by genre was to downgrade the plot from state level to a more neighbourly or individual level. A cattle feud had been the situation of *Broken Lance*, in which an old cattle baron struggled against the mining expansion of a new era. Dmytryk's film even seems to provide *King of Texas* with one of its secondary plots. When Emmett falsely accuses his brother of stealing his father's horses, this echoes a scene in *Broken Lance* where two of Devereaux's sons steal some cattle from their father and get caught red handed.

The genre change also necessitated a shift from issues of lineage and monarchy to more domestic reflections on family and father/child relationships. Both films add a fourth child – a son – who draws all the father's affection. In *Broken Lance*, Joe is Devereaux's favourite son from a second marriage. In *King of Texas*, Lear still grieves for a son lost in the massacre of Goliad, and when Susannah finally tells the naked truth to her father, she confronts him with his unfair preference: 'All you cared about was your son, and after he died all you cared about was Claudia.'

From Class Struggle to Race Conflict

The Western genre is emblematic of a more general perception of American culture as race sensitive rather than class sensitive.[28] This shift of perception accounts for the major changes in plot and characters of *King of Texas*, which displaces some of the social tensions of *Lear*. This is apparent in two characters who undergo a significant transformation in *King of Texas* and whose reworkings are co-dependent.

In condensing *King Lear* to fit the 90-minute format, and for financial reasons, the character of Kent disappears in *King of Texas*. Also gone is Edgar's transformation into Poor Tom, whose only trace is the fact that Edgar's name is changed to Thomas. In the Shakespearean hypotext, both characters constitute nobles disguising themselves as common men for self-preservation, in the process of which their true natures are revealed. Edmund's soliloquies and Tom's mad ravings, elements that reflect on and question the construction of social status as acquired by birth, are thus absent in *King of Texas*.[29]

Just as 'Poor Tom' vanishes, Kent's character is displaced onto Mr
Tumlinson, transforming the latter's character in the process. Unlike the
evolving Albany, whose conscience asserts itself as the play unfolds,
Tumlinson's character is depicted as righteous from the start, when he
listens disapprovingly to his wife during her flattering speech to her father.
Since Tumlinson is given some of the traits and scenes from the character
of Kent, it is thus he who tries to reason with Lear in the division scene
when the latter disinherits Claudia.

Tumlinson's moral superiority is further conveyed by his clothes, as he is
the only character who always appears in business suits, even when riding
for a long journey, while others – Lear included – regularly switch between
riding outfits and evening suits or dresses. Tumlinson seems to represent
the new generation of civilized citizens as opposed to the old ranching
world. Such a sartorial characterization arguably offers a glimpse of the
European vision of the American West that inflects the project. A similar
dichotomy is suggested in *Broken Lance* in the struggle between a cattle
baron and new mining businessmen, but in that case the modern, urban
generation is not depicted as morally superior.

Perhaps the most original transformation in *King of Texas* is the shift of
the Fool into the black slave Rip,[30] and once again *Broken Lance* offers an
illuminating precedent for the introduction of race. In both films, Lear's wife
is reintroduced either in the flesh or as a memory. In *Broken Lance*, after the
death of his first wife, Matt Devereaux married a Native American woman
who gave him another son. There are several scenes in which Devereaux has
to defend his marriage against an intolerant society, as well as references to
the law that treats Native American women unfairly. In fact, the gist of the
tragedy in Dmytryk's film (unlike Mankiewicz's source) lies in the problem
posed by a mixed marriage. Joe falls in love with the daughter of his father's
governor friend, and because the latter is opposed to the very notion of such
a marriage, he refuses to help Devereaux with his legal problems, which
precipitates the tragic outcome. In *King of Texas*, as in *King Lear*, there is no
wife, but her memory haunts the film, together with the ghost of his beloved
son. When Claudia seeks asylum at Menchaca's hacienda, the two evoke the
pleasant past they shared when her mother helped his mother. The added
presence of the mothers in the two films provides the sons or the daughters of
the Western Lears with clear psychological reasons for hating and betraying
their fathers.

Setting the film's time period in the young Republic of Texas locates the
action three decades before the abolition of slavery in the USA and the civil
war that ensued. In contrast, Mexico had abolished slavery even before its

independence in 1810, and then as a sovereign state in 1813 and in 1820. Slaves were effectively freed with the new constitution of 1824, a process that lasted till 1829.[31] The following year, Mexican president Anastasio Bustamante ordered Mexican Texas to abolish slavery, but the Anglo-American settlers converted their slaves into 'indentured servants for life'.[32] When the Republic of Texas became independent in 1836, slavery was legalized again. It is within this shifting, unstable context that Harrigan chose to recast the Fool as blacksmith Rip: 'Rip, Lear's slave, who is a version of the Fool in Shakespeare's play, is modeled after Joe, the slave of Alamo commander William Travis and the only known combatant who survived the battle . . ..'[33]

Joe was spared, along with some women and children, so that they could spread the news of Santa Anna's victory. This historical intertext is important in a scene in which we see an aspect of Kent displaced onto Lear. During the round-up on which Rip accompanies his master, Rip is separated from Lear, and when he comes to a well to water his horse, he meets Susannah's henchman, who allows only the horse to drink. Rip does not comply and the man recognizes him ('You're the son of a bitch from Alamo') and then knocks Rip out with a stone. When Rip regains consciousness, he is tied up to a dead tree, and the henchman whips him, accusing him of being a runaway slave. It is then that Lear comes to his rescue and whips and beats up the man, as disguised Kent does to Oswald (2.2.1–37).[34] Although Rip refuses to consider himself a slave, during the beating, Lear cries out to the henchman: 'You're gonna interfere with my property again?' The timing is important here since, between the Battle of Alamo (1831) and the independence of Texas (1836), Rip had been a free man, or more likely made an 'indentured servant for life' by Lear.

Although a slave, Rip is the only one allowed to speak his mind and criticize Lear, as with Shakespeare's Fool. This is also reminiscent of *Broken Lance*, where Lear's Native American wife is one of the few people who dare speak their minds and criticize Devereaux. Moreover, Lear's splitting of his ranch is due to the fact that, according to the law, a Native American woman could not hold property.[35] In the two films, such changes bring more nuanced portraits of Lear, who is depicted as opposing customs and laws that a modern audience finds repugnant. Thus in both *Broken Lance* and *King of Texas*, the element of race is highlighted in the adaptation process, suggesting that, in an American context, Shakespeare's discourses on social class and legitimacy only retain currency in terms of race.

To conclude, the production contexts of *King of Texas* provide evidence that the adaptation was the product of an international 'creative cartel'. Each of the creative figures brought their own perspectives and influences to the process of making the film. Stewart brought his experience and authority as an RSC actor to shape his version of *Lear*; Edel's directorial experience, including in the Western genre, left his print on the film; Harrigan's expertise as a Texas historian facilitated reshaping the characters and plot; and Halmi enabled the project to become a reality. Harrigan's input was decisive in transposing the play's early modern social preoccupations into the film's contemporary concerns of slavery and race, and thus shifting the traditional Western's focus on Native Americans to enslaved African Americans. From this perspective, *King of Texas* anticipated a new trend in Hollywood, which reintroduced black cowboys into the Western genre that had been almost exclusively white for many decades.[36] *King of Texas* came barely a decade before the revival of the Western genre that entrusted the main parts to black characters, as in Quentin Tarantino's *Django Unchained* (2012), Jeymes Samuel's *They Die by Dawn* (2013) and Steve McQueen's *Twelve Years a Slave* (2013). Thus *King of Texas*, with its various traces and negotiations, a work by multiple authors, not only resonates with its early modern hypotext, and earlier Westerns, but also with significant future shifts in film history.

Notes

1. E. Walker, 'Getting back to Shakespeare: Whose Film Is It Anyway?', in D. E. Henderson (ed.), *A Concise Companion to Shakespeare on Screen* (Malden and Oxford: Blackwell, 2006), 13, quoting from W. B. Worthen, *Shakespeare and the Authority of Performance* (Cambridge: Cambridge University Press, 1997), 60.
2. Quoted in R. Burt, 'Shakespeare, "Glo-cali-zation," Race, and the Small Screens of Popular Culture', in R. Burt and L. E. Boose (eds.), *Shakespeare, the Movie, II: Popularizing the Plays on Film, TV, Video, and DVD* (London: Routledge, 2003), 23.
3. Casting: Lisa Freiberger; editing: Marc Conte.
4. Robert Halmi Sr: executive producer, Hallmark Entertainment.
5. W. Harris, 'A chat with Patrick Stewart', 28 April 2010, www.bullz-eye.com/television/interviews/2010/patrick_stewart.htm (accessed 2 June 2016).
6. C. Rawson, 'Patrick Stewart transports "King Lear" to Texas', 2 June 2002, http://old.post-gazette.com/ae/20020602stewart0602fnp5.asp (accessed 2 June 2016).
7. The novel received a Western Writers of America Spur Award and a National Cowboy and Western Heritage Museum Western Heritage Award.

8. J. D. Boggs, 'King of Texas', *True West*, 1 July 2002: www.truewestmagazine .com/king-of-texas (accessed 2 June 2016).

9. C. Jess-Cooke, 'Screening the McShakespeare in Post-millennial Shakespeare Cinema', in M. T. Burnett and R. Wray (eds.), *Screening Shakespeare in the Twenty-first Century* (Edinburgh: Edinburgh University Press, 2006), 179.

10. C. Lehmann, 'The Passion of the W: Localizing Shakespeare, Globalizing Manifest Density from *King Lear* to Kingdom Come', *Upstart Crow* 25 (2006), 26.

11. Rawson, 'Patrick Stewart transports "King Lear" to Texas'.

12. According to IMDB: www.imdb.com/title/tt0282659/releaseinfo?ref_=tt_d t_dt (accessed 2 June 2016).

13. Lehmann, 'The Passion of the W', 28.

14. Between 1998 and 2004, 1954 people were officially reported to have died along the US–Mexican border.

15. Quoted in Burt, 'Shakespeare, "Glo-cali-zation"', 22.

16. Winnetou, a fictional Native American character, was created by the German writer Karl May in the late nineteenth century. The stories were adapted for film in the 1960s in Germany and the former Yugoslavia.

17. Quoted in Burt, 'Shakespeare, "Glo-cali-zation"', 22–3.

18. J. Basinger, *Anthony Mann* (Middletown: Wesleyan University Press, 2007), 191.

19. J. McBride, *Hawks on Hawks* (Lexington: University Press of Kentucky, 2013 [1982]), 72.

20. *Broken Lance*, 1:01:15–25.

21. Boggs, 'King of Texas'.

22. Rawson notes that Harrigan was signed to write the screenplay subsequent to his research, in Rawson, 'Patrick Stewart transports "King Lear" to Texas'.

23. Boggs, 'King of Texas'.

24. Later Rebecca alludes to 'the men who captured Santa Anna' (29:50). See Harrigan's interview in *True West*: 'Shakespeare's character of Gloucestor (*sic*) has been reinvented in this movie as the man who captured Santa Anna at San Jacinto' (Boggs, 'King of Texas').

25. Boggs, 'King of Texas'.

26. *Ibid.*

27. Walker, 'Getting back to Shakespeare', 14.

28. See E. Buscombe, *The BFI Companion to the Western* (New York: Da Capo Press, 1988); M. Carter, *The Myth of the Western: New Perspectives on Hollywood's Frontier Narrative* (Edinburgh: Edinburgh University Press, 2014). I would like to thank Hervé Mayer (University Paul-Valéry Montpellier 3) for pointing out these references to me.

29. Emmett and Thomas are first introduced as brothers and Emmett's bastardy is mentioned only when Henry rides home with Emmett: 'I learnt to live with the pain of a bastard a long time ago'.

30. For another take on the character of Rip, see Courtney Lehmann's chapter in this volume.

124 PIERRE KAPITANIAK

31. During this period several US states also freed their slaves, such as New York in 1827.
32. P. Reid-Merritt, *A State-by-State History of Race and Racism in the United States*, vol. 2 (Santa Barbara: Greenwood, 2018), 844.
33. Boggs, 'King of Texas'.
34. Once again, the whip used by Lear (0:26:30) might also be an echo of the whip used by Devereaux (Spencer Tracy) in *Broken Lance* (0:19:10).
35. *Broken Lance*, 0:55:45.
36. A significant instance of earlier mainstream productions featuring black cowboys is Mario Van Peebles's *Posse* (1993).

WORKS CITED

Basinger, J., *Anthony Mann* (Middletown: Wesleyan University Press, 2007).
Boggs, J. D., 'King of Texas', *True West*, 1 July 2002: www.truewestmagazine.com /king-of-texas (accessed 2 June 2016).
Burt R., 'Shakespeare, "Glo-cali-zation," Race, and the Small Screens of Popular Culture', in R. Burt and L. E. Boose (eds.), *Shakespeare, The Movie, II: Popularizing the Plays on Film, TV, Video, and DVD* (London: Routledge, 2003), 14–36.
Buscombe, E., *The BFI Companion to the Western* (New York: Da Capo Press, 1988).
Carter, M., *The Myth of the Western: New Perspectives on Hollywood's Frontier Narrative* (Edinburgh: Edinburgh University Press, 2014).
Jess-Cooke, C., 'Screening the McShakespeare in Post-millennial Shakespeare Cinema', in M. T. Burnett and R. Wray (eds.), *Screening Shakespeare in the Twenty-first Century* (Edinburgh: Edinburgh University Press, 2006), 163–84.
Lehmann, C., 'The Passion of the W: Localizing Shakespeare, Globalizing Manifest Density from *King Lear* to Kingdom Come', *Upstart Crow* 25 (2006): 16–32.
McBride, J., *Hawks on Hawks* (Lexington: University Press of Kentucky, 2013 [1982]).
Reid-Merritt, P., *A State-by-State History of Race and Racism in the United States*, vol. 2 (Santa Barbara: Greenwood, 2018).
Walker, E., 'Getting back to Shakespeare: Whose Film Is It Anyway?', in D. E. Henderson (ed.), *A Concise Companion to Shakespeare on Screen* (Malden and Oxford: Blackwell, 2008), 8–30.

CHAPTER 8

Romancing King Lear: Hobson's Choice, Life Goes On *and Beyond*

Diana E. Henderson

No, Lear is easy. He's like all of us, really: he's just a stupid old fart.

Laurence Olivier[1]

For me the tragedy's most important act is the sixth:
  the raising of the dead from the stage's battlegrounds,
  the straightening of wigs and fancy gowns,
  removing knives from stricken breasts,
  taking nooses from lifeless necks,
  lining up among the living
  to face the audience.

Wislawa Szymborska[2]

Shall we continue to sit upon the ground and tell sad stories of the death of kings? A long line of adaptations reform – or revert to the origins of – Lear's story in order to make some space for futurity, and even consolation.[3] For literary scholars, such notes of consolation have long been the cue for accusations of sentimentality triumphing over sterner stuff. Nonetheless, at an angry, violent historical moment when apocalyptic fantasies and regressively patriarchal politics have seen a resurgence on national stages, it seems important at least to entertain the possibility of something other than a copout in the *Lear* spinoffs that turn away from the stark cruelty of Shakespeare's fifth act. Elsewhere I have argued that Nahum Tate's historical moment and contextual assertions encourage a more robust interpretation of his tragicomedy than is usually countenanced.[4] Closer to our own time, if my epigraph from Olivier is not just the consummate performer's tongue-in-cheek sprezzatura, perhaps Lear as a character (for all the monumentality of his rhetoric and of the play itself) is not so very far from the everyday. Ultimately, as Nobel laureate Szymborska implies, resurrecting life at that more familiar scale after human tragedy has its own heroism.

Indeed, it may be just as bold and more creative to try to think beyond the death of patriarchs or the revenge of youth in a world where inter-generational relations and the normative boundaries of gender and sex, while not free of patriarchal inheritances from the time of Shakespeare, have shifted radically. How can modern collaborations with the *Lear* story function anew, or help us see Shakespeare's own playwriting trajectory past tragedy in a different light? Here I examine two films that refuse one (tragic) form of sentimental relations in favour of a more progressive one. Their particular choices, moreover, gesture beyond themselves to a larger landscape of creative collaborations and (as a footnote) might feed back into the professional practices of Shakespeareans as well. The first of these films has been underappreciated as a *Lear* spinoff, and thus what follows analyses the particular filmic choices (focused on the Lear figure) that establish that connection, as well as pursuing the narrative alterations contributing to its optimism. The second film announces its ancestry more directly, though with less visual invention (not surprisingly, being a directorial debut juxtaposed with the work of an established master of the medium). Nonetheless, its use of flashback and cross-cutting, as well as modern narrative variation, contributes to its multi-layered, socially resonant performance.

At the comic end of the spectrum lies David Lean's marvellous – and by Shakespeareans under-acknowledged – 1953 remediation of *Hobson's Choice*, based on the 1915 play by Harold Brighouse in which some of *Lear*'s themes are transferred to a Lancastrian bootmaker of a tyrannical and incontinent disposition. *Lear* and *Hobson* share structural, character-ological and, through Lean's *mise-en-scène*, aesthetic affinities. In this film version (the third, indicative of the story's enduring popularity),[5] the monumental Charles Laughton stars as late-Victorian Henry Hobson, widowed father of three marriageable daughters, who precipitates the erosion of his authority by the ever-responsible Maggie, his most valued eldest daughter (Brenda De Banzie). As Marisa Fryer notes, Hobson 'does not want to do the work required of his position and relies ungraciously on the support of his daughters. He behaves rashly when he doesn't feel respected', and creates the conditions that lead to that perception. Like Cordelia, 'Maggie leaves her father when his demands become unreason-able and returns only after he has been humbled by his own failures'.[6] Primarily a rollicking satirical comedy, *Hobson's Choice* reworks aspects of *Lear* that are now – and have been for the past century – showing their age.

The shift of narrative focus from the youngest to the eldest daughter immediately signals the most obviously 'modern' dimension of this film: its protofeminist critique of male domination and corresponding celebration of a progressive woman's power, even within a heteronormative comic genre. Rather than follow the familiar fairytale trope of oppressive elder sisters and a more vulnerable 'good' third child, Brighouse's play (written in the wake of the suffrage movement) allows Maggie to challenge the notion that a thinking woman, who (at 30) is no longer an ingénue's age, can be reduced to her father's 'spinsterish' aide or an impediment to the younger sisters' marital desires. Nor is her success the stuff of poignant last-chance romance or monetary inheritance. Rather, fusing the more sympathetic dimensions of Goneril's situation with the forthright integrity of a Cordelia, Maggie revises the usual romance plot by actively employing her wits and the business sense her father has been relying upon while he has been self-indulgently holding court with his surrogate 'knights' over pints at the Moonrakers Inn.[7]

Indeed, the fusion of Brighouse's playtext, the adapted screenplay by Lean, Norman Spencer and Wynyard Browne, Lean's filming and De Banzie's performance effectively queers the Pygmalion myth. Recognizing the special shoemaking ability of Will Mossop, a lowly work-man (quite literally, labouring in the cellar underneath the shop and meekly peering up from a trapdoor in its floor), Maggie decides to ally herself with Will in a joint venture of wedlock and rival shoe business. Under her tutelage this illiterate 'rabbit' of a man gains confidence and rises socially as well as physically, ultimately fulfilling her hopes for a marriage of respect *and* affection (a possibility that her father had peremptorily dismissed). Brilliantly rendered by John Mills and benefiting from Lean's meticulous shot composition, Will Mossop grows from a reluctant, fearful human tool (whom Maggie calls, to his face, a 'business idea in the shape of a man' as well as her marital 'best chance') into a proud husband and full business partner. In terms of Cinderella narratives, this film puts the shoe on the other sex's foot.

Moreover, while achieving her own goals, Maggie shows good will – as well as tough love – not only to her father but also to her sisters. Refusing the easy antagonisms of the *Lear* tradition and indeed of her Victorian milieu, Maggie helps her more conventionally aspiring sisters (a very young Prunella Scales as Vicky, alongside Daphne Anderson as Alice) to wed the professional men they desire: the corn merchant Freddy Beenstock and solicitor Albert Prosser respectively. Because Hobson refuses to provide his daughters with either wages for their shop labour or with marriage settlements (these men are no Kings of France), this requires finding the money. As in her own case, Maggie does so by using her head and a pragmatic ability to work with events as they arise. In this aspect of the plot, as in *Lear*, the pivotal action is initiated by the father's appalling and unruly behaviour, at and after another evening holding court at the pub – in which Hobson plays both irrational deposed authority and (inebriated) fool.

Despite the film's windy opening shots that imply trouble ahead at the sign of the swinging boot, this later sequence is truly Laughton's 'storm' scene, and its dramatization springs from the black-and-white expressionist artistry of David Lean rather than the play itself (in which, as befitted theatrical conventions for domestic comedies of the time, both Hobson's visits to the pub and their consequences are merely narrated). As in *Lear*, the scene is prompted by Hobson's dissatisfaction with the way his two remaining daughters treat him, once left to manage the home and shop after he has violently driven away Will, and with him Maggie. Disgusted at Alice's midday dinner of cold 'jellied tongue' and the two daughters' accompanying vocal complaints, Hobson flounces out of his 'castle' to Moonrakers for an all-day bender; en route, he violently scatters a paperboy's stack of advertisements for the opening of Mossop's new shop and, with that action, initiates a wild wind that mimics the thunder's uncanny arrival during Lear's symbolically as well as affectively heartbreaking 'Reason not the need' speech (2.4.257–79; '*Storm and tempest*' at 276).[8]

At the Inn, facing his friends' laughter aimed at his daughters, Hobson proceeds to insult each member of that remaining 'wonderful little band' and storms out of his last sanctuary into the night. As Alain Silver and James Ursini note in their DVD commentary, Lean's creative use of point-of-view shots here allows to come to the fore both the preposterousness of Hobson's indulgence and also viewer identification with his unhinged subjectivity.[9] Whereas the film previously has looked *at* rather than *with* Hobson, repeatedly displacing his authority through camera identification with Maggie and then also, increasingly, Will Mossop, now we see the doubled images that the drunken Hobson experiences in his final moments in the pub, and teeter through the puddled streets of Salford as he does (clearly the wind had led to 'the rain that raineth' as he drank) – shifting up and down repeatedly among the actual moon, its reflection in puddles and then Hobson's reflected face in the water and shop window where the moon had been.[10] As Fryer observes, 'the external elements represent Hobson's internal instability. The camera switches between high and low angle shots, and between the sky and the street. As Hobson struggles to focus on signs and objects, the camera zooms in and out, distorting the image'.[11] The soundtrack compounds the disorientation, shifting between the familiarly comic, brass-heavy music hall orchestration and the eerie, seemingly spiritual vibrations of a musical saw, as Hobson becomes enchanted and (like Act 3's Lear) confused by the blurring of cosmic nature, its images and himself. Whereas the film's first scene concluded with Laughton drunkenly charging up his own stairs to bed while still the authority figure in his home (despite all his self-indulgence), now we see him topple down both figuratively and literally, complete with a slow-motion downward tracking shot that similarly deceives the viewing audience as to the distance of his fall. Having attempted to skulk away past a shop sign's command to 'defy the demon drink', through his own unrelentingly misguided actions Hobson finally careens into the grain cellar of none other than Beenstock & Son (the elder being a firm 'Temperance man'), from whence Hobson will awaken next noon to be confronted with a legal action of trespass and damages.

The ignominy of his fall conflates the absurdity of Gloucester's imaginary tumble from Dover cliff with the ravings of Lear on the heath, recalling those high winds that initiated the fuller episode.[12] Whereas Hobson in his rage had scattered advertising flyers for the rival bootery, now it is legal papers, filed on behalf of Beenstock, that undo his attempts to restore his dignity. Hobson's humiliation is compounded when he must again literally descend to Maggie and Will's basement-level shop to seek her help. The court action, we begin to glean through intercutting with Maggie's wedding day, is in fact her swiftly improvised solution to gain marriage settlements for her sisters, concocted with help from the younger Beenstock and Prosser during Hobson's unconsciousness: this leads to the first proverbial 'Hobson's choice' with which she then confronts her father.

As with *Lear*, however, the story ends neither with the patriarch's encounter with the harsh elements nor even with a chastened return to the most dutiful daughter – although the plot easily could have. While the film's comic arc clearly diverges in the latter scenes' second 'Hobson's choice' that heralds the restoration of (a revised) order, even here cinematic as well as narrative specifics recall aspects of the fourth and fifth acts of Shakespeare's tragedy transformed. Most surprising in a film whose exterior shooting in Salford has been extolled as characteristic of Lean's 'hyper-realism' is the sudden subjective shift back into Hobson's altered state when he awakens from another bout of drinking, the sequence being yet another creation of Lean's without precedent in the play;[13] even after the drunken 'heath scene', nothing quite prepares one for the jump cut to swarming abstracted mosquitos assaulting the viewer – nor to the fantastic appearance of a spectral, human-sized feathery rat nonchalantly leaning over the bottom of Hobson's bedstead.[14] This is all the more surprising since the last we had heard from Hobson was on Maggie's wedding evening, when having submitted to the daughters' plans he exited, saying of married life and family, 'I've suffered [through it] for thirty years and more, and I'm a free man [from] today'.

Now we rejoin him with eyes closed, hearing a croak on the soundtrack and then buzzing that spurs him to swat before his eyes open: the film audience is left uncertain until the mosquito assault that we have shifted to a subjective perspective with 'matter and impertinency mixed,/ Reason in madness' (4.5.166–7). Hobson proceeds to rise (fearfully) and confront in the mirror not his own face but that of one of his Moonrakers drinking companions, shocking him into dropping a water pitcher. Its shattering in turn alerts his shopworkers, who summon both a doctor and Maggie.[15] Although Hobson refuses to see the doctor in his bedroom at his most vulnerable, the stage is set for the Lear-like reunion of father and daughter with doctor present, in this case marking her homecoming as well as the occasion when she receives instruction in how to help restore him at least temporarily (the doctor has warned that he is presently 'within six months of the grave'). While far from the wrenching pathos of *Lear*'s fourth act, this is Hobson's closest brush with torment and death, and leads to a final reunion with the three sisters in which the younger two again reveal that only Maggie can be relied upon.

More could be said about the artfulness of Lean's remediation and its Shakespearean echoes in *Hobson's Choice*, at least a trace of which has been acknowledged recently (in the wake of the 2009 release of the BFI's well-restored print on DVD and even more notably the film's sixtieth anniversary DVD and Blu-ray, 2014): the 1954 reviews I have recovered said nary a word about *King Lear*. But even when intertextual connection is mentioned now, the analysis seldom extends beyond recognition of the three-daughters-with-a-tyrannical-father intergenerational plot with marital consequences. One exception is Norman H. Holland, who writes:

> Hobson follows a tragic downward arc in this film. He is King Lear, an angry, impotent old man boasting of his power ... He has a kind of mad scene, when he tells his cronies in the pub what he really thinks of them ... Like *King Lear*, *Hobson's Choice* gives us a battle of the generations. And the younger generation triumphs, as, in comedy, it always must.[16]

I would emphasize not only this overarching generic departure but the significance of the film's specific forms of divergence which encourage us to reflect back upon *King Lear* somewhat differently, seeing even within the latter's relentless suffering its early modern investment in, and deep identification with, the lost patriarch as sustaining and pivotal, thereby rendering the young (women especially) merely the human wreckage that follows from his displacement. Removing Shakespeare's subplot and his schematic opposition between the sisters increases the emphasis on the gendered generational difference in the Hobson household, and thus the marginalizing of women's lives upon which the patriarch's order is constructed.

Perhaps even more consequentially, and unlike most other modernizing collaborations with *Lear*, Lean's film reinforces the benign necessity of generational collaboration and progress. Lean creates scenes that align the camera with Hobson's perspective almost exclusively when his disorientation and vulnerability come to the fore – and quite importantly *not* at the film's conclusion. There, the final words and tracking shot go to a triumphant Will joining Maggie and Hobson as they nonetheless all voluntarily head to the lawyer's office together to transform 'Hobson's' into 'Mossop and Hobson's'.[17] As well as recognizing certain aspects of a patriarchal Bard, then, this film's playfulness with genres, texts and media makes visible the opportunities for 'late moderns' to collaborate creatively whenever performing or invoking *King Lear*; it models selectivity, affective reworking and departure from (to cite only the most salient thematic strands) the earlier play's fears, constraints and sentimentality associated with femininity and the younger generation assuming power.

As regards its significance in allowing us to rethink our performative relationships with *Lear*, Lean's *Hobson* remains oddly marginalized. Although the film anticipates more obviously inverted feminist reworkings such as *Lear's Daughters* and *A Thousand Acres*, perhaps *Hobson*'s comic genre obscures its more substantial dimensions. Perhaps it also reveals the residual gender assumptions of much film genre theory and practice. Yvonne Griggs, who in 2009 claimed 'there are only six populist genre reworkings of the text' on film, cites among them only Jocelyn Moorhouse's 1997 remediation of Jane Smiley's novel *A Thousand Acres* as 'female-centred melodrama' with the rest 'male-centred' gangster and Western examples – including the far less directly connected *Godfather* trilogy.[18] Nowhere in sight is Lean's *Hobson*, despite its being populist to the core, and having received the BAFTA Award for Best British Film and the Golden Bear at the Berlin Film Festival. Even had it not been directed by the man who edited the first British Shakespeare sound film[19] nor starred a legendary actor who regarded playing *King Lear* at Stratford-upon-Avon in 1959 as a long-sought pinnacle of his career,[20] Lean's

Hobson's Choice surely should have earned a place on any such list of creative collaborations with Shakespeare's *Lear* – and it nicely complicates binary gender and genre assumptions in the process.

Since Griggs's book first appeared, another more obviously *Lear*-inspired British film has joined *Hobson* in challenging those particular boundaries, and more, this time both written and directed by a woman. Set in pre-Brexit London and focusing on an affluent family within its transplanted Bengali community, Sangeeta Datta's 2009 *Life Goes On* similarly refuses to divide-and-conquer the three British-born daughters, while strengthening the woman's part in a different way: through greater emphasis on the mother's importance – *this* mother whose sudden death initiates the narrative and leads to the (temporary) unravelling of the family.[21] As such, the film confronts mortality far more directly and extensively than does *Hobson's Choice*.

Life Goes On lingers with the consequences of mortality, using its filmic resources to disrupt the linearity of its narrative; indeed, it revives as well as mourns the mother, Manju Banerjee, through the flamboyantly self-conscious use of flashback and imaginary slow-motion sequences that intercut with present-tense actions and grieving. The film thereby redirects its pathos not only to honour a figure notably absent from both plots of *King Lear* but also to embrace the positive aspects of Indian cultural inheritance she had sustained and thus symbolizes; the music and poetry of Rabindranath Tagore (among others) recurs throughout the film, including her repeated singing of Tagore's 'remember me'. The choice of actress Sharmila Tagore to play the mother adds obvious performative layers (as a star of both Bengali and Hindi cinema, and grand-niece of Rabindranath Tagore). Casting Sharmila Tagore's real-life daughter Soha Ali Kahn as the youngest child Dia further compounds the fluidity between life and art – especially given that Dia's becoming pregnant by a Muslim fellow-student resembles Tagore's own religious boundary-crossing to marry Ali Kahn's father. In thus enlarging and diffusing its elegiac mode through allusion, casting and filmic flashbacks, as well as in the particulars of its representation of gender, social perspectives and power, *Life Goes On* arguably lays claim to a different ancestry than melodrama: the retrospectively constructed, aesthetically self-conscious generic category of Shakespearean romance.

At the same time, *King Lear* is overtly the play haunting this family and film. The successful doctor-father Sanjay Banerjee (Girish Karnad) loves Shakespeare's tragic play, quoting *King Lear* when Dia is doubting whether to continue playing Cordelia – crucial for her acting degree – during the week of her mother's funeral. From the opening credits onward, we hear lines from Dia's opening scene intercut with establishing shots of her family members' lives, including their work around London and a televised cricket victory for India. Later we learn in flashback from Manju that the two elder daughters call their father 'King Lear' because of his paternal indulgence of Dia, the third. The narrative extends the *Lear* analogies (and overt quotation of the 3.2 'Blow, winds' speech) when the Hindu father, appalled to learn belatedly that this daughter is pregnant by a Muslim, leaves the house to wander all night through London in what the director consciously constructs as his heath scene. Datta also incorporates repeated shots of a picnic on Hampstead Heath as a pivotal memory for Sanjay, capturing the triad of himself, Manju and the non-Bengali family friend who plays the truth-telling Fool as well as avuncular jokester, Alok (Om Puri). The final twist in the film's narrative involves Alok's revelation of what (else) Sanjay had 'ta'en/ Too little care of' (3.4.32–3) in those earlier days, with further use of those heath location shots. But before that, we hear Sanjay speak Lear's 'foolish, fond old man' speech in Dia's presence after his stormy night outdoors, although in private voiceover – reinforcing his difficulties in overcoming his pride (and prejudice) to share his own childhood trauma with his daughters.

In addition to personal losses and the revelation of guilt and betrayals, the painfulness of the larger context of modern India's state formation lies behind the father's Hindu intolerance, offsetting the nostalgia and apparent sentimentality that hovers around the figure of the Bengali-identified mother. As director Datta recently put it, for her own Punjabi relatives just as for the fictional Banerjees (and as Sanjay eventually articulates within the film), immigration to England is always the second journey, the first being the violent upheavals of Partition that displaced and killed so many on the subcontinent in 1947.[22] The doctor's personal history of double displacement (from Dhaka to Kolkata to London, again reanimated into the present via flashback sequences) thus converges with a broader context of terrorism and increasing Islamophobia within twenty-first-century London (and of course well beyond, as a classic-era Hollywood newspaper montage within the film swiftly rehearses) – two overlapping horrors that the film acknowledges but in no way excuses or endorses. Instead, it turns primarily to the seeming Fool Alok (originally from Lahore) to reveal the limited perception of the Bengali doctor as regards both the broader Indian subcontinental realities and his intimate familial ones. Sanjay, like Hobson, must let go of his paternal authority and accept the younger generation's more progressive, category-crossing attitudes – though his route is obviously a more profound one. Not only does it involve recalling and publicly sharing his traumatic early history (which the film renders present in his mind and to our eyes through flashbacks), but also realizing the cost of his idealized vision of himself as patriarch and leader in his community: he must ultimately face his own role in unwittingly creating mixed bloodlines and paternity out of wedlock, as well as accepting these realities along with religious and cultural difference.

The radical nature of this change, especially for a man of his status and background, stands out against the Indian cultural – and filmic – heritage that plays just as important a role here as does the politically ambivalent inheritance of British Shakespeare.[23] As Jonathan Gil Harris has recently observed, most inter-faith Indian *Romeo and Juliet* films present a Hindu Romeo and reduce the Juliet-figure's active desiring, so that the sexually assertive character (and the paternity of any imagined offspring) sustains the nation's majority religion;[24] in this context, the inversion in *Life Goes On* of a young Muslim father and Hindu mother-to-be becomes all the more potent and challenging. And indeed, neither Dia's child nor Sanjay's other grandchildren (in a surprising twist that compounds their obvious interracial paternity) will perpetuate his illusion of Bengali Hindu 'purity' in his adopted country. Nevertheless, in keeping with the dominant refusal of tragic endings in Hindi cinema and also with the semi-allegorical politics of Datta's collaboration,[25] Sanjay's journey leads ultimately to a vision of acceptance, and a highly non-traditional family renewed.

In the process, *Life Goes On* makes space for affect often associated with women's stories and melodrama but here involving both men and women, and with a forward-looking or indeed antilinear rather than nostalgic temporality.[26] Like the Tagore song that provides its most insistent musical motif and derives from the Vedas, the film departs from tragedy; it favours mixed emotions and transcendent forgiveness, more akin to the forms of resolution expressed in late Shakespearean romance. Thus, when at the conclusion we hear the final *Lear* quotation from the 'Come, let's away to prison' speech (5.3.8ff), it is accompanied by the release of white balloons into the sky honouring (and then filmically recalling a nonetheless visually departing) Manju, and we see the surviving Banerjee clan all standing together, embodying sexual, racial and religious differences in a semi-allegorical reformed community. Beyond death come memory, acceptance and further life.

Not that this formal conclusion erases the earlier strains of realism, any more than Maggie's actions in *Hobson's Choice* undo the marital order and class divisions of Victorian England. Despite Sanjay's exceptional wealth and success, in flashback Manju had called attention to the high price for his Kolkata relatives of his refusal to allow the sale of his father's house there: even if traumatic memories motivate that resistance, the effect nonetheless is to expose the selfishness and even hypocrisy of his putative Bengali loyalties. Whether Sanjay's cross-generational acceptance will end his impoverishment of those Indian lives remains unresolved, just as the death of Mamillius remains to haunt the reunions that conclude Shakespeare's *The Winter's Tale*. Nonetheless, this ending at least resists (what strike me as) the reactionary gender implications of separating the sisters from one another and having the 'good' daughter return with her father and British-Indian childhood sweetheart to Kolkata itself – a conclusion represented in the aligned (and in other ways progressive) earlier television movie *Second Generation* (dir. Jon Sen, 2003).

More difficult to counter is the objection that both films I have analysed uphold a (British) neoliberal consensus which naturalizes individualism, gendered differences and capitalist privilege and inequity. These are far from overtly revolutionary texts, though arguably satire and subversion can aid in advancing nonviolent change more broadly than do works professing to render – rather than tentatively imagine – a more benign future. The comedy of *Hobson's Choice* and the romance of *Life Goes On* each imagine a space in which daughters need not be victimized or ruled by division, nor fathers be unable to accept (grudgingly or not) their daughters' agency. For many present-day viewers, such imaginings are neither a given nor trivial. Furthermore, these genres continue to require advocacy as sites for serious reflection. In a recent discussion of *Othello*, Christopher Pye argues that when Shakespeare chooses to build a tragedy on a comic structure, he makes clear its aesthetic autonomy as a creative work. Moreover, this reveals the conventional rather than natural logic that associates tragedy with greater ontological truth or profundity.[27] I would argue that the generically inverted choices in these two films similarly attest to their being acts of aesthetic autonomy, with equal validity – and no less 'truth value' as reflections upon ontological reality.

I have highlighted some of the filmic, gender-related and other cultural alterations that allow homage to avoid mere monumentalization of *King Lear*, reiteration of its seventeenth-century societal presumptions or simple inversion by 'reading against the grain'. In analysing these alternatives, we might also consider how their visions do – or do not – feed back into our scholarly cross-generational stories as well.

And thus, a coda. Who do we cite as our own collaborators? In this essay, I have consciously included quotations from an unpublished essay written for an MIT undergraduate seminar by a former student, because I know part of my thinking derives from her responses and, indirectly, the then-junior colleague who taught her film studies, Eugenie Brinkema. Similarly, the four conference organizers of Indian Shakespeares on Screen named in note 22 – at the time all graduate students and untenured instructors – brought *Life Goes On* to my attention, and provided responses to my questions and early formulations: all these young women could easily be credited as co-authors for portions of this essay.

I am no King (or even Queen) Lear, yet it is still easy in published scholarship to overlook the people and places where one actually gets ideas. Nonetheless, learning from the younger generation is not confined to genre films, nor need we continue to round up the 'usual suspects' as footnoted proof that we have listened to our elders – unless they truly helped us on the scholarly journey. In those moments we must cite them, and acknowledgement becomes authentic and a pleasure. But as with our reading, so too with our talking and teaching: we who are now ourselves elders might do well to pay a bit more public (and published) attention to those who will benefit from that recognition now, as well as remembering those who have long received it. And so here explicitly, at the close, I name them again: Marisa Fryer, Thea Buckley, Koel Chatterjee, Varsha Panjwani and Preti Taneja. Because life indeed goes on.

Notes

1. L. Olivier, *On Acting* (London: Weidenfeld and Nicolson, 1986), 93. A shorter version of my argument appeared as 'Genre and Modernity in *Hobson's Choice* and *Life Goes On*', *Litteraria Pragensia: Studies in Literature and Culture* 26.52, Special Issue (December 2016): 49–57.
2. W. Szymborska, 'Theatre Impressions', in her *Poems New and Collected 1957–1997*, trans. S. Baranczak and C. Cavanagh (New York: Harcourt, 1998), 114.
3. It is worth recalling that, even in Shakespeare's sources, the future for the surviving Cordelia includes her eventual imprisonment by her nephews, ending in suicide. The folk tale of the princess who values her father like salt is more benign.
4. See 'Alternative Collaborations: Shakespeare, Nahum Tate, Our Academy, and the Science of Probability', in D. E. Henderson (ed.), *Alternative Shakespeares 3* (London: Routledge, 2008), 243–63.
5. Most recently, a production by the Theatre Royal Bath returned to London's West End (the Vaudeville Theatre on the Strand) in the summer of 2016, with

Martin Shaw as Hobson and Naomi Frederick as Maggie, directed by Jonathan Church; it marked the 100th anniversary of the first British production in 1916, the play having debuted in New York. The story was also made into the Broadway musical *Walking Happy* (1966–1967).

6. M. Fryer, 'Abstract Storms: Reinventing Storms from Elizabethan Theater', undergraduate essay, MIT, 2015, 5–6.

7. The establishing shot for Moonrakers fittingly features a 'Walker's Falstaff Ales' placard.

8. The stage direction is from the First Folio. Lear, having similarly tried to deny his vulnerability ('You think I'll weep;/ No, I'll not weep'), is interrupted by the elements that enact his fracture; he then proclaims 'but this heart/ Shall break into a hundred thousand flaws/ Or ere I'll weep' (2.4.275–79), even as this context encourages most performers to motivate his imagined audience response with angry, frustrated tears.

9. Criterion Collection DVD, audio commentary by A. Silver and J. Ursini, co-authors of *David Lean and His Films* (London, Frewin, 1974; Los Angeles: Silman-James Press, 1991).

10. In a classic instance of projection, Hobson has just slandered Maggie and Will's intention of succeeding with a rival shop as being 'just talk', indeed, 'moonshine'. N. H. Holland, 'David Lean, *Hobson's Choice*, 1954', discusses the origins of 'moonraker' as relevant here: www.asharperfocus.com/Hobson.html (accessed 12 July 2016).

11. Fryer, 'Abstract Storms', 6.

12. Hobson's narration in Brighouse's play provides verbal inspiration for these associations with *Lear*, and another Goneril/Maggie connection: blaming his fall on Maggie, he admits he stayed too long at Moonrakers 'To try to forget that I'd a thankless child' – 'And the result, the blasting, withering result? I fell into that cellar'; Harold Brighouse, *Hobson's Choice: a Three-act Comedy* (London: Constable and Company, 1916), 82.

13. 'Hyperrealism' is the term used by Armond White in his essay 'Custom-Made' in the booklet included with the Criterion Collection DVD cited above, n.p. Lean's dedication to capturing the ugliness of late Victorian industrialism included dumping waste into the river where Maggie 'woos' Will; the sustained rendering of class distinctions adds a more serious context to her refusal of those boundaries.

14. I am indebted to my undergraduate research student Casey Crownhart for prompting me to consider further Hobson's rat.

15. The film here departs most obviously from the play, in which Hobson is irascible at his illness but admits no vulnerability (Brighouse, *Hobson's Choice*, 101).

16. Holland, 'David Lean'. He adds, in tones that resonate with my epigraph from Olivier, 'Hobson is really a dreadful human being'.

17. Here again Lean's film departs from the Brighouse play, in which the final decision is solely the younger generation's and allows Hobson no final bluster nor illusion of his continuing agency, even in reduced form: his last words

there are the submissive '(meekly) Yes, Maggie' (Brighouse, *Hobson's Choice*, 128). Thus differentiation from both earlier plays, though for opposite reasons, is required in order to reach the film's comic intergenerational rapprochement.

18. Y. Griggs, *Shakespeare's 'King Lear': the Relationship between Text and Film* (London: Methuen Drama, 2009), 28. The three *Hobson* films appear, albeit very briefly, in D. M. Lanier's capacious 'Film Spin-offs and Citations' survey in R. Burt (ed.), *Shakespeare after Shakespeares: an Encyclopedia of the Bard in Mass Media and Popular Culture* (Westport: Greenwood Press, 2007), 189, 186.

19. Lean edited the 1936 *As You Like It* featuring Laurence Olivier (who also worked with Lean as narrator for *This Happy Breed*, released the same year as Olivier's *Henry V* and also starring John Mills).

20. The BBC feature on Charles Laughton written and narrated by Barry Norman (dir. Margaret Sharpe, 1978, included on the Criterion Collection DVD) mentions Laughton's life-long obsession with playing Lear; although it shifts fairly swiftly from his performance as Hobson to his 1959 Lear, it makes no direct connection between the two.

21. Datta previously worked as associate director on both *Brick Lane* (2007) and Rituparna Ghosh's 2007 Indian film *The Last Lear*, both relevant here.

22. Sangeeta Das speaking at the Indian Shakespeares on Screen Conference, Asia House, London, 29 April 2016. I am indebted to the conference organizers, Varsha Panjwani, Koel Chatterjee, Preti Taneja and Thea Buckley, for introducing me to Datta and helping me contextualize this film.

23. On the larger topic of Shakespeare, politics and Indian film, see (among many) the groundbreaking work of Poonam Trivedi and the new work of Preti Taneja cited below.

24. 'Why Art Thou Romeo?', *Indian Express*, 2 April 2017: 'If the Hindu Romeo is embraced as a figure of eve-teasing [*sic*] fun, the Muslim Romeo is a clear and present threat. This much is evident in the political panic created around the alleged figure of the Muslim "love jihadi" who schemes to seduce Hindu women.' Harris's intended title was 'Wherefore art thou anti-Romeo?', explicitly addressing the BJP's 'anti-Romeo police squads' in Uttar Pradesh; see www.indianexpress.com/article/lifestyle/life-style/why-art-thou-romeo-4595 484 (accessed 1 May 2019).

25. As Preti Taneja notes, Dia means 'holy light' and in the 'highly modern' unusual Banerjee family, 'it is also Dia whose aberration is held worse than her sisters' mixed-race or lesbian relationships'; that Dia's mother and sisters knew of her pregnancy and the father did not 'is a betrayal to the patriarchal order in and of itself'; '*King Lear* in India – the Playing Out of "Divide and Rule" Politics in State and Family', presentation at the Shakespeare Adaptations and Appropriations Conference, Cambridge University, 2011. Taneja's 2017 novel *We That Are Young* builds on these insights to create her own powerful rewriting of *Lear* as a modern Indian tragedy.

26. See K. Földváry, 'Postcolonial Hybridity: the Making of a Bollywood *Lear* in London', *Shakespeare* (British Shakespeare Association) 9.3 (2013): 304–12, which discusses the mother and lesbian figures in complementary ways to my own.
27. C. Pye, *The Storm at Sea: Political Aesthetics in the Time of Shakespeare* (New York: Fordham University Press, 2015).

WORKS CITED

Brighouse, H., *Hobson's Choice: a Three-act Comedy* (London: Constable and Company, 1916).

Földváry, K., 'Postcolonial Hybridity: the Making of a Bollywood *Lear* in London', *Shakespeare* (British Shakespeare Association) 9.3 (2013): 304–12.

Fryer, M., 'Abstract Storms: Reinventing Storms from Elizabethan Theater', undergraduate essay, MIT, 2015.

Griggs, Y., *Shakespeare's 'King Lear': the Relationship between Text and Film* (London: Methuen Drama, 2009).

Henderson, D. E., 'Alternative Collaborations: Shakespeare, Nahum Tate, Our Academy, and the Science of Probability', in D. E. Henderson (ed.), *Alternative Shakespeares 3* (London: Routledge, 2008), 243–63.

'Genre and Modernity in *Hobson's Choice* and *Life Goes On*', *Litteraria Pragensia: Studies in Literature and Culture* 26.52, Special Issue (December 2016): 49–57.

Holland, N. H. 'David Lean, *Hobson's Choice*, 1954': www.asharperfocus.com/Hobson.html (accessed 12 July 2016).

Lanier, D. M., 'Film Spin-offs and Citations' in R. Burt (ed.), *Shakespeares after Shakespeare: an Encyclopedia of the Bard in Mass Media and Popular Culture* (Westport: Greenwood Press, 2007), 132–365.

Olivier, L., *On Acting* (London: Weidenfeld and Nicolson, 1986).

Pye, C., *The Storm at Sea: Political Aesthetics in the Time of Shakespeare* (New York: Fordham University Press, 2015).

Silver, A. and J. Ursini, *David Lean and His Films* (London: Frewin, 1974; Los Angeles: Silman-James Press, 1991).

Szymborska, W., 'Theatre Impressions', in her *Poems New and Collected 1957–1997*, trans. S. Baranczak and C. Cavanagh (New York: Harcourt, 1998), 114.

CHAPTER 9

'Easy Lear': Harry and Tonto *and the American Road Movie*

Douglas M. Lanier

King Lear has long been regarded as infertile territory for mainstream American film, particularly after the advent of the talkie. Many of the American films included in lists of *Lear* screen spinoffs are second-order adaptations – that is, works based upon novels or plays themselves often loosely based upon Shakespeare's play. Though *House of Strangers* (dir. Joseph L. Mankiewicz, 1949, a melodrama about an immigrant banking family), *Broken Lance* (dir. Edward Dmytryk, 1954, a Western) and *The Big Show* (dir. James B. Clark, 1961, a melodrama about a circus family), all works about tyrannical fathers and the passing of their business empires to their children, are regularly listed as *Lear* spinoffs, their immediate source is Jerome Weidman's 1941 novel *I'll Never Go There Any More.*[1] The Western *The Man from Laramie* (dir. Anthony Mann, 1955) is also often listed as a *Lear* adaptation on the basis of motifs from the Gloucester subplot, but screenwriters Philip Yordan and Frank Burt based the film not on Shakespeare but on a 1954 short story, 'The Man from Laramie', by Thomas T. Flynn. While *Rosie!* (dir. David Lowell Rich, 1967), a comedy involving a madcap matriarch and children greedy for her fortune, bears many resemblances to *Lear*, it is in reality an adaptation of Ruth Gordon's 1965 play *A Very Rich Woman*, itself an adaptation of Philippe Hériat's 1960 play *Les Joies de la famille*. More recent *Lear* cinematic analogues like *The Substance of Fire* (dir. Daniel J. Sullivan, 1996) and *A Thousand Acres* (dir. Jocelyn Moorhouse, 1997) follow the same pattern, *The Substance of Fire* being based upon Jon Robin Baitz's 1996 play and *A Thousand Acres* upon Jane Smiley's 1991 novel. The roster of American films that draw more directly upon Shakespeare's play is considerably shorter. John Boorman's *Where the Heart Is* (1990) uses the basic narrative structure of *Lear* as part of a yuppie revenge comedy in which an arrogant property developer forces his children to live in urban squalor only to find himself homeless and unexpectedly dependent upon

140

their kindness. *King of Texas* (2002), a TV movie produced towards the end of the millennial Shakespeare film boom, transfers the action of *King Lear* to a Texas ranching empire – one of the few American film adaptations of *Lear* that retains the play's tragic ending, perhaps because, as a television film on a cable network, it did not have to navigate the commercial film marketplace.[2]

If one compares this short list to the lengthy lists of American films that draw upon other major Shakespearean tragedies like *Romeo and Juliet*, *Hamlet*, *Macbeth* and *Othello*, one is immediately struck by the disparity. One explanation may be found in genre, for adapting Shakespeare to the American screen has typically involved finding a suitable film genre into which Shakespearean material might be transposed.[3] Though filmmakers have been able to cultivate affinities between other Shakespearean tragedies and well-established mainstream genres – *Hamlet* with the revenge thriller, *Macbeth* with the gangster epic and the horror film, *Othello* with romantic melodrama – *King Lear* has proved far more difficult to affiliate with a particular genre. *Lear* has been filmed as family melodrama,[4] Western,[5] business saga, madcap comedy and more, yet none of these genres seems an especially comfortable fit with Shakespeare's play for Hollywood film-makers. More fundamentally, Hollywood has struggled with transposing *King Lear* to an American context, for, although a number of filmmakers have sought to make elements of the *Lear* narrative relevant to the American experience, the relentlessly tragic, even nihilistic nature of the play ill sorts with the dominant ideological orientations of American culture, with its emphasis on optimism and youthful possibility, the efficacy of personal agency, freedom and self-reliance. Here I want to address the challenge of an American screen *Lear* by examining *Harry and Tonto* (1974), a *Lear* adaptation by American screenwriter-director Paul Mazursky. *Harry and Tonto* has now largely been forgotten by Shakespeare film historians,[6] but in 1974 it was something of a hit for Mazursky, garnering him and his writing partner Josh Greenfeld a 1975 Oscar nomination for best original screenplay and a surprise Oscar for best actor for Art Carney, who played the title character.[7] It has the distinction of being the most commercially successful American film yet made from *King Lear*. *Harry and Tonto* adapts Shakespeare's play to that quintessentially American film genre, the road movie. As a number of commentators have suggested, the road movie is in many ways heir to the Western, with life in a car travelling between destinations – or without destination – serving as the new fantasy incarnation of American liberty in a post-frontier society. Like Shakespeare's play, the road movie, at least in its 1960s and

1970s incarnations, conceives of self-exile and rootlessness as existential states of freedom. Those states are by turns exhilarating and riddled with despair; filled with possibility and constrained; countercultural and deeply American. The uneasy fit between Shakespeare's play and Mazursky's film, I will argue, illustrates the difficulty of bringing Shakespeare and modern cinematic genres into dialogue, but also, and more importantly, the challenge this particular play poses to Hollywood screen adaptation.[8]

While *Harry and Tonto*'s borrowings from *King Lear* are certainly recognizable, Mazursky substantially alters and re-orientates many of the characters, relationships and motifs. The film's Lear figure is Harry Coombes, an elderly ex-teacher who is evicted from his New York apartment to accommodate urban renewal. As the film begins, Harry, like Lear, lives under an illusion of stability and control. His 'kingdom' is his long-time New York neighbourhood, which he navigates with a sardonic familiarity. His apartment, seemingly frozen in time since the forties, provides him an oasis from the changing streets outside, a bubble (like Lear's court) that shields him from engaging with loss and change and allows him to indulge nostalgia for the long-past joys of his youth. Even so, early on Harry encounters signs that control over his neighbourhood kingdom is illusory: on the way home from the grocer he is nearly run down by a speeding car, he is mugged outside his building and he learns that he has only weeks until he must vacate his apartment. He and his companion Jacob also register their sense of waning power in terms of anxieties about lost virility, a recurring topic among the ageing men in the film (and a source of gentle comedy involving bananas as aphrodisiacs). Urban life, the film repeatedly demonstrates, involves dealing with a loose system of rule-bound bureaucrats and martinets who subject Harry to various indignities – he cannot get a new apartment because he has a pet, and he struggles to get past a paper-pushing attendant to see the body of his friend Jacob at the morgue.

This inchoate system of what Jacob calls 'capitalist bastards' – one target of social critique in the film, albeit an oblique one – also lies behind the destruction of Harry's home. When the authorities come to evict Harry, he tries to deny the reality of impending loss by holing up in his apartment and indulging his routine of sipping tea and reading the newspaper. Soon enough, however, he is forcibly removed, carried outside while still sitting in his old easy chair. It is at this moment that Harry identifies himself explicitly with Lear, for as he is deposited on the stoop, he quotes Lear's raging lines from the storm scene: 'Blow, winds, and crack your cheeks! Rage, blow,/ You cataracts and hurricanos, spout/ Till you have drenched our steeples, drowned the cocks!/ You sulph'rous and thought-executing fires,/ Vaunt-couriers to oak-cleaving thunderbolts,/ Singe my white head' (3.2.1–6).⁹ To add to the indignity of his eviction, Harry spies his mugger running free as he is manhandled by the police, an instance of injustice thematically akin to Lear's discovery of Kent in the stocks. After this moment, Harry is, like Lear, dispossessed of the supports for his former identity. Rendered homeless, he is forced by his circumstances to confront the depredations of ageing and the existential instability of life. After the wrecking ball demolishes his building, Harry underlines the similarity between himself and Lear: 'He gave up his real estate too. Know what happened to him, what they did to him? They foreclosed. That's life. An old man loses his home, he's just a wanderer.' Notably, Harry's fall is not precipitated by hubris or an engulfing desire for love, though, like Lear, Harry does seek in his retirement to hang on to the stability of his former life: his creature comforts, his dapper dress, his 'retinue' of elderly compatriots from the neighbourhood, his cat Tonto. With the loss of his home, Harry hits the road, traversing the United States, from New York to Los Angeles, in the course of the film.

Like Lear, Harry has three children, and his journeys between them provide the film its basic structure. The first of them is his son Burt, who, like Cordelia, shows constant love and protectiveness towards his father. Burt rescues Harry when he is evicted and provides him a room in his suburban home, but, in one of the film's many re-orientations of Shakespeare's scenario, Harry's blunt manner in the already fractious household adds tension to Burt's family, much as Lear disrupts Goneril's. The loving union between the Lear and Cordelia figures of this film is not possible, and so Harry, seeking personal independence, decides to strike out on his own, ostensibly to visit his daughter Shirley in Chicago, from whom he has become estranged. Shirley is a sharp-tongued bookstore owner who shares with her father a literary bent but who invariably ends up quarrelling with him. When, lamenting his lack of grandchildren from her, Harry references *Lear* again – 'I loved her most, and thought to set my rest/ On her kind nursery' (1.1.116–17) – Shirley tartly retorts, 'Please, Harry, no Shakespeare, huh?', an exchange that in many ways sums up their argumentative relationship. She disapproves of Harry's willingness to drift after his eviction, even though it is apparent from her four divorces that she is as romantically unrooted as Harry has become geographically and psychologically. Harry's third child is his son Eddie, a would-be Los Angeles playboy who is secretly unemployed and, despite his veneer of wealth, is on the brink of homelessness himself. Like his sister, he is divorced, and in his desperation he is all too willing to exploit his father financially to address his prodigality. Shirley and Eddie correspond very roughly to Regan and Goneril as their father's alienated children, although neither Shirley nor Eddie exude the greed, cruelty or manipulativeness of their Shakespearean counterparts. Indeed, in the course of his short stays with both, Harry manages to strike tentative rapprochements with them, agreeing to disagree with Shirley about his pursuit of independence and comforting Eddie about his fears of failure, not so much repairing the relationships as accepting his children's flaws. Harry's children represent various versions of flawed bourgeois conventionality, all shown to be wanting. His decision not to live with any of them picks up and recodes Lear's choice to venture out on the heath alone rather than to accept the terms of life his children are dictating. Unlike Lear, he does not leave their company because they mistreat him. Rather, on the road he finds independence and dignity in old age, a renewed sense of possibility in the final chapter of his life.

As is typical of the counterculture road movie of the 1960s and 1970s, life on the road affords Harry alternatives to bourgeois American culture. Just as Lear's wandering upon the moors puts him in contact with Poor Tom, 'unaccommodated man', and thereby transforms his perspective, so Harry's cross-country journey puts him in contact with representatives of America's underclass and counterculture – a hitchhiking Jesus freak; a runaway girl headed for a commune; a black family; Burt's alienated son Norman who experiments with drugs, macrobiotics and Buddhism; an eccentric itinerant salesman; a hooker; a Native American medicine man. While this contact involves an element of social critique of mainstream America, as it so often did in the countercultural road movies of the period, in *Harry and Tonto* that element is considerably muted, treated more as a source of offbeat humour than as a potential set of alternative lifestyles for Harry. This lack of political critique may spring from the fact that by the early 1970s faith in a counterculture alternative had largely faded as a result of the events of 1968 and after.[10] Indeed, references to the commune to which the runaway girl Ginger and Norman are heading are decidedly mixed and cautionary, a world away from the commune scenes in *Easy Rider* (dir. Dennis Hopper, 1969) just a few years earlier. Instead, the figures Harry encounters on the road function as symbols of a depoliticized and rather vague counterpoint to traditional social norms, more invigorating for Harry than the bourgeois lives represented by his children but not entirely coherent or viable alternatives for him. What unites these figures is their willingness to wander and be open to contingency, a lack of anxiety about their own directionlessness and an acceptance of the non-bourgeois identities they encounter. Though Harry himself exudes some of that openness early in the film – his best friends are Jesus, the local Hispanic grocer, Jacob, an old Polish Jew, and Leroy, a black janitor who lives in his building – his time on the road in the company of these drifters amplifies that native trait, so that he becomes increasingly willing to suspend caution and try, for example, a rubdown from the vitamin salesman or a healing spell from the Native American with whom he shares a jail cell. Harry's encounter with the American counterculture and underclass is, in short, more personally therapeutic than it is political in its effect – a journey of existential awareness rather than of social rebellion.

Crucial to Harry's growing openness to contingency is for him to accept the inevitability of mortality and loss: as Harry himself confesses in a moment of candour with his daughter, 'I think I remember the past too much.' Harry's cross-country journey, like Lear's wandering on the stormy heath, brings him in contact with the painful realities of loss, realities Harry has long kept at bay through routine and memory. At the start of his journey – and perhaps its immediate catalyst – is the death of his long-time friend Jacob who, as a Polish Jewish immigrant, is himself something of a wanderer. Harry responds to seeing his dead friend's corpse with barely controlled tears, and a poignantly comical epitaph that memorializes Jacob's (and by extension his own) lost virility: 'he had his first affair', he tells the morgue attendant, 'when he was 14'. Later, when Harry speaks to Ginger about a memorable affair he had with a free-spirited dancer named Jessie, Ginger insists that he search her out. When Harry does (fearing all along that she might be dead), he discovers her in a nursing home. While Jessie retains her spirited personality and seems at first to recognize Harry, it soon becomes apparent that she, in the early stages of dementia, has mistaken him for someone else – she doesn't remember him at all. The dance that Harry and Jessie share marks a change in Harry's response to loss, for although his eyes well up with sadness, he also takes pleasure from their dancing, as a fleeting reliving of a past he knows is now irretrievably lost. After this point, Harry no longer tells stories about his past, especially those of his beloved wife Annie, as if he is becoming reconciled to living in the present. Eventually, Harry loses even the company of his travelling companions Ginger and Norman, giving them his car and abandoning himself entirely to life on the road, hitchhiking his way across the West to Los Angeles. Notably, his leave-taking of Ginger and Norman is sudden and matter-of-fact, without tears or regrets.

Though Norman declares, 'I feel weird leaving you here' at a parking lot of an Arizona hotel, Harry's reply suggests how fully he has embraced the contingent existence of life on the road: 'Norman, for the first time in my life, I'm west of Chicago and I love it. It's splendid, it's amazing, and it's beautiful. I'm feel fine, I'm happy and I just want to spend some time by myself.'[11]

Throughout his journey, Harry's travelling companion is his cat Tonto, Mazursky's equivalent for Lear's Fool. Tonto[12] is named after the Lone Ranger's Native American tight-lipped, stoic sidekick from the old radio show, and that name hints at how Harry has seen his solitary existence – in this case, as the Lone Ranger – through myths of the past rather than realities of the present. This reference also allows Mazursky to recode Harry's solitary 'ranging' as an updated version of a classic Western myth, a tale of virtue and not irresponsibility. Tonto is the creature for whom Harry shows the most affection and, though Tonto cannot, like Lear's Fool, give voice to his master's subconscious fears of mortality and dependency, he becomes the catalyst for Harry to reveal his memories of the past and anxieties about death in long, one-sided conversations and snippets of Tin Pan Alley songs. Most importantly, Tonto is metonymically linked to Harry's dead wife Annie – a remnant of and substitute for their relationship (much as the Fool functions for Lear in relation to Cordelia). Tonto is the primary means by which Harry keeps full acceptance of his wife's loss at bay. Tellingly, Harry keeps him on a leash much of the time. When early in his journey Tonto briefly runs away from Harry in a cemetery, Harry's evident panic underlines just how psychologically dependent he is upon his cat and how unable he is to address loss. A whirling 360° shot of the graveyard as he desperately searches for Tonto communicates Harry's existential vertigo as he is left alone – or so it momentarily seems – to confront the reality of mortality. This is Harry's one moment of madness, akin to Lear's scenes of mad anguish on the heath, and when Tonto returns it quickly passes. Even so, it is with this incident that Harry's road trip properly starts, for Harry immediately afterwards buys a car and begins to drive himself and Tonto cross-country.

Tonto's death, the last and most devastating of Harry's losses, is the culminating event of the film, akin in emotional weight to Lear's final scene with the dead Cordelia. It is a final test of how fully Harry has come to accept the inevitability of death and loss. Interestingly, Mazursky plays the scene not for tragedy but for understated poignancy. Unlike Harry's parting with Jacob, Harry's parting with Tonto is quiet and barely tearful. As Tonto dies, Harry carries on the routine he has conducted with the cat throughout the film, singing to him and asking, 'who's that, Tonto?' In this case, the song is the old standard 'Roamin' in the Gloamin''[13] about walking at sunset with one's beloved, and the lines 'When the sun has gone to rest,/ That's the time we love best./ O, it's lovely roamin' in the gloamin'' articulate Harry's now active embrace of ineluctable loss as a principle of life. Throughout the film he has been 'roamin' in the gloamin'' without fully recognizing it, until this moment. His gentle parting from Tonto, with no more than a 'so long, kiddo' and a quick exit in long shot, provides the full measure of his changed perspective. The final sequence of the film reinforces the point of this scene. At the sea, Harry falls into conversation with an elderly woman who feeds feral cats, and she, providing the potential for a new chapter in Harry's life, spontaneously offers to share her apartment with him. As she feeds her cats, Harry sees a tabby who looks very much like Tonto, and, excited and agitated, he chases the cat onto the beach. This scene replays Harry's earlier pursuit of Tonto in the cemetery but with a difference, for although Harry soon catches the cat, picks it up and pets it, even calling it 'kiddo', he simply lets it go rather than adopting it to replace his beloved Tonto. In that gesture, Harry resists the temptation to return to his former existence and his former denial of mortality. Instead, Harry wanders over to a girl[14] building a sand castle and watches her work as the sun slowly sets. The sand castle aptly symbolizes Harry's recognition of the inescapable evanescence of life. Alluding back to the demolished building that is the catalyst for his journey on the road, the sand castle is, like human life itself, destined to be swept away, and Harry's long pause before it suggests his acceptance of the pain (and pleasures) of contingency and the inevitability of loss as reigning principles of existence.

The hardly obvious resemblances between *King Lear* and the American road movie are nonetheless potentially quite productive. The genre has a long pedigree in the nation's film history, its emergence coinciding with growing urbanization and the new importance of the automobile in American culture. In its classical manifestations (*It Happened One Night*, dir. Frank Capra, 1934, *The Grapes of Wrath*, dir. John Ford, 1940, *Sullivan's Travels*, dir. Preston Sturges, 1941), the protagonist journeys outside the enclaves of bourgeois or urban America into the countryside, where he or she has a series of encounters with the nation's own version of 'unaccommodated man' – the inhabitants of working-class, rural America. Typically the protagonist, dislocated from his or her sheltered native milieu, often involuntarily so, becomes through contact with this 'real' America spiritually renewed, or at least more independent of blinkered bourgeois ossification. Often the classic road movie has a journey-and-return structure, in which the protagonist, after a series of picaresque adventures, returns to the point of departure with new knowledge of the core values of American society. In the case of *The Grapes of Wrath*, the film's journey does not start from a site of social privilege but rather from a perspective of political naïveté, from which protagonist Tom Joad comes to a progressive awakening brought about by his contact with social injustice and New Deal aid to the poor. This transformative encounter with the 'real' America also springs, so the genre suggests, from contact with the open landscape of rural America itself, photographed with attention to its rustic charm and experienced with the unfettered freedom offered by car travel. For that reason, the road movie can be thought of as an ideological heir to the Western, since in both genres the American landscape itself promises liberation from overcivilization and bourgeois constraint, the possibility of ever-new horizons and personal renewal through self-reliance and endurance of adversity (in road movies typically protagonists at some point must get by without enough money).

The genre saw a renewal in the late 1960s in such films as *Bonnie and Clyde* (dir. Arthur Penn, 1967) and *Easy Rider* (1969), where life on the road came to represent for youth culture a life of independence, rebellion against social convention and bourgeois entanglements and the romantic search for a real, countercultural America unrepresented by the mass media. By the early 1970s, however, faith in the liberatory potential of the counter-culture had soured and so life on the road in films of that period came to be characterized, so argues David Laderman, by 'drift': an aimless, apathetic detachment from both the norms of mainstream America and the utopian ideals of the counterculture. 'Laden with psychological confusion and wayward angst', road movies like *Zabriskie Point* (1970), *Five Easy Pieces* (1970), *Two-Lane Blacktop* (1971), *Badlands* (1973) and *Alice Doesn't Live Here Anymore* (1974), to name a few, turn away from sociopolitical critique and focus instead as on 'existential loss'; driving on the road becomes a psychological journey inward, 'an allegory of a personal search through life's meaningless landscape'.[15] While the genre retains a sense of rebellion in its resistance to 'the ideology of American enterprise and the dominant "affirmative" classical Hollywood narrative',[16] by the early 1970s its focus turned decisively towards existential crisis, cynicism about 'goal-oriented moral trajectories'[17] and the psychological experience of Heideggerian 'thrownness'.

The idea of 'drift' provides a noteworthy point of conjunction between *King Lear* and the 1970s road movie. *Lear* evinces a deep loss of faith in mainstream institutions, in this case the patriarchal monarchy, but a just-as-savage critique of the Machiavellian alternative epitomized by Edmund, Cornwall and Cordelia's two sisters. Like the protagonists of 1970s road movies, Lear moves from the comfortable security of life at court to the life of a dislocated wanderer, newly vulnerable to the vagaries of fortune, forced to experience an existential crisis that in Lear's case comes in the form of confrontation with the realities of mortality. Yet though Lear might be viewed as a 'drifter', he experiences his encounters with contingency and loss as unremittingly painful, a searingly tragic coming-to-knowledge about human vulnerability that is almost too much to bear. In the final scene of the play, Lear's response to his greatest loss – the death of Cordelia – alternates between rage, anguish and desperate denial. In his final moments, faced with the terrifying 'Never, never, never, never, never' (5.3.282) of his beloved daughter's loss, he tries to spy signs of life in her dead body. Whether Lear dies with full tragic recognition of the existential weight of mortal vulnerability or, finding it too much to bear, dies in denial, Shakespeare leaves ambiguous. No matter which text of *King Lear* we choose, Shakespeare offers very little sense of a new social or metaphysical order emerging from the ashes of the old. At the end of *King Lear*, we are left with the survivors in crisis without resolution. Though the road movie of the early 1970s does not share the searing tragedy of *King Lear*, it does share the sense that its characters are set adrift without formerly secure moral or social bearings. The one reigning compensation for the road movie's overwhelmingly young protagonists was that 'drifting' had the connotation – if not exactly the substance – of youthful rebellion and so was coded as 'cool', providing a form of affective triumph.

What is striking about *Harry and Tonto*, then, is its desire to recast its intertexts – *King Lear* and the 1970s road movie – in more positive terms, in an effort to bring both better in line with what Thomas Elsaesser has called the 'affirmative-consequential' nature of classic Hollywood narrative. Elsaesser defines that narrative structure and its ideological orientation in this way:

> the scenes fitted into each other like cogs in a clockwork, and all that visual information was purposive, inflected towards a plenitude of significance ... Out of conflict, contradiction, and contingency the narrative generated order, linearity and articulated energy. Obviously, at a deeper level such a practice implied an ideology: of progress, of forging in the shape of the plot the outlines of a cultural message, understood and endorsed by Hollywood's audiences as the lineaments of a pragmatism in matters moral as well as practical ... Ideological critics have therefore detected in the classical

cinema a fundamental affirmative attitude to the world it depicts, a kind of a-priori optimism located in the very structure of the narrative about the usefulness of positive action.[18]

Such a narrative structure and the distinctively American ideology it purveys is, as Elsaesser points out, fundamentally at odds with the aimless structure of the 1970s road movie, with its pervasive atmosphere of unrooted malaise and vague rebelliousness. In a very characteristically American approach to *King Lear*, then, *Harry and Tonto* takes up the tragic or defeatist journey narrative and reimagines it as a tale of triumph without sacrificing the aleatory structure of *Lear* and the 1970s road movie. What in *Lear* might have challenged the values of can-do American optimism and control of one's destiny becomes in Mazursky's hands the story of Harry's growing assertion of personal freedom, resilience and self-reliance, central US values recoded as an internal victory over the forces of ageing and bourgeois conventionality.[19] Harry's psychological journey may be poignant, but it is never tragic or defeatist. Although he is plunged into something of an existential crisis by losing his home, he accommodates the experience of homelessness with wry humour, curiosity, tolerance and, with only a few exceptions, aplomb. In fact, he comes to find life on the road interesting, revitalizing and, most importantly, therapeutic. Because Harry eventually embraces the experience of being nomadic, the narrative can find resolution in his growing internal centredness without his leaving nomadism behind, without having him, as we might well expect, establish a conventional life with a new cat on the West Coast, the American locale for new beginnings. To be sure, the knowledge that Harry gains about loss and his own mortality involves some pain, but the film's ending stresses bittersweet acceptance of the principle of existential 'drift' rather than tragic devastation. Mazursky makes that acceptance more palatable by aestheticizing it, by rendering it in terms of the film's lovely final shot of Harry at the shore during a beautiful California sunset. In short, *Harry and Tonto* reconciles *King Lear* and the 1970s road movie – and the darker vision of the principle of 'drift' they share – to the protocols of mainstream American cinema and ideology. Mazursky's writing partner Josh Greenburg quips that while writing the project they called it 'Easy Lear', a melding of *Easy Rider* and *King Lear*.[20] Though clearly Greenburg did not intend it, perhaps an apt way of understanding that ironic title is to note that *Harry and Tonto* makes psychologically easy – or at least more palatable – what is in Shakespeare's play unremittingly difficult, irresolvable and emotionally devastating.

As one of the very few versions of *King Lear* to make it to the American screen, *Harry and Tonto* illustrates why *Lear* has been so rarely adapted in

America: the play poses simply too great a challenge to the protocols of classic American film and its underlying ideological armature. Whereas American film has tended to focus on youthful protagonists, with the promise of their futures before them, *King Lear* focuses on the tribulations of the elderly and the underclasses, and their narrowed field of action; whereas the affirmative nature of classic American film narrative stresses the efficacy of action and the drive towards resolution in even tragic circumstances, *King Lear* suggests the futility of agency and the vulnerability of humankind within a chaotic, even actively hostile universe; whereas American film tends to portray freedom as a condition of expansive, optimistic possibility, *King Lear* portrays freedom in existential or psychological terms amid conditions of loss, deprivation, suffering and confinement – the hovel on the heath, the cage-like prison from which Lear imagines he and Cordelia might observe the instabilities of court life. *Harry and Tonto* seeks to negotiate these formidable formal and ideological gaps by turning its Lear-like protagonist's homelessness into its own kind of existential virtue and an active choice, providing a distinctly American ideal of freedom with a vaguely countercultural twist by means of the mediating genre of the 1970s road movie. What *Harry and Tonto* finds more difficult to do is to engage the darkly tragic dimensions of Shakespeare's play, its portrayal of despair and unrestrained cruelty, the terrible yearning for love and the irremediability of death. That difficulty, rooted deep in Hollywood's ideological unconscious, suggests why in America *Lear* has seemed such inhospitable material for screen adaptation.

Notes

1. In all these films (as well as in Weidman's novel), the protagonist is not the Lear-figure but rather the Cordelia-figure, the faithful son who takes a fall for his father only to learn years later that his siblings have, out of greed, betrayed him and his father. The focus falls less on the father-figure's descent than on the faithful son's vengeance. That is to say, these films fall somewhere between family melodramas and revenge thrillers.
2. On *King of Texas* (2002), see Chapter 7 of this volume.
3. Harry Keyishian makes a form of this argument for screen adaptation of *Hamlet*: 'Shakespeare adapts to the authority of film more than film adapts to the authority of Shakespeare', and the authority of film is mediated through cinematic genre, its 'specific subject matters and settings, recurrent narrative patterns and themes, characteristic techniques and tones', 'Shakespeare and Movie Genre: the Case of *Hamlet*', in R. Jackson (ed.), *The Cambridge*

Companion to Shakespeare on Film, 2nd edition (Cambridge: Cambridge University Press, 2007), 73–4. I would add that generic mediation is especially crucial for Shakespeare films aimed at popular audiences.

4. On melodrama, see Diana Henderson's contribution in this volume.

5. On Western, see Pierre Kapitaniak's contribution in this volume.

6. *Harry and Tonto* appears not at all or only in passing in major discussions of the road movie. See P. Biskind, *Easy Riders, Raging Bulls: How the Sex-Drugs-and-Rock-'n'-Roll Generation Saved Hollywood* (New York: Simon and Schuster, 1998); S. Cohan and I. Rae Hark (eds.), *The Road Movie Book* (New York: Routledge, 2002); M. Hammond, 'The Road Movie', in L. R. Williams and M. Hammond (eds.), *Contemporary American Cinema* (London: Open University Press, 2006), 14–20; K. Mills, *The Road Story and the Rebel: Moving through Film, Fiction, and Television* (Carbondale: Southern Illinois University Press, 2006).

7. Carney was best known (and much beloved) for his role as Ed Norton on the television show *The Honeymooners* (1955–1956). For his role in *Harry and Tonto*, Carney beat Albert Finney, Dustin Hoffman, Jack Nicholson and Al Pacino to the Oscar.

8. Another set of intertexts are important to this film – works concerned with ageing protagonists, a topic quite rare in Hollywood films. The three most immediate intertexts are Vittoria de Sica's neorealist study of ageing *Umberto D.* (1952), John Steinbeck's travelogue *Travels with Charley: In Search of America* (1960) and Ruth Gordon's counter-cultural comedy about a January–May romance, *Harold and Maude* (1971). De Sica and Steinbeck's works involve elderly male protagonists whose only companions are pets. Gordon's film, a cult hit, was instrumental in convincing studios that a film featuring an old protagonist might have commercial potential, so long as that protagonist was aligned with the counterculture. Mazursky and Greenfeld acknowledge knowing about *Umberto D.* and *Travels with Charley* (see S. Wasson and M. Brooks, *Paul on Mazursky* (Middletown: Wesleyan University Press, 2011)) but both deny any direct influence.

9. The Cambridge University Press edition reads 'Vaunt-couriers *of* oak-cleaving thunderbolts' (emphasis added).

10. See D. Laderman, *Driving Visions: Exploring the Road Movie* (Austin: University of Texas Press, 2002), 82–6; J. R. Taylor, *Directors and Direction: Cinema for the Seventies* (New York: Hill and Wang, 1975); D. A. Cook, *Lost Illusions: American Cinema in the Shadow of Watergate and Vietnam, 1970–1979* (New York: Charles Scribners, 2000).

11. Harry's stress upon the pleasure of drifting, something he increasingly comes to embrace on the road, recalls the link between the pleasures of the road typical of 1960s and 1970s road movies (D. Orgeron, *Road Movies: from Muybridge and Méliès to Lynch and Kiarostami* (New York: Palgrave Macmillan, 2008)) and Barthes's discussion of the pleasure of the text. Both, Orgeron argues, involve the indulging of isolated or disconnected delights rather than maintaining respect for goal-orientated order.

12. The word 'Tonto' means 'fool' in Spanish, a fact that Mazursky and Greenfeld may or may not have known. It is likely that Tonto in *The Lone Ranger* was named after the Tonto Apache tribe, and that the name was not intended as an ethnic slur.
13. See the video at www.youtube.com/watch?v=pudhooCsKLs (accessed 20 August 2017).
14. In an interview, Mazursky revealed that the girl was in fact his own daughter (Wasson and Brooks, *Paul on Mazursky*, 80).
15. Laderman, *Driving Visions*, 83.
16. *Ibid.*, 86
17. T. Elsaesser, 'The Pathos of Failure: Notes on the Unmotivated Hero [1975]', in T. Elsaesser, N. King and A. Horvath (eds.), *The Last Great American Picture Show* (Amsterdam: Amsterdam University Press, 2004), 279.
18. *Ibid.*, 280–1.
19. Reviewer Gary Arnold puts the matter more directly: '"Harry and Tonto" more or less reverses the geography, philosophy and generational bias of the defunct and dated youth culture movies symbolized most conspicuously and effectively by "Easy Rider" ... The prevailing mood of "Easy Rider" was a fatalistic sense of despair. In "Harry and Tonto" that mood is replaced by a modest sense of optimism' (*'Harry and Tonto* and . . .', *The Washington Post*, 25 September 1974, D11).
20. Wasson and Brooks, *Paul on Mazursky*, 88.

WORKS CITED

Arnold, G., '*Harry and Tonto* and . . .', *The Washington Post*, 25 September 1974: D1, D11.

Biskind, P., *Easy Riders, Raging Bulls: How the Sex-Drugs-and-Rock-'n'-Roll Generation Saved Hollywood* (New York: Simon and Schuster, 1998).

Cohan, S. and I. Rae Hark (eds.), *The Road Movie Book* (New York: Routledge, 2002).

Cook, D. A., *Lost Illusions: American Cinema in the Shadow of Watergate and Vietnam, 1970–1979* (New York: Charles Scribners, 2000).

Elsaesser, T., 'The Pathos of Failure: Notes on the Unmotivated Hero [1975]', in T. Elsaesser, N. King and A. Horvath (eds.), *The Last Great American Picture Show* (Amsterdam: Amsterdam University Press, 2004), 279–92.

Greenfeld, J. and P. Mazursky, *Harry and Tonto* (New York: E. P. Dutton, 1974).

Hammond, M., 'The Road Movie', in L. R. Williams and M. Hammond (eds.), *Contemporary American Cinema* (London: Open University Press, 2006), 14–20.

Keyishian, H., 'Shakespeare and Movie Genre: the Case of *Hamlet*', in R. Jackson (ed.), *The Cambridge Companion to Shakespeare on Film,* 2nd edition (Cambridge: Cambridge University Press, 2007), 72–84.

Laderman, D., *Driving Visions: Exploring the Road Movie* (Austin: University of Texas Press, 2002).

Mills, K., *The Road Story and the Rebel: Moving through Film, Fiction, and Television* (Carbondale: Southern Illinois University Press, 2006).

Orgeron, D., *Road Movies: from Muybridge and Méliès to Lynch and Kiarostami* (New York: Palgrave Macmillan, 2008).

Taylor, J. R., *Directors and Direction: Cinema for the Seventies* (New York: Hill and Wang, 1975).

Wasson, S. and M. Brooks, *Paul on Mazursky* (Middletown: Wesleyan University Press, 2011).

PART IV

Lear *on the Loose: Migrations and Appropriations of* Lear

CHAPTER 10

Relocating Jewish Culture in The Yiddish King Lear (1934)

Jacek Fabiszak

On 1 March 2018, the TV movie *The Yiddish King Lear* was released in the USA, directed by David Serero, who is also credited as a co-writer of the adaptation and plays the lead role of Dovidl Moysheles, the Lear figure.[1] This adaptation is the most recent node of a rhizomatic thread, to draw from Douglas Lanier's metaphor of Shakespearean adaptation, of Yiddish *Lear*s that has its origins in the late nineteenth century.[2] This chapter examines an earlier screen adaptation, *The Yiddish King Lear* (1934) (also known as *Der Yiddishe Koenig Lear* and *Der Yidishe Kenigen Lir*),[3] directed by Harry Thomashefsky, a film version of Jacob Gordin's play *The Yiddish King Lear* (1892) (also known as *The Jewish King Lear*).[4] I will outline some of the historical and production contexts of the 1934 film, its engagement with *Lear* and the 1892 play, and how it can be classified in terms of contemporary adaptation theories, before concluding with some observations on the most recent 2018 adaptation. I argue that firstly Gordin, the playwright, and then Thomashefsky and Joseph Seiden, producer of the 1934 film, transposed and indigenized *Lear* to the needs of Yiddish-speaking audiences in New York. Gordin's aim was to change the nature of Yiddish drama and address pertinent social issues; Seiden and Thomashefsky's task was to salvage Gordin's play as a forgotten classic of Yiddish culture.[5] The 1934 film is generally referenced in the context of Yiddish stage or film history but rarely in the context of *Lear* on screen.[6] This chapter thus aims at positioning the film in its historical and theoretical contexts and as a significant aspect of *Lear* on screen.

Jacob Gordin (1853–1909) was a Russian-born American playwright, and his 1892 play is considered by theatre historians as a landmark of early Yiddish drama, in that it introduced realism and reduced elements of song, dance and improvisation.[7] At the same time, when it was staged in America, especially by theatre company owner Jacob Adler (who also played the lead role), the result was a kind of compromise between

Gordin's realistic image of the Jewish community in Eastern Europe and the melodramatic demands of Yiddish theatre.

Gordin's play focuses on one of the central themes of Shakespeare's *Lear* – parent–child relationships. As Ruth Gay and Sophie Glazer observe, this theme resonated particularly with immigrant New York audiences:

> this tale reflected the far more complex struggle taking place in the families of his audience, families in which parental power was already compromised by the exigencies of the immigrant experience. American-born children challenged the authority of their immigrant parents in countless ways; the children's mastery of the language in which their parents struggled and their confident understanding of the new culture which baffled their parents led these American-born offspring to reject the notion that their parents had anything to teach them. To Gordin's audience, the sufferings of parents whose children no longer honor them was a powerful theme indeed.[8]

Other themes that Gordin's play addresses include the position of women in traditional Jewish society as well as the issue of secularism versus religion. In the play, the Orthodox Jews, Dovidl Moysheles and his Misnagid son-in-law Avrom, and the Hasidic Jew[9] (Dovidl's other son-in-law Moshe) oppose the enlightened Jew, Yaffe, and the liberated Jew and woman, Dovidl's youngest daughter Taybele. The action is situated in Vilna (today's Vilnius, the capital of Lithuania), home city of Dovidl Moysheles, a prosperous Jewish merchant.[10] The play opens with a celebration of the feast of Purim, part of which is a gift-giving ceremony. Dovidl has prepared jewels for his three daughters: Etele (the eldest, equivalent of Goneril; wife of Avrom, equivalent of Cornwall), Gitele (the middle daughter, equivalent of Regan; wife of Moshe, equivalent of Albany) and Taybele (the youngest, equivalent of Cordelia). Etele and Gitele thank their father with formulaic expressions, accepting the gifts; Taybele refuses them, arguing that her body does not need any ornaments. This of course enrages Dovidl, who starts ranting about the required position of women in a Jewish family: 'As long as I live, you will all do only that which I demand. If I say that it is day, you must all also say that it is day. If I say that it is night, then it must be night ... And if I say that is absolutely not Trytel [his servant] over there but a horse, then you must all agree ... even Trytel himself'.[11] This antifeminist and misogynistic speech is reminiscent of Petruchio's manner of disciplining Katherina in *The Taming of the Shrew*. Most likely, *Lear* was not the only Shakespearean inspiration for Gordin.

This is not the only 'mistake' that Dovidl makes: the other, more grievous, after which he will send the protesting Taybele away, is his decision to devote the rest of his life to the study of holy books in Israel and divide his fortune between the three daughters. He establishes his eldest son-in-law, Avrom, as the administrator and executor of his decision. Taybele, who, like Cordelia, speaks the truth compulsively, protests against being supervised by the Orthodox Avrom, who would choose a husband for her. When she announces that she wants to study medicine in St. Petersburg, Dovidl tells her to 'get out of [his] sight'.[12] Predictably, Dovidl's stay in Israel is soon over because Avrom stops sending him money. Dovidl, his wife Hanne Leah and his servant Trytel (an equivalent of the Fool) return to Vilna and lead a poor life in the house of Avrom. Avrom and his wife Etele do not feed them properly, which sends the proud Dovidl begging in the streets.

The title of the production clearly signals Shakespeare's play as intertext. In this, Gordin actually draws from nineteenth-century Russian literary traditions in which titles of novels or short stories allude to Shakespearean drama and characters, for instance Nikolai Leskov's novel *Lady Macbeth of the Mtsensk District* (1865) or Ivan Turgenev's novella *King Lear of the Steppes* (1870).[13] In Gordin's play, *Lear* is not only referenced in the construction of the plot and characters but is explicitly discussed towards the end of Act 1. Yaffe, an enlightened German Jew, tells Dovidl, the old, traditional patriarch, about Shakespeare's tragedy and makes an overt comparison between the patriarch and Lear, exclaiming: 'Yes, you are a Jewish King Lear! May God protect you from such an end as that to which King Lear came. May you be healthy and happy.'[14] Yaffe's warning is significant in that it will eventually be heeded, albeit in an unexpected way. Dovidl does not avoid Lear's mistakes, but Gordin provides a happy ending whereby Dovidl, his wife and his servant, and, importantly, his youngest daughter Taybele and her husband Yaffe will be reunited. Dovidl even regains his failing eyesight, thanks to his daughter's and his son-in-law's medical expertise. The phrasing of Yaffe's explicit warning is important too. Although himself an enlightened Jew, considered an atheist by the Orthodox community, he addresses Dovidl in a traditional Jewish way, evoking divine protection and God's will and ending with a wish typical of the feast of Purim that the family is celebrating in Act 1. Yaffe is aware that, in order to communicate with Dovidl, he needs to use language that the patriarch understands. At the same time, the young Jew realizes that Dovidl is as stubborn and proud as Lear, and nothing but fate, or experience, can change Dovidl's decisions. It is a bitter realization, since Dovidl eventually adheres to those fateful decisions even in his most adverse situation, when begging on the streets of Vilna.

Yaffe reminds Dovidl of the Lear figure again in Act 2: 'You, Reb Dovidl, are still playing the role of King Lear and don't want to understand who is your true friend, who really loves you!'[15] Dovidl can admit his mistake but cannot take back his decision – it would ruin the world he believes in. He would rather play the part of the Shakespearean character. In Act 2 he blames himself and tells his wife: 'Don't be silent. Remind me at every moment of what foolishness I engaged in. Draw my blood from me drop by drop'.[16] Gordin clearly alludes to the image of the pelican daughters but distorts its application. Furthermore, Dovidl explicitly 'takes on' the role of King Lear when he turns to the streets to beg: 'Make way for King Lear! ... A vivat for King Lear! A vivat for the new, for the blind King Lear' [*He goes out with Trytel, striking loudly with his stick*].[17] Here, King Lear becomes a symbol of pride and stubbornness, a grotesque figure to which Gordin adds one more motif from Shakespeare's play: as there is no Gloucester-figure in the play, blindness is transferred onto Dovidl. However, the fallen patriarch's blindness is caused by cataracts so it is curable, and at the play's end, Dovidl's eyesight is restored.

Gordin thus radically changes Shakespeare's tragedy by turning it into a comedy, at least in terms of giving it a happy ending, not unlike the tradition established by Nahum Tate. What Gordin adds, however, is a metadramatic dimension: the play not only follows the plot of *King Lear* but also contains overt references to the tragedy.

Gordin's work was soon given a special position in Yiddish theatre and was chosen to be filmed pursuant to a government project assisting unemployed actors during the Great Depression. As Joel Schechter outlines:

> The United States government bankrolled some of the most innovative Yiddish stage productions in the 20th century when it paid the salaries of actors, writers and directors under the auspices of the Works Progress Administration in the 1930s. One of the first plays funded by the WPA [was] the 1935 production of prominent Yiddish playwright Jacob Gordin's 1892 play 'The Yiddish King Lear' ... Although Joseph Seiden supervised the film's production, the cast in this 'Lear' was directed in New York by Harry Thomashefsky, son of the famous Yiddish actor Boris Thomashefsky. The 1935 film captures a performance by actors who were part of the Federal Theatre Project's Yiddish Unit, created under a plan to put unemployed Yiddish actors back to work at the height of the Great Depression. The FTP, part of the WPA, sponsored a free touring stage production of Boris Thomashefsky's adaptation of Gordin's 'Lear,' as well as Harry Thomashefsky's English version of the play, 'Another King Lear'.[18]

The filmic adaptation was thus the result of political and economic action taken by the US government. Gay and Glazer highlight the economic underpinnings of the project.[19] Subsequently, an effort was made to produce a film in Yiddish with Jewish actors, preferably a version of a well-known text in Yiddish. Gordin's play was probably filmed due to its fame and position in Yiddish theatre, especially its career on the New York stage at the turn of the nineteenth century; its artistic merits were of less significance. The fact that it was a loose adaptation of Shakespeare's play was also unimportant: in the opening credits, it is Gordin's play, not Shakespeare's, that is referenced as 'the immortal classic'.

This paratextual element that centres the Yiddish play and decentres Shakespeare is significant. As Gérard Genette asserts, the paratext '*make*[s] *present* . . . [and] ensure[s] the text's presence in the world, its "reception" and consumption'.[20] Similarly, as Christy Desmet, Natalie Loper and Jim Casey point out, 'paratextual' elements . . . shape the readers' experience of the text'.[21] The opening credits of the 1934 film shape the viewer's experience of the film: not as an adaptation of a play by Shakespeare, but as an adaptation of Gordin's drama. This evidences that what the film attempted to achieve was to revive Yiddish dramatic culture in the United States.

An important aspect of the film is the context of Yiddish cinema history, a context that was not limited to the USA but also relevant to Poland. In 1935, according to Eric A. Goldman's census, four Yiddish films were produced – three in the USA and one in Poland.[22] This ratio would change as more and more films were shot in Poland until 1939. What this implies is that, in the 1930s, there were two major centres for Yiddish films: the USA and Poland. This is also true of Yiddish theatre: the tradition goes back to before the outbreak of the First World War. Yiddish cinema, in a way, grew out of Yiddish theatre.

E. A. Goldman calls the latter half of the 1930s 'The Golden Age of Yiddish Cinema'.[23] Yiddish films in Poland had their heyday in the years 1936–1939 when as many as nine feature films were shot.[24] Tadeusz Lubelski notes that the Jewish producers and directors in Poland did not hesitate to invite international stars – for example, renowned Jewish actress Molly Picon as the cross-dressed fiddler in *Jidl mit'n fidl* (*Jidl with a fiddle*, dir. Józef Green and Jan Nowina-Przybylski, 1936) – on location in Kazimierz Dolny in Poland, a favourite setting for many films in Yiddish. The most memorable production of the time was *Der Dibuk* (dir. Michał Waszyński, 1937).[25] Yiddish cinema thus often reached for well-known plays for screen adaptation, although films based on original screenplays were also shot. Whereas in Poland Yiddish cinema produced remarkable works, in the USA the situation was not so favourable for artistic development. Frank Manchel notes that 'contemporary melodramas with convoluted plots, singing, religion and the requisite ending'[26] were typical of Yiddish films produced in America. In fact, they resembled films produced in the Russian partition of Poland before the First World War. As Natan Gross observes, Yiddish films made in this era were shot on a limited budget. For example, producer Mordek Towbin chose the following method of filming:

> he taped a performance with the help of a single, stationary camera, whose lens was directed at the actors. Such films were directed by Marek Arnsztejn or Abraham Izak Kamiński. The task of the director was to prepare the production/performance, make the cuts as well as prepare the credits and intertitles . . . Out of more than ten films shot in such a way in 1912–14, six were based on Jacob Gordin's plays . . . these plays were performed by the Jewish theatre belonging to the Kamiński family.[27]

Thomashefsky's film appears to conform to this practice, even under the supervision of the rather experienced producer Seiden. As a result, it has generally attracted negative criticism. James Hoberman comments on the film's merit, ignoring Thomashefsky's contribution and recalling the political agenda behind the filming: 'Joseph Seiden's inept recording of *Der Yidisher Kenig Lir* is at once an abysmal movie and a singular record of the Yiddish section of the Federal Theater Project.'[28] However, Thomashefsky and Seiden did not limit themselves to a mere recording of a stage production; there are filmic expansions in the form of additional shots on location, and the editing is quite dynamic, which helps quicken the pace of the action.

The screenplay was written by Abraham Armband, who drew mainly from Jacob Adler's stage adaptation but without doggedly following it. Consequently, the screenwriter, like Adler, did not include Gordin's criticism of Yiddish theatre, even removing the Purim play from Act 1. Likewise, the film does not end with an operation on Dovidl's eyes but with a doctor's diagnosis that his eyesight can be restored. Armband's ending is significantly different from both Gordin's and Adler's versions, and more melodramatic. The director and producers decided to change and/or modernize some of the names of the characters – Dovidl becomes David Moshele Lear, his wife is Hanna Lear, the Fool figure, Trytel, is called Shomoi, etc. The change of names, especially the identification of the eponymous figure with the Shakespearean character, is significant and may have resulted from the fact that the audience of the American mid-1930s, especially the Yiddish-speaking one, was familiar with Shakespeare's oeuvre, and was able to draw comparisons with Shakespearean Lear when watching the movie.²⁹ The film thus creates more overt links to Shakespeare's original than Gordin's play. At the same time, the names of both the protagonist and his wife, as well as the other characters in the play, appear to be 'americanized', as it were: a kind of compromise between the Yiddish/Jewish origin and its more anglicized version, more suitable for the 1930s audiences.

The film shows a number of locations. It opens with a shot of a shop window in a street in Vilna with a sign above which reads in Polish and Yiddish (but not Russian): 'Candies, food and spices, tobacco, cigarettes, Aranowicz [*Sprzedaż cukierków, artykuły kolonialne, tytoń I papierosy, Aranowicz*]'.³⁰ Then the camera cuts to the interior of David's house, the dining room, where his family is gathered around the table, celebrating the feast of Purim. This is the main location for most of the scenes, yet it is not as dominating as in Gordin's play. The blocking of actors is static but is made more dynamic through camera work: shots showing all the characters seated around the table, with David Lear in the middle, are intertwined with close-ups of particular figures. Thomashefsky and Seiden also introduce two more locations: one is St. Petersburg, where Toibele and Joffe (respectively, the play's Taybele and Yaffe) study medicine; here, the set design shows just a student's room. While David and Hanna's stay in Jerusalem is only mentioned in the play, the film reveals David and Hanna's house in Israel, which is introduced in a sequence that shows the streets and hills of Jerusalem – a man riding a donkey in the streets, Jews praying at the Wailing Wall, etc. One more location shot is added to the production – David and Shomoi begging in the streets of Vilna.

These street shots have an important function in the film. On the one hand, the scene where David and Shomoi are on the street in horrible weather conditions becomes the equivalent of the storm scene in Shakespeare's play. On the other, it serves as a counterpoint to the events occurring in David's house, as well as in the house of Toibele and Joffe on their wedding day. When David is forced to beg outside and leave his former home, a symbol of familial unity and lasting patriarchal Jewish values, he does not move to an inferior place since the streets of Vilna are as indifferent, lonely and foodless as his house, now governed by his son-in-law. Incidentally, Gordin, and Thomashefsky after him, makes the sons-in-law more influential than David's/Lear's daughters – they take decisions which their wives only follow. This is typical of patriarchal cultures – one may recall here Kurosawa's decision to replace daughters with sons in *Ran*, as only male heirs could inherit a lord's wealth and title(s). Such a change on the one hand shifts the focus from the fraught parent/child relationships in *Lear*; on the other, diminishing the position of women in a traditional Jewish family emphasizes the contrast with the new, independent woman – the youngest daughter.

David/Lear, indirectly forced by his eldest daughter Etelle and her husband Chariff,[31] leaves the household on his own, still trying to maintain the illusion that he is in control of his fate. In the film, David bitterly realizes his situation, recalling the wisdom of Joffe, the modern Jew, whom he rejected before: 'I will ask the good people to give to David Moshele charity . . . give charity . . .',[32] adding: 'Respect for the King . . . make way for the King . . . play a hymn for the new king beggar' and 'Give charity to the Jewish King Lear'. This announcement strengthens the association between *Lear*'s heath and storm and the streets of Vilna.

During the scene of Toibele and Joffe's wedding, the unwelcoming and cold street, where David is deprived of all his dignity, pride and family, is melodramatically contrasted with the happy, warm and cosy home of the newlyweds, but the sequence paves the way for the final happy ending. The *new* house of Toibele and Joffe, with Hanna happily making arrangements for their wedding, becomes a place for the family reunion, which is not postponed by Etelle and Chariff's unwelcome visit. Joffe refuses to accept a present from them and they leave. Interestingly enough, Gittele and Chariff do return and complain that Chariff's brother, to whom Chariff signed over his wealth in order not to share it with David's family, threw them out of David's house. Their return is preceded by Shomoi leading David (against the latter's will) to Toibele and Joffe's house, where the old patriarch is reconciled with his daughters (Gittele and Moshe also join them for the wedding) and his wife. With the promise that his eyesight can be restored, happy to have his family together again (even Etelle and Chariff), he forgives everybody and asks that peace be restored in the family to the cheers of everybody. The melodramatic, happy ending is highly conventional, which is emphasized by equally conventional camera work: the camera lens captures the gathered figures in a long-distance shot, with David in the middle, thus providing a framework for the whole of the movie.

In terms of theorizing the 1934 film, it constitutes a 'recontextualization', according to Kenneth Rothwell's classification of Shakespeare spinoffs/ derivatives as it 'keep[s] the plot but move[s] Shakespeare's play into a wholly new era and jettison[s] the Elizabethan language'.[33] As a screen adaptation of a play that itself adapts *Lear*, it also meets the criteria of what Douglas Lanier terms 'second-order adaptations', i.e. an 'adaptation of earlier Shakespearian adaptations or performances'.[34] The theatrical adaptation, Gordin's play, had already radically altered Shakespeare's text, turning a tragedy into a comedy.[35] Although shot in the USA in 1934 the film evokes the culture of a far-away land (Eastern Europe), from the previous century: 1892. The culture of traditional Judaism, Hassidism, is contrasted with the spreading 'modern', or enlightened, anti-religious movement among the European Jews, in the play personified by Joffe (the German Jew). The 1934 film is characterized by the explicit referencing of its hypotext, and by applying aspects of Shakespeare's tragedy to the characters of Gordin's play and Thomashefsky's film and the social issues they face. First, Joffe compares David's social conduct to that of Lear, his division of the family, the mistakes that he makes and their consequences; then, David stigmatizes himself as Lear, who has lost everything and, more importantly, has no hope, he believes, of regaining his family and position. He thus plays the *social* role of Lear – a man utterly deprived of his full identity.

The film also exemplifies Hutcheon's 'creative *and* interpretative act of appropriation/salvaging'[36] and Julie Sanders's idea of 'embedded and sustained appropriation'.[37] In terms of Hutcheon's concept of salvaging, what the film salvages – or saves from oblivion – is, on the one hand, Gordin's play and the memory of its stage history and, on the other, traditional, patriarchal Jewish culture, which New York, or in general American, spectators were not familiar with in the 1930s; paradoxically and sadly, this Eastern European culture and language would be completely obliterated by 1945. Although part of the play's aim was to critique this traditional culture through the intertext of *Lear*, the film does not seem so critical of the world of nineteenth-century Jewish urban culture and is certainly a great celebration of Yiddish, a language that had grown less popular among younger generations of Jewish immigrants in America.

Significantly, the film, while explicitly referencing Shakespeare's play in the title, names of characters and dialogue, places emphasis not on the Shakespearean original but on its rewriting through Gordin's play and its stage history. It is Gordin, not Shakespeare, who is considered canonical in this case. In terms of the radical shift in genre from tragedy to comedy, as Douglas Lanier observes, 'the narrative deviates from Shakespeare's ending in order to mute the inescapability of tragedy and to demonstrate the value of family solidarity and forgiveness'.[38]

While Gordin's play constitutes an indiginized text,[39] the film resists such pigeonholing. The film was not screened in a very different culture from the one that admired Gordin's play in early-twentieth-century New York. It is likely that the memory of Gordin's text and its stage versions was still quite fresh among the spectators. Yet, for the new generations of Eastern European Jewish immigrants already born in the USA, the culture the movie replicated may have appeared alien, both linguistically and socially.

Contemporary adaptation theories recognize the complex interrelations that govern Shakespearean hypotexts and their hypertexts, imagined in terms of a rhizomatic model (Lanier), with networks of intertextual dialogues conceived in non-binary terms.[40] These concepts enable us to consider adaptation as an ongoing process in which multiple texts are engaged. *The Yiddish King Lear* constitutes a product of a complex process and network of relations: including Shakespeare's play; seventeenth-century adaptations that shifted tragic genres to comedic; Shakespearean appropriations in nineteenth-century Russian fiction; adapting Shakespeare in late nineteenth-century Yiddish drama; adapting Gordin's play in American theatre in Yiddish; and then screen adaptation of Gordin's play in 1930s Yiddish cinema. Paradoxically, the screen adaptation – perhaps for reasons linked with the project's financing and its production contexts – turned out to be a typical melodrama, perhaps even more melodramatic than Gordin's play. It lacked formal innovations and did not draw from the achievements of cinema, being no match for the masterpieces in Yiddish shot either in the USA or Poland in that period. At the same time, the film presented, with some nostalgia, a world that in 1935 already belonged to the past.

David Serero's TV adaptation of Gordin's play, released on 1 March 2018, is based on a stage reading performed by Serero at the Angel Orensanz Foundation in New York on 30 January and 1 February 2018. It is characterized by the incorporation of songs in Yiddish, performed by Serero, who is also an opera singer. The songs contribute to the movie's celebration of Jewish culture and revival of the Yiddish legacy which, in 1934, before the Holocaust, was thriving in Eastern Europe and became gradually forgotten with the disappearance of native speakers of Yiddish. Gordin's critique of the Yiddish theatrical tradition, and Thomashefsky/Seiden's focus on melodrama, are replaced in Serero's work with an appreciation of, and longing for, a world long gone, with Shakespeare's presence marginalized. In each case, the key hypotext for Thomashefsky/Seiden and Serero is not Shakespeare's *Lear*, but rather Jacob Gordin's playtext and the Yiddish culture it represents.[41]

Notes

1. See IMDB: www.imdb.com/title/tt7762360/?ref_=nv_sr_2 (accessed 9 November 2018).
2. D. M. Lanier, 'Shakespeare/Not Shakespeare: Afterword', in C. Desmet, N. Loper and J. Casey (eds.) *Shakespeare/Not Shakespeare* (Cham: Palgrave Macmillan, 2017), 295.
3. See IMDB: www.imdb.xcom/title/tt0026010/?ref_=nv_sr_1 (accessed 9 November 2018).
4. Gordin also wrote a later play adapting *King Lear*, but this time with a female Lear figure, *Mirele Efros* (1898) (also known as *The Jewish Queen Lear*). This play was adapted for the screen in 1912 in Warsaw, directed by Andrzej Marek, in 1913 in Moscow and in 1939, directed by Josef Berne. Also see Victoria Bladen's chapter in this volume.
5. On salvage, see L. Hutcheon, with S. O'Flynn, *A Theory of Adaptation*, 2nd edition (New York and London: Routledge, 2013), 8.
6. Jeffrey Kahan mentions Gordin's play and its theatrical history in *'King Lear': New Critical Essays* (New York and London: Routledge, 2008). Michael Moon focuses on potential links between queer theatre and Yiddish theatre, including discussing Gordin's play: 'Tragedy and Trash: Yiddish Theater and Queer Theater, Henry James, Charles Ludlam, Ethyl Eichelberger', in D. Boyarin, D. Itzkovitz and A. Pellegrini (eds.), *Queer Theory and the Jewish Question* (New York: Columbia University Press, 2003), 266–84. Iska Alter is more concerned with Gordin's *Mirele Efros* (1898), yet references *The Yiddish King Lear* in a survey of Jewish dramaturgy in the American context: 'Jacob Gordin's *Mirele Efros*: King Lear as Jewish Mother', in *Shakespeare Survey 55: 'King Lear' and its Afterlife* (2002): 114–27. Barbara Henry analyzes theatrical reform in Gordin's plays, including *The Yiddish King Lear*, in *Rewriting Russia: Jacob Gordin's Yiddish Drama* (Seattle: University of Washington Press, 2011). The film is only mentioned in the context of Shakespeare on screen in the entry by Douglas Lanier in Richard Burt's encyclopaedic *Shakespeares after Shakespeare*, D. M. Lanier, 'Film Spin-offs and Citations', in R. Burt (ed.), *Shakespeares after Shakespeare: an Encyclopedia of the Bard in Mass Media and Popular Culture* (Westport: Greenwood Press, 2007), 186–7.
7. The history of staging the play in New York theatres began on 21 October 1892 and continued well into the 1930s – in 1932 the play saw its own stage adaptation, or even parody: at the Yiddish Art Theatre, Maurice Schwartz put on *Legend of the Jewish King Lear*. See J. Berkowitz, *Shakespeare on the American Yiddish Stage* (Iowa City: University of Iowa Press, 2002), 70. This testifies to the significance of *The Jewish King Lear* on the New York Yiddish stage even forty years after its premiere.
8. R. Gay and S. Glazer, 'Introduction', in J. Gordin, *The Jewish King Lear: a Comedy in America* (New Haven and London: Yale University Press, 2007), x–xi.
9. As Gay and Glazer observe, Misnagid and Hasidic 'represent the two chief branches of Jewish thought. Avrom ... is ... committed to Torah study and the minute observance of fine distinctions, while ... Hasidism was a more

personal, intuitive, mystical Judaism and stressed exuberant celebrations, with singing and dancing' ('Reading *The Jewish King Lear*', in J. Gordin, *The Jewish King Lear: a Comedy in America* ed. R. Gay and S. Glazer (New Haven and London: Yale University Press, 2007), 145).

10. Moysheles is also called a 'scholar' (J. Gordin, *The Jewish King Lear: a Comedy in America* ed. R. Gay and S. Glazer (New Haven and London: Yale University Press, 2007), 2).

11. *Ibid.*, 10.

12. *Ibid.*, 18.

13. Berkowitz mentions this novella in his discussion of the popularity of *Lear* adaptations in Russian letters in the nineteenth century, indicating Turgenev's work as a predecessor and inspiration for Gordin. See Berkowitz, *Shakespeare on the American Yiddish Stage*, 238–9.

14. Gordin, *The Jewish King Lear*, 19.

15. *Ibid.*, 28.

16. *Ibid.*, 24.

17. *Ibid.*, 47.

18. J. Schechter, 'Yiddish King Lear on the Relief Roll', *Forward*, 8 December 2009, http://forward.com/culture/120500/yiddish-king-lear-on-the-relief-roll/ (accessed 20 January 2016).

19. Gay and Glazer, 'Introduction', xv.

20. G. Genette, *Paratexts: Thresholds of Interpretation*, trans. J. E. Lewin (Cambridge: Cambridge University Press, 1997), 1. Also see M. Pfister, *The Theory and Analysis of Drama*, trans. J. Halliday (Cambridge: Cambridge University Press, 1993), 13–14.

21. C. Desmet, N. Loper and J. Casey, 'Introduction', in C. Desmet, N. Loper and J. Casey (eds.), *Shakespeare/Not Shakespeare* (Cham: Palgrave Macmillan, 2017), 14.

22. E. A. Goldman, *Visions, Images and Dreams: Yiddish Film – Past & Present* (Teaneck: Holmes & Meier, 2011), 49–72.

23. *Ibid.*, 72.

24. This was in addition to documentaries showing 'portraits' of Polish cities with the largest number of Jewish inhabitants: Białystok, Kraków, Lvov, Łódź, Warszawa and Vilnius.

25. T. Lubelski, 'Historia Kina Polskiego. Twórcy, Filmy, Konteksty [History of Polish Film. Artists, Films, Contexts]', *Videograf II* (2009), 105–8. *Der Dibuk* was actually a version of a Russian play by Shloyme Zanvl Rappoport (known as Shimon Ansky), who first wrote it in Russian (1914) and then produced a version in Yiddish (1917). Similarly to Thomashefsky's film, Waszyński's movie is also based on a play composed by a Russian Jew, which points to the significance of Russia as a source of texts in Yiddish.

26. F. Manchel, *Film Study: an Analytical Bibliography*, volume 1 (London and Toronto: Associated University Presses, 1990), 846.

27. N. Gross, *Film żydowski w Polsce [Yiddish film in Poland]* trans. from Hebrew by A. Ćwiakowska (Kraków: Rabid, 2002), 134–5.

28. J. Hoberman, *Bridge of Light: Yiddish Film between Two Worlds* (Hanover and London: University Press of New England, 2010), 363.
29. The new generations of Americans of Jewish descent watched films, spoke English, were educated at American schools and must have read Shakespeare, unlike the first generation of Yiddish-speaking immigrants.
30. Lack of Russian inscriptions can be explained by the fact that, in the 1930s, Vilnius was a city in Poland and one would encounter shop signs in Polish or Yiddish (more specifically, in the Hebrew alphabet) but not in Russian.
31. The middle daughter (Gittele) and her husband (Moses) do not have much to say about David's fate.
32. Similarly, in Jacob Adler's version, one reads 'Alms! Alms!'.
33. K. S. Rothwell, *A History of Shakespeare on Screen: a Century of Film and Television*, 2nd edition (Cambridge: Cambridge University Press, 2004), 209.
34. D. M. Lanier, *Shakespeare and Modern Popular Culture* (Oxford: Oxford University Press, 2002), 104–5.
35. On the issue of altering the genre of Lear from tragedy to comedy, see Diana Henderson's chapter in this volume.
36. Hutcheon, *Theory of Adaptation*, 8.
37. J. Sanders, *Adaptation and Appropriation* (London and New York: Routledge, 2006), 26.
38. Lanier, 'Film Spin-offs and Citations', 187.
39. Hutcheon, *Theory of Adaptation*, 145, 149.
40. Lanier, 'Shakespeare/Not Shakespeare: Afterword', 295, 297; J. Bruhn, A. Gjelsvik and E. F. Haussen, '"There and back Again": New Challenges and New Directions in Adaptations Studies', in J. Bruhn, A. Gjelsvik and E. F. Haussen (eds.), *Adaptation Studies: New Challenges, New Directions* (London: Bloomsbury, 2013), 8.
41. See D. E. Henderson, *Collaborations with the Past: Reshaping Shakespeare across Time and Media* (Ithaca and London: Cornell University Press, 2006), 2.

WORKS CITED

Alter, I., 'Jacob Gordin's *Mirele Elfros*: King Lear as Jewish Mother', in *Shakespeare Survey 55: 'King Lear' and its Afterlife* (2002): 114–27.
Berkowitz, J., *Shakespeare on the American Yiddish Stage* (Iowa City: University of Iowa Press, 2002).
Bruhn, J., A. Gjelsvik and E. F. Haussen, '"There and back Again": New Challenges and New Directions in Adaptations Studies', in J. Bruhn, A. Gjelsvik and E. F. Haussen (eds.), *Adaptation Studies: New Challenges, New Directions* (London: Bloomsbury, 2013), 1–16.
Desmet, C., N. Loper and J. Casey, 'Introduction', in C. Desmet, N. Loper and J. Casey (eds.), *Shakespeare/Not Shakespeare* (Cham: Palgrave Macmillan, 2017), 1–22.
Genette, G., *Paratexts: Thresholds of Interpretation*, trans. J. E. Lewin (Cambridge: Cambridge University Press, 1997).

Goldman, E. A., *Visions, Images and Dreams: Yiddish Film – Past & Present* (Teaneck: Holmes & Meier, 2011).

Gordin, J., *The Jewish King Lear: a Comedy in America*, ed. R. Gay and S. Glazer (New Haven and London: Yale University Press, 2007).

Gross, N., *Film żydowski w Polsce [Yiddish film in Poland]*, trans. from Hebrew by A. Ćwiakowska (Kraków: Rabid, 2002).

Henry, B., *Rewriting Russia: Jacob Gordin's Yiddish Drama* (Seattle: University of Washington Press, 2011).

Henderson, D. E., *Collaborations with the Past: Reshaping Shakespeare across Time and Media* (Ithaca and London: Cornell University Press, 2006).

Hoberman, J., *Bridge of Light: Yiddish Film between Two Worlds* (Hanover and London: University Press of New England, 2010).

Hutcheon, L. with S. O'Flynn, *A Theory of Adaptation*, 2nd edition (New York and London: Routledge, 2013).

Kahan, J. (ed.), *'King Lear': New Critical Essays* (New York and London: Routledge, 2008).

Lanier, D. M., *Shakespeare and Modern Popular Culture* (Oxford: Oxford University Press, 2002).

'Film Spin-offs and Citations', in R. Burt (ed.), *Shakespeares after Shakespeare: an Encyclopedia of the Bard in Mass Media and Popular Culture* (Westport: Greenwood Press, 2007), 186–7.

'Shakespeare/Not Shakespeare: Afterword', in C. Desmet, N. Loper and J. Casey (eds.) *Shakespeare/Not Shakespeare* (Cham: Palgrave Macmillan, 2017), 293–306.

Lubelski, T., 'Historia Kina Polskiego. Twórcy, Filmy, Konteksty [History of Polish Film. Artists, Films, Contexts]', *Videograf II* (2009), 105–8. www.aka demiapolskiegofilmu.pl/pl/historia-polskiego-filmu/artykuly/film-zydowsk i-w-polsce-1930–1939/266 (accessed 15 January 2016).

Manchel, F., *Film Study: an Analytical Bibliography*, volume 1 (London and Toronto: Associated University Presses, 1990).

Moon, M., 'Tragedy and Trash: Yiddish Theater and Queer Theater, Henry James, Charles Ludlam, Ethyl Eichelberger', in D. Boyarin, D. Itzkovitz and A. Pellegrini (eds.), *Queer Theory and the Jewish Question* (New York: Columbia University Press, 2003), 266–84.

Pfister, M., *The Theory and Analysis of Drama*, trans. J. Halliday (Cambridge: Cambridge University Press, 1993).

Rothwell, K. S., *A History of Shakespeare on Screen: a Century of Film and Television*, 2nd edition (Cambridge: Cambridge University Press, 2004).

Sanders, J., *Adaptation and Appropriation* (London and New York: Routledge, 2006).

Schechter, J., 'Yiddish King Lear on the Relief Roll', *Forward*, 8 December 2009, http://forward.com/culture/120500/yiddish-king-lear-on-the-relief-roll/ (accessed 20 January 2016).

The Trump Effect: Exceptionalism, Global Capitalism and the War on Women in Early Twenty-first-century Films of King Lear

Courtney Lehmann

Humanity must perforce prey on itself,
Like monsters of the deep.

King Lear (4.2.47–8 Q1)

This essay explores three turn-of-the-century spinoffs of *King Lear*: Kristian Levring's *The King Is Alive* (2000),[1] Don Boyd's *My Kingdom* (2001) and Uli Edel's *King of Texas* (2002). Each of these films takes for its point of departure a world in which the 'state of exception', as Giorgio Agamben describes it, is universal and the predatory instincts of late capitalism have been globalized. *King Lear*, with its Hobbesian vision of early capitalism, thus becomes a particularly apt play for tracing the apocalyptic arc of a society in which humanity must consume or be consumed and, indeed, 'prey on itself' (4.2.47 Q1). Ultimately, all three adaptations with which I am concerned here position the King Lear figure as an accessory to what Slavoj Žižek has called the 'new racism of the developed world', a phrase coined to characterize a society in which the fundamental divide is economic in theory but unabashedly racist in practice because it entails 'the construction of *new* walls safeguarding prosperous Europe from the immigrant flood'.[2] In the end, however, I will argue that the most pernicious form of racism, in the Foucauldian sense of the term, is, in fact, sexism.

The King Is Alive, My Kingdom and *King of Texas*, all spinoffs of *King Lear* directed by men, feature interpolated scenes of violence against women. Yet what concerns me is not that the violence is gratuitous but that it is somehow *structural* – that is, necessary – to the broader cultural project in which these films participate. In these *fin de siècle* versions of *Lear*, the wounded female body rises to the level of a hermeneutic, becoming the privileged object of predation, punishment and biopolitical control – a phenomenon that I am calling, proleptically, the 'Trump effect'. More specifically, I will explore the ways in which women are positioned in these films as 'precarious life', in Judith Butler's words,[3] or, in Agamben's phrasing, 'bare life' – also known as *homo sacer*. Shorthand for a person whose killing is unpunishable and whose life is deemed unworthy of sacrifice, *homo sacer* is an apt ontological designation for women wherever resurgent, or emergent, tribalisms dispossess them of their fundamental rights, including access to education, healthcare and a safe workplace – from East to West, to the Global North and South. This essay is dedicated to Jo Cox, the British MP who was the face of the pro-immigration 'Remain' campaign in the lead-up to the UK's Brexit referendum in 2016 until she was assassinated by a far-right crusader. After seeking to open national borders to the 'immigrant flood' of Syrian refugees, Cox was shot and stabbed to death. Her killer shouted, 'This is for Britain!' and Brexit went forward; Cox died for nothing, the epitome of *homo sacer*.

A film about British and American tourists whose bus runs out of gas in the middle of the Namib desert, *The King Is Alive* is a spinoff of Shakespeare's play in which the stranded travellers undertake a production of *King Lear* as an exercise in dignity that fatally backfires. With only a stash of canned carrots for food and an abandoned diamond mine for shelter, the privileged Westerners are progressively reduced to 'poor, bare, forked animal[s]' (3.4.96), whose battle over scarce resources becomes a parable of predatory capitalism run amok – until, that is, they come to identify *themselves* as *homo sacer*. A deceptive word, 'sacer' means both 'sacred' and 'damned', a duality that accounts for the paradoxical status of *homo sacer* as a life that can be killed but not sacrificed. Long removed from its redemptive role in ancient socio-religious rituals such as scapegoating, *homo sacer* has evolved into a juridico-political entity, functioning as the means by which sovereign power reinforces its own exceptionalism vis-à-vis the law. The conversion of *homo sacer* to a purely secular identity is, according to Agamben, the founding gesture of modern political power.[4]

Producing a subject whose murder can be neither punished nor celebrated, *homo sacer* thus refers to a category of being that is purely performative, invoking a species of life that has been engineered, paradoxically, for death. In the first half of the twentieth century, this classification corresponds to the figure of the Jew, 'the representative par excellence of ... the bare life that modernity necessarily creates within itself, but whose presence it can no longer tolerate in any way'.⁵ What distinguishes the second half of the twentieth century, as well as the early twenty-first century, is the increasingly indiscriminate nature of this process, which is the hallmark of the extra-legal phenomenon that Agamben identifies as the 'state of exception' – a condition wherein the gap that separates the political subject from *homo sacer* narrows to the point of indistinction.

The King Is Alive slouches towards this apocalyptic scenario as the tourists invest in *King Lear* in an effort to reassert all that separates them from the '[p]oor naked wretches' (3.4.28) who are indigenous to this virtually uninhabited landscape. Made possible by Henry's painstaking act of memorial reconstruction (and his conviction that 'good old *Lear*' will redeem 'all those lost souls' from spiritual death), the play is indeed the thing that replaces relations between people in *The King Is Alive*, as Shakespeare soon becomes an excuse for the very savagery that the tourists perform towards one another in the name of perfecting their parts. More specifically, it is over the abused and, eventually, dead body of the Cordelia character, Gina, that the egregious violence in the film is wrought, the most disturbing example of which occurs when the production of *King Lear* is threatened by Charles's refusal to supply the missing role – presumably, the part of Gloucester. Forcing Gina into a Faustian bargain, the nasty old man agrees to perform only on the condition, he insists, that 'I get to fuck you – fuck you till this madness ends'. Too horrified to reply, Gina stares at him in disgust, as Charles chortles: 'Well, isn't that what you're supposed to do? Sacrifice yourself for your art?' But whereas we expect Gina's bodily sacrifice to sustain this community of would-be thespians by allowing the show to go on, the rehearsals progressively dissolve into disunity, mirroring the betrayals, adultery and, even, murders featured in the play itself.

Gina's increasingly violated body documents this devolution, as the camera repeatedly highlights the complete denigration of her humanity, showing Charles – wrinkled, obese and grunting like an animal – as he sweats over her and subjects her to his sexual whims. That Gina is dying in her new role is reflected in her increasing loss of affect and deteriorating morale during rehearsals, as she lives in daily dread of her serial rapist. She is also quite literally dying at the hands of Catherine, who has been feeding her carrots from cans tainted with botulism, jealous of the fact that Gina, like Lear's Cordelia, is Henry's favourite protégé. In the absence of an indigenous population to exploit, it is Gina, a white, Western woman, whose body becomes a map of global capitalism's endgame of consuming its own – in the name of art or any other presumably noble cause. Worse, she is subject to further desecration when Charles urinates all over her corpse and then hangs himself above it. Despite Dogme 95's self-proclaimed commitment to minimalist filmmaking – what they refer to, somewhat ironically, as their cinematic 'Vow of Chastity' – gratuitous displays of female abjection prove to be the exception to the rule.[6]

Only at the end of the film, when the tourists gather around the fire to burn their dead, do they recognize that, like Charles, they too are unexpected casualties of the 'new racism of the developed world'. The nature of this revelation is epitomized by the words of a teacher from nearby Congo, who, when asked to explain why the human rights violations in his country go unnoticed by the rest of the world, describes to reporters a state of exception: 'Our misfortune is that we have gold, diamonds and precious wood, but, unfortunately, no white farmers'.[7] Unable to reach into the deep pockets of their own favoured nation status, the Anglo-American tourists discover that they are not 'white' – farmers or otherwise – either, for their production of *King Lear* leads only to the production of themselves as bare life; indeed, as *homo sacer*.

My Kingdom, starring the legendary Richard Harris, documents the rise of a generalized state of exception, depicting a war of all against all in which the Lear character, Sandeman, is at its epicentre. Tracing the phenomenon of exceptionalism back to its imperial origins in the figure of the monarch, Michael Hardt and Antonio Negri explain that the king once served as the singular embodiment of the 'sovereign exception', or the notion that the one who commands need not obey.[8] At least at the start of *My Kingdom*, Sandeman, the last of Liverpool's great crime bosses, is exclusively identified with this privilege. Indeed, his 'kingdom', which is financed largely by heroin trafficking and, therefore, dependent on the city's most desperate population, is the lone exception to Liverpool's otherwise vast geography of disadvantage. Appropriately, Sandeman is introduced hunched over a hand of solitaire, poised to play a king. A game in which one person literally holds all the cards, solitaire also points to his status as a figure who lives outside the boundaries of – or, indeed, serves as the 'sovereign exception' to – traditional jurisprudence.

In the state of exception, however, the situation is far more ambiguous. As Agamben observes, 'a person who goes for a walk during the curfew is not transgressing the law any more than the soldier who kills him is executing it' – precisely because the state of exception is marked by a 'law' that 'is in *force* but does not *signify*'.[9] Sandeman learns this lesson the hard way when he takes a shortcut with his wife, Mandy (played by Lynn Redgrave), through Granby-Toxteth, the ghetto with the highest crime rate in Liverpool. Moments later, a hooded black youth in search of fast cash and a quick fix pulls a gun on Mandy and demands her purse. While she remains frozen with fear, Sandeman, utterly convinced of his ability to tour the city's meanest streets with impunity, incredulously stares back at the teenager and repeatedly demands: 'Do you have *any idea* who I am?' Although as king of Liverpool's organized crime scene Sandeman has long served as the singular embodiment of – and exemption from – the law, the fact that his assailant does not know who he is indicates that times have changed. Blithely guiding the mugger's gun away from Mandy so that it points directly into his eyes, Sandeman taunts: 'That's better. Now be sure you don't miss'. When the junkie fires two blanks, Sandeman laughs and instructs Mandy to give the kid her purse with a dismissive wave of his hand, grazing the tip of the revolver in the process. This time it fires, point-blank, into Mandy's head and kills her instantly.

In the absence of the self-sacrifice that the Cordelia character typically embodies, Mandy occupies the role of the subject engineered for death in *My Kingdom*. But Sandeman refuses to acknowledge Mandy as *homo sacer*. Instead, he endeavours to master his loss through recourse to religious ritual. Emulating ancient theistic practices, he makes a ceramic death mask of Mandy's face, converting her into an object of idolatry even as her mortal body is shown engulfed in flames inside the crematorium. Sandeman even goes so far as to fashion Mandy as a kind of martyr; by claiming that the bullet that killed her was really intended for him, Sandeman spins his personal tragedy into a city-wide conspiracy against his life. Yet the fact that everyone else, including his own family members, assert that the episode was 'just a mugging' is no subtle indication that Mandy's death does not reflect the workings of a divine plan but, rather, the capricious laws of the market, or *lex mercatoria*. Appropriately, the only ordering principal that springs from the interpolated murder of Sandeman's wife is an economic one, for his daughters quickly discover that Mandy's name is on the bank account containing all of the family's assets – a disturbing linkage that associates localized violence against the female body with access to global stores of capital. In this spirit, Boyd's film is a nihilistic parable of private ownership that takes place over Mandy's dead body, as every family member (save Jo, the compromised Cordelia figure who rejects the family fortune derived from her father's multinational drug cartel)[10] lays claim to the dubiously derived income at each other's expense.

In *My Kingdom*, this is the defining moment of what Hardt and Negri classify as the *self-rule* of capital, and with it, the shift from *lex mercatoria* to *rex mercatoria* – the sovereign market.[11] Recalling Marx's nightmarish vision of a world in which 'people' and 'things' become interchangeable, Žižek argues that 'despite the much celebrated free circulation opened up by global capitalism, it is "things" (commodities) which freely circulate, while the circulation of "persons" is more and more controlled'.[12] *My Kingdom* explores the ways in which this phenomenon affects migrant women in particular, through a scene that takes place in the archetypal space in which people are consumed as things: a brothel, run by Lear's eldest daughter, Kath. In an effort to land a new client who appears unimpressed with the local merchandise, Kath calls to another employee and exclaims: 'Yolanda, can you bring us the drinks?' 'Yolanda?', the customer gasps, with a mixture of disdain and intrigue. With smug satisfaction, Kath replies: 'Fresh from the Balkans'.

Despite the fact that 'the Balkans' invoke a number of different countries in the former Soviet bloc – nations so wedded to their differences that nothing shy of ethnic cleansing could define their borders upon the collapse of the Soviet Union – such details are of no concern to Yolanda's 'importers'. Rather, Yolanda is simply 'from the Balkans', a region so poor that one of its principal contributions to the global economy is indeed young girls, whose desperation makes them easy targets for the tightly organized gangs who traffic in them. As the boss of one such operation observes in an interview, although most women from the Balkans are sold for an average of 2500 to 3000 euros, there are some cases where, 'if the girl is fresh, very young and not used, the price is higher' – rhetoric that seeks to normalize paedophilia and child rape by likening women and girls to meat. In such an environment it is fitting that the only excerpt from *King Lear* cited in Boyd's film is the prophecy that 'humanity must perforce prey upon itself,/ Like monsters of the deep' (4.2.47–8 Q1). Not unlike the hawkish culture featured in *The King Is Alive*, this line, with its audible pun on 'prey' and 'pray', inaugurates a new world order in which the consumption of people as things is elevated to a sacramental rite.

It is perhaps little surprise, then, that when Sandeman's thugs apprehend Mandy's incidental murderer (who turns out to be the son of an old friend), the revenge scene takes place in another privileged locus of consumption: a restaurant kitchen. Splayed on a stainless steel, industrialized kitchen table, the nameless black youth is naked, bound and progressively anatomized to death by Jug, the Cornwall character. Though the actual violence occurs off screen, there can be no doubt that the black body – and black masculinity in particular – is the target of a unique, spectacularizing violence in this scene which, I would argue, shares a tragic affinity with the condition of female characters like Yolanda and Mandy. More than chronicling the regime change from *lex mercatoria* to *rex mercatoria*, Boyd's film renders visible the often invisible but 'inextricable link', in Saidiya Hartman's words, 'between racial formation and sexual subjugation'.[13]

King of Texas, starring Patrick Stewart as the maverick cowboy John Lear, is a western set in 1842 on Texas Independence Day. The film begins with a tableau of two lifeless bodies hanging from a lone tree; banished to the more arid land beyond the Texas Republic, the starving Mexican *vaqueros* have been caught butchering one of Lear's cows. When the 'enemy', the Mexican leader Menchaca (who has formed a romantic and political alliance with Claudia, the Cordelia character), learns that Lear has imposed capital punishment for a petty crime, his incredulous response – 'You hung two men for one cow!' – attests not only to the status of the Mexicans in Lear's imagination as *homo sacer* but also to Lear's God-like ability to preside over life and death as the lone king of the frontier. By the end of the film, however, the tables have turned: when Lear learns that Menchaca has rescued him not only from the raging elements on the heath but also from his predatory family, Lear must choose either to ally himself with 'the enemy of our blood', as he describes the Mexican general to Claudia, or to fight against his own flesh and blood. In choosing the former, Lear takes the path of most resistance, which is to cross over to the other side and to side with the Other, in order to undertake the passage from *homo sacer* to neighbour – by acknowledging that either we are all full members of the polity or none of us are.[14]

Although such a position is, arguably, the only ethical stance available to post-9/11 culture, the fact remains that the violence inherent in the state of exception affects some more than others; in *King of Texas*, these 'others' are none other than female, brown and black. John Lear may be a man of few words, but when he uses them he makes them count, punishing his daughters' alleged ingratitude by imagining them raped by Mexicans: 'when you scream for your Daddy', he shouts, furious at their defiance, 'when those *vaqueros* have you on your back, their knives at your throat, when you're screaming for John Lear, I won't hear you; I'll be deaf to your cries'. Here Edel leaves room for the possibility that Lear has sexually abused his daughters – a twist that may account for the nihilism of the film's conclusion, where the Goneril character, Susannah, rides away from her pursuers only to shoot and kill herself while still on horseback. Lear's relationship with the Fool, who is his slave, forces these toxic gender and generational dynamics into a provocative triangulation with race.[15]

In *King of Texas*, Rip (David Alan Grier) is a slave who also serves as Lear's sidekick and black 'buddy' in this hybrid version of the western and buddy film genres. Rip is the only individual who can make John Lear laugh and the only figure whose counsel he takes seriously. Although the brusque affection they share is obvious, it would be a mistake to romanticize their relationship as somehow progressive, since Lear is quick to identify Rip as his property to others. What is especially curious about the representation of Rip as the Fool in this film is the fact that he is the character who is vested with the traumatic memory of the Alamo, one of the most tenacious scars in US history – especially in Texas. For example, when Rip is mistaken for a runaway slave, he is tied to a tree and whipped with a cactus branch, as his assailant growls: 'You're that son of a bitch from the Alamo, aren't you?' Later, when war is fast approaching, Lear marvels at his companion's unflappability; with his expression frozen in a perpetual smirk, Rip nonchalantly explains that he was ''posed to die in the Alamo', adding that 'all the fear got scared out of me at the Alamo'. Thus, it is as if by compulsion that, after Lear and Menchaca have consolidated their powers and the first shots are fired, Rip shakes his head and exclaims: 'looks like the damn Alamo all over again'.

To represent the final battle in *King Lear* as the Alamo 'all over again' is inauspicious to say the least. The phrase 'remember the Alamo', which refers to the overnight stand waged by William 'Buck' Travis and his band of some 200 rag-tag men against the Mexican General Santa Anna's nearly 1800 troops, has long served as a nationalistic rallying cry in the US and in Texas lore in particular. However, to 'remember the Alamo' is a profoundly ambivalent injunction, invoking the homicidal combination of unilateral decision-making and bureaucratic impasse that spelled the doom of the poorly manned outpost, despite its strategic positioning along the Camino Real that led north from Mexico to Texas. When, for example, Santa Anna urged the grossly under-manned Texas garrison to surrender peacefully, Colonel Travis replied with a blatant breach of the rules of engagement, launching a cannon ball along with the infamous rejoinder: 'Victory or death!' And to be sure, death carried the day, with every man – save the women, children and slaves – perishing in the ill-fated effort. Perhaps it is true, then, as Elizabeth Bronfen argues of the subject, that nationhood, too, 'can be constructed only over a narcissistic wound'.[16] The memory of the Alamo is precisely the memory of a narcissistic wound – indeed, of self-inflicted historical trauma supported by American exceptionalism. Repetition compulsion is always an effort to master trauma and, in this respect, the compulsive repetition of the phrase 'remember the Alamo' suggests an effort to smooth over the compromised flesh of the nation during a crucial turning point in America's coming-of-age story. It is little wonder that Freud ultimately aligned the compulsion to repeat with the death drive.

A narcissistic wound demands a sacrifice to shore up, retroactively, the fraying mythology that undergirds it. In Shakespeare's *King Lear*, it is Cordelia, Christ-like, who is sacrificed as an act of substitutionary atone-ment – dying for the sins of others – to bring about the play's dramatic resolution. But in *King of Texas*, this role is supplied by the interpolated character of John Lear's dead son, whose sacrifice for his country is acknowledged in Lear's anguished recollection that he was 'martyred at Goliad', invoking the massacre in which the legendarily gallant Santa Anna made the shocking decision to transport nearly 350 prisoners of war to Goliad and summarily execute them. Following hard upon the heels of the Alamo, the Goliad massacre definitively ignited the quest for Texas inde-pendence and led to the final victory over the Mexican forces at San Jacinto in 1836 – a charge which, in Edel's adaptation, John Lear is credited with having led in the name of his son.

Unlike the more explicit forms of violence against women typified in the murders of Gina in *The King Is Alive* and Mandy in *My Kingdom*, in *King of Texas*, Claudia's death is utterly understated – perhaps despite Edel's efforts to establish a sacralizing arc to this penultimate scene. Representing John Lear as the Moses of the American West, Edel shoots from a low angle that emphasizes Lear's God-like perspective on the action as he staggers distractedly around Menchaca's camp. Replete with flowing white hair and long white robes, Lear presides over the casual slaughter with an aura of holiness as he raises his hands over his head and issues his commandments: 'No! No! Stop it! Damn it, stop!' But Lear knows not what he does, for his antics unintentionally draw Claudia out into the action. Seeking to come to her disorientated father's aid, she is gunned down by an anonymous bullet – perhaps even by friendly fire – in an off-screen moment that is registered when Rip is heard shouting 'Claudia!' immediately after a lone shot rings out. That it is Rip's, and not Lear's, perspective through which Claudia's death is revealed, is significant; so, too, is the subsequent frame that shows Rip poring over Claudia's dead body in a tableau that is suggestive of a reverse *pietà*. Rip and Claudia are, in this instance, racialized flesh, crossing over ontologically from *homo sacer* to *habeas viscus*.[17]

Up until this point I have used the term 'body' to describe the victims of male violence in early twenty-first-century *King Lear* spinoffs because they are all white, Western women – figures of relative privilege compared with explicitly racialized others from 'elsewheres' near and far. But the term 'body', as Alexander Weheliye characterizes it, is limiting, because to possess a body is to imply a certain degree of self-ownership that is available to some within the neoliberal 'free market' but not to others. Even the concept of *homo sacer* is short-sighted in this regard since, as Weheliye observes, its foil remains the white, male, liberal humanist subject. By contrast, *habeas viscus*, with its focus on mortified flesh, 'designates those dimensions of human life cleaved by the working together of depravation and deprivation'.[18] Minoritarian, contingent, messy and accretive, a politics of the flesh 'construes race not as a biological or cultural classification but as a set of sociopolitical processes that discipline humanity into full humans, not-quite-humans, and nonhumans'.[19] The fact that the 'racializing assemblage' of Rip and Claudia takes place against the backdrop of a war in which white people invade brown people's land is further demonstrative of this process of ontological stratification; moreover, as dead Mexican women and boy soldiers strew the ground, we see in their subjugated forms the disfigurations of the 'flesh', in Hardt and Negri's words, 'from which collective capital tries to make the body of its global development'.[20]

Made at the onset of the twenty-first century and wedged awkwardly between Y2K hysteria and 9/11, *The King Is Alive, My Kingdom* and *King of Texas* draw particular attention to the female body-in-pain as a vehicle for expressing the 'new racism of the developed world'. Not racist in the traditional sense of pertaining exclusively to skin colour, the new 'racism', as Žižek defines it, 'is in a way much more brutal', because

> its implicit legitimation is neither naturalist (the 'natural' superiority of the developed West) nor any longer culturalist (we in the West also want to preserve our cultural identity) but unabashed economic egotism – the fundamental divide is the one between those included into the sphere of (relative) economic prosperity and those excluded from it. What lies beneath these protective measures is the simple awareness that the present model of late capitalist prosperity *cannot be universalized.*[21]

I want to go one step further to suggest that this 'new racism' is perhaps even more fundamentally about sexism, in the Foucauldian sense of the term. Concomitantly, and by way of conclusion, I wish to underscore, as Weheliye does in *Habeus Viscus*, 'just how comprehensively the coloniality of Man suffuses the disciplinary and conceptual formations of knowledge that we labor under, and how far we have yet to go in decolonizing these structures'.[22]

For Foucault, racism goes beyond the traditional seizure of the physical body of individual subjects and instead targets entire populations – even species – 'massifying', in his words, the scope of the State. It is in this context that I pose the word 'gendercide' in an effort to invoke the long history of patriarchal oppression and institutionalized violence against women which, in its most insidious incarnations, becomes a *de facto* form of population control.[23] Whether it manifests itself in 'one child' policies in which the one child is male, in the pervasive use of rape as a political weapon, in the resurgent battle over reproductive rights in the US and around the world, or in its many other pernicious forms, this 'racism' instantiates a primal violation of the flesh – a practice personified, as my title suggests, by a US president who was elected after admitting to serial sexual assault. Perhaps, then, in the spirit of the flesh, the female body is better characterized as 'three-fifths' human. I refer here to the status assigned to black male slaves vis-à-vis white men at the Constitutional Convention of 1787; women, black or white, were not considered worthy of legal recognition – beyond Thomas Jefferson's assertion that black women were sexually preferred by the orangutan species.[24] This gross negation of the humanity of the dispossessed is what I am referring to as the 'Trump effect' and, despite the conspicuously twenty-first-century origins of this phrase, none of this is new to women – especially women of colour.

The early twenty-first-century adaptations of *King Lear* that I have examined here accentuate the ways in which the lawlessness of the global state of exception is inscribed upon distinctly feminized flesh – black, white, brown and, in the wake of male violence, too often red all over. In this razed territory, the boundaries of gender, race and class prove porous in a dance of mutual dispossession. And although Weheliye reminds us that 'most instantiations of bare life do not necessarily entail physical mortality, per se but other forms of political death',[25] there is little separation between the two for those who have yet to experience full personhood. *King Lear* is a play about political death and economic disruption, about the birth pangs of the market economy and the hypostasization of exchange value. But the fact that Shakespeare's tragedy culminates not only in the fatal clash between the old and the new orders but also in the less-remarked and distinctly unnatural deaths of all the female characters admonishes us to consider the ways in which women in *King Lear* become 'vanishing mediators' of the uneven historical transition from feudalism to capital-ism – just as women in *The King Is Alive, My Kingdom* and *King of Texas* are positioned with respect to the inauguration of *rex mercatoria*. Lost to history, they are the unremarked casualties of 'progress'.

If it is true that history, as Marx once remarked, 'repeats itself as tragedy, then as farce', then it would be hard not to associate the Trump Presidency with the latter, were it not for the fact that, despite new forms of autonomy and social organization offered by the globalization of capital, women's mobility continues to be restricted by rising rates of criminal and sexual violence, not to mention growing wage exploitation. But as countless studies have shown, failure to acknowledge the human rights of women and girls, coupled with a lack of investment in their education and healthcare, jeopardizes economic growth. Perhaps this inconvenient truth will issue the clarion call to the United Nations to treat the global war on women as a form of fascism anywhere that poses a threat to democratic futures everywhere.[26] And perhaps, more locally, we may one day have a female President of the United States. Now that would be the ultimate trump card.

Notes

1. Though Levring is credited as director, Dogme 95 is a filmmaking collective.
2. S. Žižek, *Welcome to the Desert of the Real* (London and New York: Verso, 2003), 149, his emphasis.
3. J. Butler, *Precarious Life: the Power of Mourning and Violence* (London and New York: Verso, 2004).
4. G. Agamben, *Homo Sacer: Sovereign Power and Bare Life*, trans. D. Heller-Roazen (Stanford: Stanford University Press, 1998), 85.
5. *Ibid.*, 179.
6. Indeed, Dogme 95's 'Vow of Chastity' is a collective filmmaking manifesto that follows particular rules of cinematic 'purity' (all filming must be on location; much of the camera work is hand held; artificial light cannot be used, etc.), authored by Lars von Trier and Thomas Vinterberg.
7. Quoted in Žižek, *Welcome to the Desert of the Real*, 125.
8. M. Hardt and A. Negri, *Multitude: War and Democracy in the Age of Empire* (New York: Penguin, 2004).
9. Agamben, *Homo Sacer*, 57; 51, his emphasis.
10. To demonstrate just how universal the state of exception is in *My Kingdom*, Jo – the Cordelia character – is identified as the good girl by virtue of the fact that she is a *recovering* addict, who for a time took to the streets with the paraplegic black pimp known as 'The Chair' in order to support her 'smack habit the size of Mt. Kilimanjaro'.

11. Hardt and Negri explore the transition from *lex mercatoria* to *rex mercatoria* throughout *Multitude*.

12. Žižek, *Welcome to the Desert of the Real*, 149.

13. S. Hartman, *Scenes of Subjection: Terror, Slavery, and Self-Making in Nineteenth-Century America* (Oxford and New York: Oxford University Press, 1997), 85.

14. Throughout his chapter titled 'From Homo sacer to Neighbor' in *Welcome to the Desert of the Real*, Žižek invokes the Israeli Army's 'refusniks', who consider occupants of Palestinian territories to be 'neighbors' and refuse the order to police their borders.

15. For an alternative discussion of the racial politics of *King of Texas*, see Pierre Kapitaniak's chapter in this volume.

16. E. Bronfen, *Over Her Dead Body: Death, Femininity, and the Aesthetic* (Manchester: Manchester University Press, 1992), 30.

17. A. Weheliye, *Habeas Viscus: Racializing Assemblages, Biopolitics, and Black Feminist Theories of the Human* (Durham and London: Duke University Press, 2014).

18. *Ibid.*, 39.

19. *Ibid.*, 4.

20. M. Hardt and A. Negri, *Multitude*, 101.

21. Žižek, *Welcome to the Desert of the Real*, 149.

22. Weheliye, *Habeas Viscus*, 7.

23. Jacqui True offers the long view of what I am referring to as 'gendercide', a phenomenon that proceeds along the historical continuum that 'extends from violence in the home, to the structural violence of poverty, to the ecological violence associated with the depletion of our planetary resources and natural disasters, to the violence of war and its aftermath', in J. True, *The Political Economy of Violence against Women* (Oxford and New York: Oxford University Press, 2012), 5.

24. Jefferson writes in his *Notes on the State of Virginia* (New York: Penguin, 1999 [1785]): 'Are not the infused mixtures of red and white, the expressions of every passion by greater or lesser suffusions of colour in the one, preferable to the eternal monotony, which reigns in the countenances, that immovable veil of black which covers all the emotions of the other race? Add to these, flowing hair, a more elegant symmetry of form, their own judgment in favour of the whites, declared by their preference of them, as uniformaly as is the preference of the Oran-utan [orangutan] for the black women over those of his own species' (145).

25. Weheliye, *Habeas Viscus*, 35.

26. These films were made at the same time that the UN Millennium Development Goals were drafted, targeting 2015 for the achievement of female equality and promising diminished violence against women. But in 2015, when the 2030 UN Sustainable Development Goals were written, this campaign was qualified in favour of a broader emphasis on 'people', 'prosperity' and 'planet'.

WORKS CITED

Agamben, G., *Homo Sacer: Sovereign Power and Bare Life*, trans. D. Heller-Roazen (Stanford: Stanford University Press, 1998).

Bronfen, E., *Over Her Dead Body: Death, Femininity, and the Aesthetic* (Manchester: Manchester University Press, 1992).

Butler, J., *Precarious Life: the Power of Mourning and Violence* (London and New York: Verso, 2004).

Hardt, M. and A. Negri, *Multitude: War and Democracy in the Age of Empire* (New York: Penguin, 2004).

Hartman, S. *Scenes of Subjection: Terror, Slavery, and Self-Making in Nineteenth-Century America* (Oxford and New York: Oxford University Press, 1997).

Jefferson, T., *Notes on the State of Virginia* (New York: Penguin, 1999 [1785]).

True, J., *The Political Economy of Violence against Women* (Oxford and New York: Oxford University Press, 2012).

Weheliye, A., *Habeas Viscus: Racializing Assemblages, Biopolitics, and Black Feminist Theories of the Human* (Durham and London: Duke University Press, 2014).

Žižek, S., *Welcome to the Desert of the Real* (London and New York: Verso, 2003).

CHAPTER 12

Looking for Lear in The Eye of the Storm

Victoria Bladen

> ... she was still too weak from the great joy she had experienced while
> released from her body and all the contingencies in the eye of the
> storm
>
> Patrick White, *The Eye of the Storm*[1]

Through a high-angled opening shot, we see a mature woman at the
sea's edge (Figure 12.1). The wind has calmed, and sunlight illuminates
her face. Gulls circle above and she is open to the sky, her head lifted.
Wearing a white dress, she is slightly bloodied, with a gash on her face
and stains on her dress. Appearing to have emerged from some catastrophe, she is nevertheless elated and serene, the soundtrack reflecting
her mood. What does she see? As the camera zooms in closer, we hear
a voiceover – the voice of her son reflecting on his mother's arrogance
at choosing the time of her death. Yet this voice seems an intrusion on
a profound moment, an iconic tableau. There is no reference to
Shakespeare at either the film's opening or the closing credits, thus
most viewers will not experience the film through a Shakespearean lens.
However, for those with knowledge of the link, through reading the
novel or reviews that make the connection,[2] the opening scene is
striking: can this be Lear, and if so, what new perspectives are opened
up? Such questions resonate with contemporary critical debates on
what constitutes 'Shakespeare' or 'Not Shakespeare', or, as Douglas
Lanier asks, 'Where to place the slash?'[3]

The Australian film *The Eye of the Storm* (2011), directed by Fred
Schepisi, enters into complex intertextual dialogues with both the novel
that it adapts, Patrick White's *The Eye of the Storm* (1973), and
Shakespeare's *King Lear* (1605), White's central intertext; and both film
and novel are situated within a rich Australian history of Shakespearean
adaptation and appropriation.[4] This chapter explores the film's dialogue
with *Lear*, arguing that an appreciation of this dimension has the potential

Figure 12.1: Elizabeth Hunter (Charlotte Rampling) in the eye of the storm in Fred
Schepisi's *The Eye of the Storm* (2011)

to enrich both our understanding of the film and the Shakespearean
intertext.

The film traces the final days of Elizabeth Hunter (Charlotte Rampling)
as she slips between memories of the past and the present, while the family
and household disintegrate like a crumbling empire. Elizabeth's two adult
children Basil (Geoffrey Rush), an actor who has played Lear to poor
reviews, and Dorothy (Judy Davis), who is recovering from a failed marriage to a French aristocrat, have returned to Australia, from the UK and
France respectively, expecting to benefit from their mother's death. They
are also seeking, perhaps unconsciously, some kind of resolution to the
toxic parent–child and sibling relationships between the three. While Basil
and Dorothy are ostensibly the Goneril and Regan figures, Basil's previous
acting role as Lear complicates any neat parallel, and he doubles as an
additional Lear figure shadowing Elizabeth's parallels with Lear.

In current adaptation criticism and theory, there has been a shift away
from older ideas of 'fidelity' as a relevant criterion for assessing adaptations,
as evident in the work of theorists such as Linda Hutcheon and Julie
Sanders.[5] Their work recognizes the problematics of such morally loaded
terminology, instead offering more useful ways through which we can
assess adaptations and appropriations in terms of creative dialogues with
hypotexts, and explorations of hypertexts as palimpsests that register layers
of analogue and difference. Likewise, Douglas M. Lanier has pointed out
that creative works that push against the formal and ideological limits of
Shakespearean hypotexts 'in a spirit of critique, anarchy, pleasure, recup-
eration, participation' function to relocate Shakespeare's work 'in a long

tradition of imitation and adaptation from which their status as literary monuments has tended to isolate them'.[6] More recently, Lanier has advocated a reassessment of the concept of fidelity; while acknowledging that we are in a 'putative post-fidelity moment',[7] in the 2017 *Shakespeare/Not Shakespeare* volume, Lanier argues that 'the source for any Shakespearean adaptation is best imagined as a network – or rhizome – of prior Shakespearean adaptations' and that 'it is to the Shakespeare network and not to a single originary text that a Shakespearean adaptation establishes some relationship of fidelity'.[8]

The film *The Eye of the Storm* could be described as a second-order adaptation in that it is arguably an adaptation of an adaptation.[9] At the same time, White's novel, while a recontextualization in its resituating of the hypotext, is less an adaptation than a sustained appropriation.[10] Sarah Hatchuel has highlighted the complexity of defining a 'Shakespeare film' and outlines various taxonomies, while suggesting a four-part division, pursuant to which *Eye* aligns with her third category, in that the framework is loosely inspired by Shakespeare's while the playtext is absent.[11] In addition, the fact that Basil has played Lear invokes Hatchuel's fourth category, of films in which characters play Shakespeare roles, and the idea of the mirror film, which, as Kenneth Rothwell describes, involves a metacinematic element whereby the personal lives of actors 'run parallel' to the plot of a Shakespearean play they are appearing in.[12]

We can imagine the concepts of adaptation and appropriation as two zones along a spectrum. Whereas adaptation, as Sanders describes, 'signals a relationship with an informing sourcetext or original', appropriation, on the other hand, 'frequently affects a more decisive journey away from the informing source into a wholly new cultural product and domain'.[13] Christy Desmet, Natalie Loper and Jim Casey state that one of the aims of their *Shakespeare/Not Shakespeare* volume is 'to see the realignment of Shakespearean binaries along a continuum', and this idea will likely prove influential.[14] The 'Learness' of a hypertext, its quality of connection with the Shakespearean hypotext, located somewhere on that spectrum/continuum – or in other words its 'Lear-effect' – is what as critics we seek to identify in relating films to Shakespeare's work.[15]

White's novel and Schepisi's film do not overtly signal their relationship with Shakespeare; the paratexts for film and novel are silent in this regard. As a result, while some critics and reviewers have recognized the link with *Lear*, others make no mention of Shakespeare. In assessing the film's 'Learness', it becomes apparent that various aspects of the film resonate with the hypotext while other facets signal journeys away that nevertheless

188   VICTORIA BLADEN

bring new insights, arguably rendering the film an example of what Desmet et al. recognize as paradoxically both Shakespeare and not Shakespeare.[16]

A former beauty and wealthy Sydney socialite, Elizabeth has wielded power all her life. Lear's monarchical power is translated, in modern capitalist Australia, to the weapons of money and looks. Although blind, unable to walk and in the final stages of life, Elizabeth keeps a full household staffed. She employs the housekeeper Mrs Lipmann (Helen Morse) to dance and sing for her, and has one of her nurses, Flora Manhood (Alexandra Schepisi, the director's daughter), the Cordelia figure, apply makeup, fit wigs and dress her with extravagant clothes.[17] Mrs Lipmann, who is Jewish and haunted by the atrocities of the Second World War, is a version of the Fool, Lear's entertainment. The solicitor Arnold Wyburd (John Gaden) is a version of Kent, one who has always loved Elizabeth and remains loyal to her. Tensions arise as the staff, Lear's pseudo-court, realize that Dorothy and Basil are seeking to water down the privileges of a monarch, and ultimately move Elizabeth to a nursing home. Where Elizabeth sees necessities befitting a rich society matriarch, her children, with their eyes on the inheritance, see extravagance and waste. That is not all that Basil has his eyes on, and he and Flora begin a sexual fling that, while not incestuous in itself, creates incestuous implications in terms of the *Lear* hypotext, given that Basil is a Goneril/Lear figure, and Flora the Cordelia figure. (Further suggestions of incest arise from a scene where Dorothy and Basil spend a night in the same bed when they return to the family's country property.)

Like Lear, Elizabeth is selfish and vain, which is conveyed filmically through several shots of her with mirrors. She seeks to control others and often offends, yet there is a compelling magnetism to her character that elicits strong feelings from those around her. There is also an alertness in Elizabeth, a quasi-mystical awareness of the more profound dimensions to life. As Rodney Stenning Edgecombe describes, she has a 'duality as a mystic and a hard-edged society woman'.[18] P. R. Beatson conceives of her as 'the shrine, relic, talisman or goddess lying at the centre of her mandala'.[19] The novel hints at this mystical aspect throughout, and the film articulates this quality in the eye of the storm scene. Strikingly, White chose a female Lear as the lens for his exploration of what Lear experiences on the heath.

Regendering Lear

With a female Lear as the central protagonist, *Eye* is part of a rich history of female casting of traditional male roles in Shakespearean performance. In the twenty-first century, there has been a strong trend in this regard, with examples including Julie Taymor's Prospera (Helen Mirren) in her 2010 *The Tempest* and, on stage, the RSC's 2016 production of *Cymbeline* with a female lead (Gillian Bevan), and Glenda Jackson's Lear in the 2016 production at the Old Vic, directed by Deborah Warner.[20] The 2015 Amsterdam production of *Koningin Lear* (*Queen Lear*), written by Tom Lanoye and directed by Eric de Vroedt, presented Lear (Frieda Pittoors) as a female CEO of a multinational.[21]

Early screen precedents for a female Lear are found in the film adaptations of *Mirele Efros* (*The Jewish Queen Lear*), the 1898 play by Jacob Gordin, adapted for the screen firstly in 1912 as a silent black and white film directed by Andrzej Marek, and then in 1939, directed by Josef Berne, also in black and white.[22] The play is set around 1900 in Poland and centres on the 50-year-old Mirele Efros, a successful business woman, and her sons Yosele and Daniel, and the difficult relationship with her daughter-in-law Sheyndele, Yosele's wife, and her family. There is a shift of genre, the play ending in comedy with a family reunion, facilitated through Shloymele, Mirele Efros's grandson. A more recent stage exploration of a Queen Lear in a Yiddish context is Julia Pascal's play *The Yiddish Queen Lear* (2001), centred on Esther Laranovska, a former Yiddish actress, and the relationship with her three daughters; the action takes place in New York, France and Switzerland in 1939–1940; thus the Second World War and the Holocaust are significant contexts.

As Gemma Miller argues, the cross-gender casting of early modern canonical texts in contemporary performance is 'an act of feminist activism' that can 'not only interrogate the misogyny immanent in the works themselves, but also expose the ideological structures that continue to collude with these values on the contemporary stage and in society more generally'.[23] *Lear* is notable for its angry vein of misogyny. There is no queen/mother figure and, from one perspective, the chaos that ensues appears implicitly tied to the fact that there is no male heir for a 'secure' succession. Power is divided between leaky female vessels, and the emphasis on 'no-thing' that resounds throughout the play links nihilism with female genitalia. Lear's cursing of Goneril's womb (1.4.230–44) and his rant associating the entrance to the womb with hell (4.5.120–7) reveal a misogynistic bias, giving voice to a long patriarchal tradition, while also foreshadowing the end of his lineage.

In shifting to a female Lear in *Eye*, ironically Lear's repressive anxiety about female sexuality, his 'sex nausea',[24] is replaced with a female Lear who has always revelled in her sexuality. Elizabeth remains in tune with her sexuality even in old age, and is still desired by Wyburd. She is able to talk frankly about sex, in contrast to the uptight Dorothy, who is horrified when Elizabeth mentions the word 'penis' in front of one of the nurses. While the misogynist speeches of Lear disappear, the pain of Goneril remains. In a high-angled shot, we see Dorothy, after instructing the attending nurse to leave them, curled up to her mother in the fetal position, an insight to the pain that remains unresolved. Later in the film, we gain insight into Dorothy's pain when we see Elizabeth's threatening sexuality competing with her daughter's in events just prior to the climatic storm.

A female Lear reimagines the Lear–Cordelia bond, and in this regard, Flora arguably means more to Elizabeth than her biological daughter Dorothy. Elizabeth has never developed in her maternal role; she is grateful to Flora for her nurturing but, more importantly, Elizabeth sees something of her younger self in Flora. An additional conception of their relationship, in terms of the mythic structure of the three ages of woman, is one of crone–maiden. Elizabeth is intriguing as a crone who has never relin-quished the role of sexually attractive maiden, even as she has progressed to mother and then crone. Her wearing of the virginal white dress during the storm is a symbol of this. In the passing on of the white dress (cleaned of the blood after the storm) to Flora/Cordelia, Elizabeth is finally accept-ing of letting go her sexuality, albeit only at death's door. In passing on the dress, there is a suggestion that Elizabeth is passing on to Flora her open-ness to life, the revelling in her sexuality and its experiences, since the angst-ridden Dorothy is not capable of this inheritance from her mother, as a consequence, we presume, of the psychological damage caused by Elizabeth. The dress means more, however, than a reductive conception of mere sexuality; it is a sign of a receptiveness to life and its mysteries through the conduit of the body and the senses. In a flashback in the film, when, lying on a couch, Elizabeth opens her legs to Wyburd in invitation, she is wearing the white 'storm' dress; this creates a visual linking of her sexuality to her transcendent state in the storm. The eye of the storm thus resonates with both her sexuality and her openness to mystical experience.

Parents, Children and Postcoloniality

Lear has been a play richly open to new contexts and shifts of place. Eye, in relocating Lear to Australia, enables the theme of parent–child relationships, and the questioning of monarchical status to resonate with concepts of postcoloniality and Australian national identity.[25] Whereas in Lear the king is stripped of his royal status, confronting him with the illusion of monarchy – 'They told me I was everything; 'tis a lie, I am not ague-proof' (4.5.101) – in *Eye*, the trappings of monarchy are seen in terms of performance and props. Elizabeth assumes a quasi-royal appearance through her tiara, wigs, jewels and grand entrances down the stairs; she often appears in the film to resemble the ageing Elizabeth II. Sir Basil's knighthood is for acting, while Princess Dorothy's French aristocratic title, a remnant from a failed marriage used as a shield for her fragile ego, is simply ludicrous. Furthermore, White's sense of humour is apparent in having Elizabeth's dying moment on the 'throne', Australian slang for the toilet. Thus, references to monarchy are by way of parody and serve to undermine and expose the idea of inherited status and power – suggestions relevant to Australia, which remains a constitutional monarchy despite widespread support for a republic.

The relationships between Elizabeth, Dorothy and Basil are fraught with tension, and constantly simmer with potential hostility. The camera often zooms in close to register the complexities of the reciprocal wounds they inflict on each other. Basil and Dorothy have chosen a type of voluntary exile from their 'home' Australia, attempting to tie themselves to Europe, yet neither has found themselves at home there, and despite whatever status they appear to have gained overseas, they still crave their mother's acceptance. That Basil and Dorothy have tried to escape their mother by fleeing to Europe raises the issue of Australia's relationship with Britain, often conceived historically as a quasi-parent–child relationship. *Eye*'s dialogue with Shakespeare, as an inherited British product and global icon, is bound up with Australian cultural identity and its ongoing negotiation with its past. As Philippa Kelly has observed, there is general acknowledgement that Shakespeare has 'helped to reflect, and to define, what it means to be Australian, providing fascinating dialogues with shifting cultural identities'.[26] Elizabeth has never watched Basil on stage in case he is no good, and she tells him so. In the film, Basil's face falls, his façade of the successful actor deflating, as his mother reminds him of the poor reviews for his performance as Lear. The parent withholding her approval from the grown child resonates with the notion of Australia's 'cultural cringe' – its supposed lack of cultural depth and ingrained sense of inferiority in comparison with European culture. That Basil's performance was for *Lear* also operates metafilmically, reflecting on the imagined reception of *Eye* by a British 'parent', and speaking back to the cultural monolith of Shakespeare.

Exploring 'Learness' and the Medium of Film

Several key elements of 'Learness' in *Eye* create echoes and connections
with the hypotext. In *Lear*, the stripping of the king, his descent from
power, develops into a larger confrontation with suffering and the human
condition. In *Eye*, we see the 'Lear-effect' where Elizabeth is faced with the
imminent loss of her way of life in the mansion with her servants and
beloved Fool. Dying is an escape from that stripping process, a refusal to
live in any other way than that of a queen. Her slipping between present
and past, interpreted by those around her as a type of madness, an echo of
Lear's, is a preparation for death, a sifting through memories to discern
those of most value, among which the storm stands out as the defining
experience.

The brutality of human nature presented in *Lear*, with its potential to
overwhelm the fragile ties of family, is diffused throughout *Eye* in the
pervasive hurt at the base of the parent–child relationships. Sissy Helff
links Elizabeth to the cyclone itself, observing how as soon as Elizabeth is
present in a scene, her children leave soon after: 'as if in anticipation of the
next, upcoming catastrophe, Basil and Dorothy seek shelter so that the
destructive force of the cyclone may drift past without causing too much
emotional damage'.[27] Elizabeth remains a potent threat; although she asks
Dorothy 'Come, I can't be a threat anymore, can I?', Dorothy's silence is
telling, and links her, in this moment, with Cordelia.[28] There is also
a tapping into the deep history of Jewish pain and the legacy of the
Holocaust through the character of Mrs Lippmann. For her, the dissolu-
tion of the household is not simply a case of being made redundant; it is
catastrophic because it leaves her without a home and purpose. She slits her
wrists in the bath, after the death of Elizabeth.

Another aspect of *Lear* emerges: that of empathy. In *Lear*, the king,
stripped of his kingly garb, learns at last to think of others. There is the self-
realization that he has taken 'too little care' (3.4.33) of his subjects.
Elizabeth, in her own way, has a degree of nurturing towards her staff,
particularly Mrs Lipmann, in a strange relationship of co-dependence
whereby cabaret performance for both is a way of escaping reality.
Despite failing to nurture her own children, Elizabeth has in fact nurtured
a whole household, and provided protection for the wounded Fool at a safe
distance from Europe and its charnel houses.[29]

Although it is primarily Elizabeth who we first perceive as a parallel for
Lear, 'Lear' in fact is a shifting role.[30] Basil's previous performance as Lear
haunts him, and renders him a hybrid Goneril–Lear figure.[31] Throughout

the novel, there are constant references to performance, and for Basil the lines between acting and 'reality' are constantly blurred.[32] He performs for his mother a certain role; at the same time, while he is with her, like a pelican child feeding from the parent, he is mentally gathering material for an autobiographical play he will subsequently write. Towards the end of the film we see shots from a production of Basil's play, inspired by the family dramas. This play-within-a-film, and the focus on social behaviour as performance, has a metafictional effect, and recalls Basil's voiceover at the beginning of the film. His extra-diegetic voice suggests that the whole film could be read as Basil's reconstruction of events that feed into the writing of his play, itself a processing of the failed Lear performance by dramatizing his Lear-like mother's life. The effect of the *mise-en-abyme* creates a hall of mirrors. Thus, the film is not only in dialogue with the playtext of *Lear* but also with the idea of performing *Lear*, the processes of creation and the symbiotic relationship between fictional worlds and material realities.

Further shifts of role are suggested in the scenes just prior to the storm, during a holiday on a tropical north Queensland island. Elizabeth and Dorothy stay with friends, and a man Edward Pehl (Martin Lynes) is also invited. The character's name evokes Edgar and Edmund, and Elizabeth and Dorothy compete for his affections. Elizabeth is sensuous, in touch with her body and sexually adventurous. Dorothy, on the other hand, is sexually uptight and frustrated, generally tense and awkward at even non-sexual bodily displays of affection. Dorothy has feelings for Edward but is unable to demonstrate them, and is mortified when her mother has no qualms about stepping into the breach.[33] So again the *Lear* roles shift as mother and daughter become versions of Regan and Goneril.

Given that Elizabeth is a blunt and cruel truth-teller, she also plays the roles of the Fool and Cordelia in some respects. Furthermore, when Flora wears Elizabeth's white 'storm' dress, she also in one sense puts on the dress of Lear. Further intertextual echoes arise through casting. John Gaden (Wyburd/Kent in the film) played Lear with Geoffrey Rush as the Fool in a stage production directed by Gale Edwards, the first woman to direct *Lear* in Australia, in 1988,[34] and Rush subsequently played Lear in the 2015 Sydney Theatre Company production. Thus, there is a suggestion that 'Lear' as a role is a shifting one that several of the central characters engage with.

Shakespeare often explored ideas concurrently via various characters, thus linking them through shared themes and creating a type of doubling. The blindness, literal and metaphorical, of Gloucester and Lear is one example; and ultimately both gain levels of insight on their experiences. In *Eye*, Gloucester and the different types of blindness are merged in the figure of Elizabeth – she is literally blind, while also, like Lear, blind to her failings as a parent. In her selfishness, vanity and failure to grant her children love, she has inevitably taught them likewise to be selfish, vain and emotionally constrained. Her cruelty has instructed her children to be cruel. At the same time, it is blind Elizabeth who is uniquely open to the potential for insight.

Just as the role of Lear shifts across the characters, the camera angles, points of view and screen compositions facilitate our contemplation of various perspectives and our engagement with characters. Uncomfortable close-ups of Elizabeth's heavily made-up face repel us, placing us in the position of her children, who are both drawn to and repulsed by their mother. A shot of Basil in profile on Sydney harbour, with the iconic clown face of Lunar Park in the background, suggests the idea of the monstrous mother that haunts his thoughts, someone for whom he will never be good enough. At other moments, we have the perspective of Elizabeth as dissolve shots move between present and past. As Brian McFarlane observes, the medium of film is particularly suited for articulating this process, creating a 'fluid concurrency of past and present, of here and there' since the *mise-en-scène* is able to 'reorient the viewer immediately'.[35] We shift with Elizabeth's point of view between timescapes.

In the iconic shot during the eye of the storm, the high angle of the camera places us up with the gulls initially. We are the gods or nature, looking down at the bare forked animal, the woman in the storm. We are elevated, and thus experience something of Elizabeth's moment of transcendence. In a later shot of Basil, wading in the mud of a dam at his childhood home Kudjeri ('walking not so steady now on his Shakespeare legs'), he quotes Shakespeare to the elements (Figure 12.2).[36] While in the novel, White has Basil quote from *The Merchant of Venice*, in *Eye* this is changed to *Lear*.[37] The speech is from just prior to Lear heading into the storm, ending with 'O fool, I shall go mad' (2.4.279), whereupon Basil cries 'shit, shit', as he cuts his feet on something sharp in the mud. The grand romanticism of Basil's performance is cut short when he is presented as ridiculous, recalling his prior inadequacy as Lear on stage. Like Lear, he also finds nature unaccommodating and, at a deeper level, the scene suggests non-indigenous Australians' alienation from the landscape, a sense of dislocation.

When Basil recites Shakespeare, the angle of the camera, and then the shot of him in context as diminished in the landscape, link him with the

Figure 12.2: Basil (Geoffrey Rush) quoting *Lear* in nature in Fred Schepisi's *The Eye of the Storm* (2011)

storm shot of Elizabeth; however in the Basil shot, the camera is positioned closer to the ground, so we have no moment of transcendence. The camera angles for both scenes thus subtly link and yet distinguish them. While Basil's grand gesture at using nature as a theatre for Shakespeare seems pathetic, reiterated with a close-up of the cut foot, Elizabeth's moment in the heart of the storm touches on something profound, in alliance with what Shakespeare was aiming for, a moment of insight at the heart of chaos.

The Storm

> Just as she was no longer a body, least of all a woman: the myth of her womanhood had been exploded by the storm. She was instead a being, or more likely a flaw at the centre of this jewel of light.
>
> Patrick White, *The Eye of the Storm*[38]

At the heart of *Lear* is the storm, the catalyst for Lear's searing insight into the illusion of monarchy and his lack of immunity from bodily suffering. Schepisi, in recognizing this, bookends the film with shots of Elizabeth in the eye. The harsh Australian landscape, with its unforgiving deserts, fires, floods and cyclones, is an apt stage for Shakespeare's heath scene. While, for most of the narrative, we see Elizabeth safely ensconced in her Sydney mansion, the climax and pivotal event that Elizabeth recognizes as the most important in her life takes place in the cyclone. Australia has a strong history of catastrophic cyclones, most of which hit the northern

Queensland coast.[39] Thus, to relocate Lear's storm to this region evokes a real history of devastation and loss of life.

Elizabeth emerges from the destruction, coming out from a cyclone shelter in a shot that references Lear's hovel and Dorothy in *The Wizard of Oz* (1939). She has a profoundly transcendent moment in the stillness; a shot of the circular space opened up, from her point of view, resonates with the vein of circular imagery throughout *Lear*. It is this reimagining of the storm on the heath that taps into the potential in *Lear* for redemption. Elizabeth has an epiphany, and the eerie centre of calm amid the maelstrom is symbolic of Elizabeth's insight. Thus, any simple classification of Elizabeth's character as shallow for her wealth and vanity risks misunderstanding. Whereas Lear's misogyny figures the entrance of the womb as the gates of hell and the lynchpin of chaos, here Elizabeth, as mature mother, sexual siren and mystic, is calm and centred with her 'o', open to life at the centre of the storm.[40] Intriguingly, there is a precedent for a bloodied female Lear in a white dress. In the 2002 New Zealand stage production, Leah (Geraldine Brophy) wore a white dress that was stained with menstrual blood during the heath scene. As Kelly notes, Leah's socially transgressive lack of concern was 'an ironic inversion of the manner in which blood is generally "worn" by Shakespeare's tragic figures of authority'.[41]

Any Shakespeare text is a shifting complex of ideas with myriad points of entry. When *Lear* is transposed to an Australian context, it exposes new focal points on the hypotext and Australian cultural space. The hypotext is both fractured and reconfigured as we look for 'Learness' in the hypertext, discerning layers and traces of Lear through the palimpsest. The film suggests new avenues of exploration for what appropriating *Lear* can mean in contemporary film, and how it can articulate suffering, complex relationships and the human condition. The malleability of Shakespeare's work enables it to migrate and be transposed into new contexts that shed light on the original. In the moment that Elizabeth looks up to the sky amid the eye of the storm, she connects in some profound way with what Shakespeare achieves in *Lear*.

Intertextuality is inherently unstable and, as theorists on intertextuality emphasize, meanings are created by and dependent on what a viewer/reader brings to a text; the act of encountering a text, filmic, literary or otherwise, 'plunges us into a network of textual relations'.[42] As Sanders argues, of appropriation and adaptation:

> The spectator or reader must be able to participate in the play of similarity and difference perceived between the original, source, or inspiration to appreciate fully the reshaping or rewriting undertaken by the adaptive text.[43]

In *Eye*, the shifting permutations of role and the possibilities of analogue and parallel rely on the audience's knowledge of *Lear*, and recognition of 'Learness', while also creating much of the film's appeal. While there are limits to its ability to fully bring out White's complex dialogue with *Lear*, the medium of film is able to give us other rich facets, taking us visually to the eye of the storm and inviting us to rethink what gender can be in *Lear*.

This female Lear is arguably more evolved than Shakespeare's protagonist, more in tune with her creaturely human nature, while also attuned to the physical world and its fury. This is a more mystical Lear, a Lear who, rather than railing at the heavens in the storm, has stood in wonder and acknowledgement that she has experienced something profound. Elizabeth is able to look the storm directly in the eye and embrace life and the human condition for what it is. Maurizio Calbi, in his study of Shakespeare's spectrality, has reiterated the instability and indefinability of the Shakespearean hypotext; whatever we define as Shakespeare 'cannot be clearly or absolutely separated from its afterlife', and the multiple media involved in processes of adaptation and appropriation 'put into play forms of reciprocal haunting'.[44] I would anticipate that, particularly as there are future developments in casting female or gender-diverse Lears, just as *Lear* haunts *The Eye of the Storm*, so too will Elizabeth Hunter haunt and reconstitute Lear and his/her/their future iterations.

Notes

1. P. White, *The Eye of the Storm* (Sydney: Vintage Books, 1995 [1973]), 428.
2. As one reviewer, Lisa Hill, comments on the connection, 'the book is littered with references to *Lear*, so it's not exactly revelatory. Unless you don't know *King Lear*'. L. Hill, '*The Eye of the Storm*, by Patrick White', *ANZ LitLovers LitBlog*, 15 September 2011: https://anzlitlovers.com/2011/09/15/the-eye-of-the-storm-by-patrick-white-bookreview/ (accessed 17 January 2018).
3. See D. M. Lanier, 'Shakespeare/Not Shakespeare: Afterword', in the insightful and thought-provoking volume *Shakespeare/Not Shakespeare* (Cham: Palgrave Macmillan, 2017), 295.
4. On White's engagement with Shakespeare across his œuvre, see A. Maack, 'Shakespearean Reference as Structural Principle in Patrick White's *The Tree of Man* and *The Eye of the Storm*', *Southerly* 38.2 (1978): 123–40. On Australian engagements with Shakespeare on stage, see: K. Flaherty, *Ours as We Play It: Australia Plays Shakespeare* (Crawley, W.A.: UWA Publishing, 2011) and J. Golder and R. Madelaine (eds.), *O Brave New World: Two Centuries of Shakespeare on the Australian Stage* (Sydney: Currency Press, 2001). I explore Shakespearean appropriations in Australian film in 'Antipodean Shakespeares: Quoting Shakespeare in Australian Film' in A. A. Joubin (ed.), *Cinematic*

Allusions to Shakespeare: International Appropriations (Cham: Palgrave Macmillan, forthcoming).

5. L. Hutcheon, with S. O'Flynn, *A Theory of Adaptation*, 2nd edition (London and New York: Routledge, 2013), 7; J. Sanders, *Adaptation and Appropriation* (London and New York: Routledge, 2006), 20. Also see Y. Griggs, *Shakespeare's 'King Lear': the Relationship between Text and Film* (London: Methuen, 2009), 16–17.

6. D. M. Lanier, *Shakespeare and Modern Popular Culture* (Oxford: Oxford University Press, 2002), 85.

7. D. M. Lanier, 'Shakespearean Rhizomatics: Adaptation, Ethics, Value', in A. Huang and E. Rivlin (eds.), *Shakespeare and the Ethics of Appropriation* (New York: Palgrave Macmillan, 2014), 27; Lanier, 'Afterword', 296.

8. Lanier, 'Afterword', 297.

9. Lanier, *Shakespeare and Modern Popular Culture*, 104.

10. On recontextualization, see K. S. Rothwell, *A History of Shakespeare on Screen: a Century of Film and Television*, 2nd edition (Cambridge: Cambridge University Press, 2004), 209.

11. S. Hatchuel, *Shakespeare, from Stage to Screen* (Cambridge: Cambridge University Press, 2004), 17.

12. *Ibid.*; Rothwell, *A History of Shakespeare on Screen*, 209.

13. Sanders, *Adaptation*, 26.

14. C. Desmet, N. Loper and J. Casey, 'Introduction' in their *Shakespeare/Not Shakespeare* (Cham: Palgrave Macmillan, 2017), 3.

15. On the term 'Learness', see the introduction to this volume. On the 'Lear-effect' see T. Cartelli and K. Rowe, *New Wave Shakespeare on Screen* (Cambridge and Malden: Polity Press, 2007), 154.

16. Desmet et al., 'Introduction', 2.

17. The film removes the additional characters in the novel, Sister Badgery and Flora's cousin Snow.

18. R. Stenning Edgecombe, 'Hugo, Goethe, and Patrick White: Sources for *The Eye of the Storm* and *The Vivisector*', *Antipodes* 28.2 (2014): 514.

19. P. R. Beatson, 'The Skiapod and the Eye: Patrick White's *The Eye of the Storm*', *Southerly* 34.3 (1974): 219–32.

20. On a 2002 New Zealand production with a female Lear, see P. Kelly, 'Performing Australian Identity: Gendering *King Lear*', *Theatre Journal* 57.2 (2005), 224. She also mentions an Australian *Queen Leah* staged at Newcastle, for which there are no reviews. On cross-gender casting, see E. Klett, *Cross-Gender Shakespeare and English National Identity: Wearing the Codpiece* (New York: Palgrave Macmillan, 2009); J. C. Bulman (ed.), *Shakespeare Re-Dressed: Cross-Gender Casting in Contemporary Performance* (Madison and Teaneck: Fairleigh Dickinson University Press, 2008), and G. Miller, 'Cross-Gender Casting as Feminist Interventions in the Staging of Early Modern Plays', *Journal of International Women's Studies* 16.1 (2014): 4–17.

21. P. Franssen, review of *Koningin Lear, Blogging Shakespeare*, 25 March 2015: http://bloggingshakespeare.com/reviewing-shakespeare/queen-lear-tom-lano ye-toneelgroep-amsterdam-stadsschouwburg-utrecht-netherlands-2015/?ut m_source=Blogging+Shakespeare+RSS-Email&utm_campaign=03aebf2ffa-RSS_EMAIL_CAMPAIGN&utm_medium=email&utm_term=0_9b7c91ae e0-03aebf2ffa-242117881 (accessed 23 November 2017).

22. Thanks to Nahma Sandrow for providing me with a copy of an unpublished English translation of the play *Mirele Efros*, translated from the Yiddish. Jacob Gordin also wrote the earlier play *The Yiddish King Lear* (1892), adapted for the screen in 1934 and directed by Harry Thomashefsky; see the chapter by Jacek Fabiszak in this volume.

23. Miller, 'Cross-Gender Casting', 4.

24. C. Hoover, 'Women, Centaurs, and Devils in *King Lear*', *Women's Studies* 16 (1989): 350.

25. On the issues at stake in postcolonial texts, see the seminal study: B. Ashcroft, G. Griffiths and H. Tiffin, *The Empire Writes Back: Theory and Practice in Post-Colonial Literatures*, 2nd edition (London and New York: Routledge, 2002).

26. Kelly, 'Performing Australian Identity', 207.

27. S. Helff, 'Patrick White-Lite: Fred Schepisi's Filmic Adaptation of *The Eye of the Storm*', in C. Vanden Driesen and B. Ashcroft (eds.), *Patrick White Centenary: the Legacy of a Prodigal Son* (Newcastle: Cambridge Scholars Publishing, 2014), 190–1.

28. *Ibid.*

29. On Jewish immigration to Australia escaping from Nazism see http://ijs .org.au/Jewish-Immigration-after-the-Second-World-War/default.aspx (accessed 24 November 2017).

30. Maack observes that, in the novel, there are two Lears – Elizabeth and Basil – and that Basil also compares himself to Edmund and Goneril; Maack, 'Shakespearean Reference', 133–4.

31. Graeme Sharrock notes, Basil 'knows he is not mature enough to play Lear'. G. Sharrock, 'Patrick White and Iris Murdoch – Death as a Moral Summons in *The Eye of the Storm* and *Bruno's Dream*', *Antipodes* 11.1 (1997), 42.

32. Performance is also an important element of the novel. Sharrock notes the 'parade of metaphors from the theater' and some parts are written as a play. *Ibid.*

33. As Maack observes, Dorothy undergoes no process of maturity throughout the narrative and at the end leaves Australia intending to '[protect] herself now from all possibility of experience'. Maack, 'Shakespearean Reference', 137.

34. Kelly, 'Performing Australian Identity', 213.

35. B. McFarlane, 'The Filmmaker as Adaptor: Fred Schepisi Takes on Patrick White in *The Eye of the Storm*', *Senses of Cinema* 60 (2011): http://sensesofci nema.com/2011/60/the-filmmaker-as-adaptor-fred-schepisi-takes-on-patrick -white-in-the-eye-of-the-storm/ (accessed 23 November 2017).

36. White, *The Eye*, 493.
37. *Ibid.*, 492. P. Conrad, 'Shakespeare in Australia: Fred Schepisi's *The Eye of the Storm*', *The Monthly*, 71, September 2011: www.themonthly.com.au/issue/2011/se ptember/1316152404/peter-conrad/shakespeare-australia (accessed 24 November 2017).
38. White, *The Eye*, 424.
39. On Australia's worst cyclones see www.abc.net.au/news/2011-02-02/austra lias-worst-cyclones/1926526 (accessed 25 November 2011).
40. McFarlane notes Elizabeth experiences 'something approaching a state of enlightenment' in 'The Filmmaker as Adaptor'.
41. Kelly, 'Performing Australian Identity', 225.
42. G. Allen, *Intertextuality*, 2nd edition (London and New York: Routledge, 2011), 1.
43. Sanders, *Adaptation*, 45.
44. M. Calbi, *Spectral Shakespeares: Media Adaptations in the Twenty-First Century* (New York and Basingstoke: Palgrave Macmillan, 2013), 18, 19.

WORKS CITED

Allen, G., *Intertextuality*, 2nd edition (London and New York: Routledge, 2011).
Ashcroft, B., G. Griffiths and H. Tiffin, *The Empire Writes Back: Theory and Practice in Post-Colonial Literatures*, 2nd edition (London and New York: Routledge, 2002).
Beatson, P. R., 'The Skiapod and the Eye: Patrick White's *The Eye of the Storm*', *Southerly* 34.3 (1974): 219–32.
Bladen, V., 'Antipodean Shakespeares: Quoting Shakespeare in Australian Film', in A. A. Joubin (ed.), *Cinematic Allusions to Shakespeare: International Appropriations* (Cham: Palgrave Macmillan, forthcoming).
Bulman, J. C. (ed.), *Shakespeare Re-Dressed: Cross-Gender Casting in Contemporary Performance* (Madison and Teaneck: Fairleigh Dickinson University Press, 2008).
Calbi, M., *Spectral Shakespeares: Media Adaptations in the Twenty-First Century* (New York and Basingstoke: Palgrave Macmillan, 2013).
Cartelli, T. and K. Rowe, *New Wave Shakespeare on Screen* (Cambridge and Malden: Polity Press, 2007).
Desmet, C., N. Loper and J. Casey (eds.), *Shakespeare/Not Shakespeare* (Cham: Palgrave Macmillan, 2017).
Flaherty, K., *Ours as We Play It: Australia Plays Shakespeare* (Crawley, W.A.: UWA Publishing, 2011).
Golder, J. and R. Madelaine (eds.), *O Brave New World: Two Centuries of Shakespeare on the Australian Stage* (Sydney: Currency Press, 2001).
Griggs, Y., *Shakespeare's 'King Lear': the Relationship between Text and Film* (London: Methuen Drama, 2009).
Hatchuel, S., *Shakespeare, from Stage to Screen* (Cambridge: Cambridge University Press, 2004).

Helff, S., 'Patrick White-Lite: Fred Schepisi's Filmic Adaptation of *The Eye of the Storm*', in C. Vanden Driesen and B. Ashcroft (eds.), *Patrick White Centenary: the Legacy of a Prodigal Son* (Cambridge: Cambridge Scholars, 2014), 181–95.

Hoover, C., 'Women, Centaurs, and Devils in *King Lear*', *Women's Studies* 16 (1989): 349–59.

Hutcheon, L. with S. O'Flynn, *A Theory of Adaptation*, 2nd edition (London and New York: Routledge, 2013).

Kelly, P., 'Performing Australian Identity: Gendering *King Lear*', *Theatre Journal* 57.2 (2005): 205–27.

Klett, E., *Cross-Gender Shakespeare and English National Identity: Wearing the Codpiece* (New York: Palgrave Macmillan, 2009).

Lanier, D. M., *Shakespeare and Modern Popular Culture* (Oxford: Oxford University Press, 2002).

'Shakespeare/Not Shakespeare: Afterword', in Desmet, C., N. Loper and J. Casey (eds.), *Shakespeare/Not Shakespeare* (Cham: Palgrave Macmillan, 2017), 293–306.

'Shakespearean Rhizomatics: Adaptation, Ethics, Value', in A. Huang and E. Rivlin (eds.), *Shakespeare and the Ethics of Appropriation* (New York: Palgrave Macmillan, 2014), 21–40.

Maack, A., 'Shakespearean Reference as Structural Principle in Patrick White's *The Tree of Man* and *The Eye of the Storm*', *Southerly* 38.2 (1978): 123–40.

McFarlane, B., 'The Filmmaker as Adaptor: Fred Schepisi Takes on Patrick White in *The Eye of the Storm*', *Senses of Cinema* 60 (2011): http://sensesofcinema .com/2011/60/the-filmmaker-as-adaptor-fred-schepisi-takes-on-patrick-white-in-the-eye-of-the-storm/ (accessed 23 November 2017).

Miller, G., 'Cross-Gender Casting as Feminist Interventions in the Staging of Early Modern Plays', *Journal of International Women's Studies* 16.1 (2014): 4–17.

Pascal, J., *The Yiddish Queen Lear/Woman in the Moon* (London: Oberon Books, 2001).

Rothwell, K. S., *A History of Shakespeare on Screen: a Century of Film and Television*, 2nd edition (Cambridge: Cambridge University Press, 2004).

Sanders, J., *Adaptation and Appropriation* (London and New York: Routledge, 2006).

Sharrock, G., 'Patrick White and Iris Murdoch – Death as a Moral Summons in *The Eye of the Storm* and *Bruno's Dream*', *Antipodes* 11.1 (1997): 41–4.

Stenning Edgecombe, R., 'Hugo, Goethe, and Patrick White: Sources for *The Eye of the Storm* and *The Vivisector*', *Antipodes* 28.2 (2014): 513–17.

White, P., *The Eye of the Storm* (Sydney: Vintage Books, 1995 [1973]).

CHAPTER 13

Between Political Drama and Soap Opera: Appropriations of King Lear in US Television Series Boss and Empire

Sylvaine Bataille and Anaïs Pauchet

Both *Boss* (Starz, 2011–2012) and *Empire* (Fox, 2015–) were conceived as modern retellings of *King Lear* according to their respective creators: Farhad Safinia presented *Boss* as 'a modern day takeoff on *King Lear*'[1] while Danny Strong, who created *Empire* with Lee Daniels, described it as '*King Lear* in a hip-hop empire'.[2] Both shows use material from *King Lear* in a loose way, significantly reworking the Lear character arc for their central male protagonists, Tom Kane (Kelsey Grammer), the corrupt mayor of Chicago in *Boss*, and Lucious Lyon (Terrence Howard), the African-American CEO of Empire Entertainment in *Empire*, both diagnosed with an incurable neurological disease at the beginning of the shows.

Beyond the many similarities appearing in the two series' handling of the Shakespearean intertext, the shows' distinctive production contexts invite comparison. *Boss*, which aired on the premium cable network Starz, smaller than the 'big players' HBO and Showtime,[3] was a typical product of the 'HBO effect', the imitation of the 'HBO formula in terms of style and content' by other channels.[4] Like HBO's critically acclaimed shows, it exploits the freedom enjoyed by cable TV in terms of violence, language and sexual content while also striving for cultural cachet and respectability,[5] as evidenced by the claim to Shakespearean inspiration and the presence of Gus Van Sant as executive producer and director of the first episode. *Boss* was rapidly compared to HBO's *The Wire*[6] and generally received favourable reviews.[7] However, it did not garner an economically viable number of viewers, even for a pay-cable channel, and was cancelled after two seasons. In contrast, *Empire* is at the time of writing in its fourth season after debuting to exceptionally high audience ratings.[8] Cinema is part of its credentials too, with filmmaker Lee Daniels and writer Danny Strong at its helm. According to Strong, the original idea was a film project, but the pair soon decided to develop it for television:

'Because it's about a family. It's *Dynasty*.'⁹ The show's success proves that it has coped well with the constraints and pressures of network television. It has been called 'the perfect show for Fox',¹⁰ a channel that has long been home to popular music shows such as *American Idol* (2002–2016) and *Glee* (2009–2015).

This article examines to what extent each show's specific production context informed its appropriation of *King Lear* aesthetically and ideologically, looking at the way each series's reconfiguring of material from *King Lear* interacts with issues of gender, race and cultural legitimacy to strike the show's own balance between family matters and political concerns.

Metaphorical Kingdoms: Chicago and Empire Entertainment

In a striking scene from the first episode of *Boss*, Tom Kane, standing on the roof of the city hall with Treasurer Zajac (Jeff Hephner), treats him to a history lesson on how Mayor Anton Cermak united the various warring ethnicities of Chicago back in the 1930s (Figure 13.1). As he points to the areas of the city occupied by the communities he mentions, his speech is accompanied by a visual effect that erases the existing view to fleetingly replace it with the buildings that could be seen in the early 1930s.¹¹ The cityscape thus becomes a dynamic three-dimensional map representing the territory of Chicago. Even though the story he tells is one of unification,

Figure 13.1: Mayor Kane commenting on his 'kingdom' of Chicago in *Boss* (Starz, 2011–2012)

Mayor Kane appears as a new Lear, designating portions of his kingdom on a map. Aerial views of the city hall alternating with medium shots and close-ups of the two men offer an arresting image of the disproportion between the 'map' and the speaker commenting on it. The roof of the city hall looks like a giant throne from which Kane rules the city, and the whole scene illustrates Kane's autocratic style of government. Kane keeps his disease a secret and remains in office, and an old map showing a bird's-eye view of Chicago can regularly be seen on the wall behind his desk. This map reminds us, as well as his visitors, of the geographical contours of his 'kingdom', a term that is occasionally used in the dialogue and recurs at the beginning of each episode in the lyrics of the old gospel song reprised by Robert Plant: 'Satan, your kingdom must come down'.

There are no such territorial representations in *Empire*, even if the name of the Lyons' hip-hop music label explicitly signals a parallel between the company and a kingdom, as do recurring words such as 'king', 'prince' or 'throne' in the dialogue and the use of a literal sceptre to symbolize corporate leadership. Lucious is a private company owner whose job is to make it profitable: the analogy relies on the similar top-down structure of power but does not cover the political stakes of governing a territory as it does in *Boss*. The term 'empire' is characteristic of the series's taste for the grandiose and is indicative of an altogether different scale, as well as a predilection for expansion. As Lucious explains in season three, episode one:[12] 'You are literally surrounded by Empire music. Everywhere you turn, there's an artist whose music is going to stream exclusively on Empire XStream. We are taking over the world!' *Empire*'s logo, appearing at the beginning of each episode and inside the diegesis itself, on posters inside the building of Empire, represents the profile of Lucious Lyon in gold against black inside a circle (Figure 13.2). This very condensed but richly suggestive image recalls a record, but also a gold coin, presenting Lucious as

Figure 13.2: Empire's logo (Fox, 2015–)

a Roman emperor, while its omnipresence evokes a personality cult. Empire Entertainment proves to be irreversibly linked to Lucious Lyon: 'I am the Empire', he declares in 2.3. This reworks Lear's inability to separate the political body of the king from his physical one. The posters featuring the logo replace the map and point to the link between Empire and its CEO, and thus to the indivisibility of the company between Lucious's three sons. However, Lucious, like Kane, never willingly retires: from the ninth episode and its plot twist revealing that he was misdiagnosed, Lucious is shown to have no intention of leaving the 'throne' of Empire. The show actually suggests that without Lucious, Empire (both the company and the television series) would cease to exist: when he goes into a coma from injuries sustained in an explosion at the end of season three, the logo of the series explodes as well, reflexively emphasizing the link between the microcosm and the macrocosm.

'The King and his Court'[13]

Both *Boss* and *Empire* offer reconfigurations of the original characters rather than modern-day equivalents. *Boss* recomposes the royal family structure, adding not only a mother, Meredith (Connie Nielsen), but also a grandfather, Meredith's father, Mayor Rutledge (Anthony Mockus Sr). Tom and Meredith only have one daughter, Emma (Hannah Ware), but Lear's two missing daughters appear in another guise.

Meredith and Kitty O'Neill (Kathleen Robertson), Kane's aide at city hall, gradually become reminiscent of Goneril and Regan when they participate in a plot supporting young, ambitious and seductive Treasurer Zajac running for mayor against Kane. Kane's overbearing attitude with the much younger, apparently docile Kitty constructs her as a daughter figure, while Meredith at first evokes Lady Macbeth, constantly working for the preservation of her husband's position. However, Tom and Meredith's marriage rapidly appears as a purely political alliance – characteristically, the representation of their intimate life as a couple includes no sex scene. By the end of episode six, Meredith secretly meets Zajac to offer to help him win against Kane, in reaction to her husband having slapped her face for organizing a meeting with a media tycoon on her own initiative, 'blind-sid[ing]' him and 'getting ahead of [her]self', in Kane's words. Kane's infantilizing gesture presents Meredith as a disobedient child undergoing corporal punishment, while his words advise her to know her place in their couple. Making Kane's wife a daughter figure brings out the incestuous undertones detected by feminist readings in the father–daughter relationship in *King Lear*.[14] To a certain extent, Meredith also literalizes the 'return' of the 'absent mother' investigated in psychoanalytical criticism of the play.[15]

Zajac's philandering is illustrated in numerous steamy intervals filmed in the explicit style characteristic of the 'HBO formula'. While the soft-porn clichés often make sex scenes appear as gratuitous spicing up of the somewhat arid political intrigue, the erotic content actually inflects the interweaving of public and private matters in the rewriting of the tragedy by expanding upon the sexuality present in Edmund's affairs with Goneril and Regan. The voyeuristic gaze of the camera suggests that there is no such thing as sexual intimacy in Kane's world.

A significant departure from the play is that all the plotters are harshly punished by Kane in a brutal reassertion of his patriarchal authority at the end of the first season: Zajac has to kneel down, Kitty is shown pictures of her lover Zajac having sex with another woman and Meredith has to offer herself sexually to an influential financier in exchange for a political favour. The series then materializes Lear's fantasies of revenge, fulfilling what in the play are only the curses and threats of the enraged Lear. Kitty's abortion after she finds out that she is pregnant, presumably by Zajac, echoes Lear's appeal to nature to punish Goneril with sterility (1.4.233–6). Conversely, Lear's decision to divest himself of 'rule,/ Interest of territory, cares of state' (1.1.44–5) becomes a deceitful utterance by Kane, one that he never actually intends to translate into fact: Kane does talk to Kitty of stepping down, but his words turn out to be only a bait to force his enemies to reveal themselves (1.7). As a Lear figure who actually clings to power, Kane makes explicit the contradictions of Shakespeare's Lear. As Kane's senior advisor Ezra Stone (Martin Donavan) points out, 'men like you never leave' (1.8).

In relation to Zajac in particular, Kane takes after both Lear and Gloucester, conflating the two figures of fathers wronged by their progeny, since he initially offers his support to Zajac in his run for governor, calling him 'this fucking kid' (1.1). Although Kane never literally loses his eyesight, he is accused of being 'blind' by Meredith (1.8), thus sharing this meta-phorical blindness with Lear. His disease also makes him see things or people not actually there, thus prolonging the theme of failing eyesight. Kane even needs additional eyes to 'see better' (1.1.152), using the built-in webcam on his laptop computer to review what has happened in his office and help him distinguish his hallucinations from reality (1.4). One of the show's signature shots, an extreme close-up of the actor or actress's eye, acts as a constant reminder of the series's reflexive obsession with vision. These shots also produce a fragmentation of the actor's face, momentarily detaching the eye from the face in a visual equivalent of Gloucester's gouged eyes.

Gloucester's mutilation is more literally evoked by Moco Ruiz's punishment for speaking too freely to the media, without first consulting the alderman representing the Latino community, Alderman Mata (1.1). After Kane violently pinches Mata's ears for being unable to control Ruiz's speech, Mata has his men cut off Ruiz's ears (off screen). Ruiz has to offer his own severed ears in a gift box to Kane, who is then seen disposing of the ears in the kitchen sink. In such scenes, the show deflects the pity aroused by patriarchal figures in Shakespeare's play towards unruly characters resisting or simply disregarding their power: disobedient women like Meredith and Kitty or undisciplined subjects like Zajac and Ruiz, in the latter case articulating the rewriting of Gloucester's plight with the politics of communities in Chicago.[16]

The second season explores new variations on betrayal and filial bonds. Among other Lear-inspired narratives and characters, it develops a subplot that was only broached in the first season. Through a number of flashbacks and hints, the series suggests that Mayor Rutledge's cerebral stroke and subsequent loss of mental and muscular functions may have been artificially induced by drugs and caused by Kane, possibly with the help of Meredith. Rutledge is thus cast as a second Lear, all the more so as Kane's memories of Rutledge (2.6) show him as an authoritarian father-in-law who did not relinquish power even after Kane succeeded him. As Meredith explains in 1.6, Rutledge wanted to be 'a sort of mayor emeritus'. Meredith has a fit of guilt at the end of 1.4, when she says to her father: 'You didn't deserve it. Everything we've done. I'm so sorry.' Rutledge then appears as a man 'more sinned against than sinning' (3.2.58), and Meredith as a repentant Goneril or Regan. In this scene, an extreme close-up of Rutledge's eyes blinking in the sun is another evocation of the theme of blindness common to the play and the series. This 'child-changèd father' (4.6.17) who has to be spoon-fed is both a remnant of the past and a living image of the future that awaits the sick Kane, his own 'promised end' (5.3.237): political eviction coupled with physical and mental degradation. Through its *mise-en-abyme* of the Lear plot, the series reflexively dramatizes its own status as a repetition of an older story.

Empire borrows from *King Lear* more obviously and explicitly than *Boss* in its portrayal of the central character and his family, at least at the beginning of the show. The parallels with Shakespeare's play are initiated in the pilot episode, when Lucious, who has just learnt of his incurable disease, gathers his three sons, Andre (Trai Byers), Jamal (Jussie Smollett) and Hakeem

Figure 13.3: 'We *King Lear* now?' in *Empire* (Fox, 2015–)

(Bryshere Y. Gray) to announce that he intends to bequeath Empire to only one of them, thus pitting them against each other (Figure 13.3). Jamal, the intellectual, sensitive son, is quick to notice the Shakespearean turn this family reunion has taken and sarcastically wonders: 'What is this? We *King Lear* now?' as a wider shot shows the three sons facing their father across the massive table. The viewers are thus rapidly informed that *Empire* will rewrite *King Lear* with black protagonists, reworking a classic of European art along the lines of the painter Kehinde Wiley, whose *Prince Albert, Prince Consort of Queen Victoria* (2013) can be spotted in the background, on the wall behind Andre.[17]

This scene presents the first of several reflexive comments on the series's appropriation of the play. The show here underlines its own resemblance to Shakespeare's *King Lear* while drawing attention to its unconventional and apparently incongruous relocation of the white English playwright's work into an African-American family and hip-hop culture. Jamal's grammar in his question 'We *King Lear* now?' is typical of (if not exclusive to) African-American vernacular English, which has the effect of further emphasizing the supposedly jarring presence of *King Lear* in this context. In fact Jamal, a hip-hop artist who belongs to a multimillionaire family, is here articulating two forms of prestige, the 'overt prestige' associated with the literary reference to Shakespeare's *King Lear* and the 'covert prestige' associated with a 'nonstandard dialect', a way for Jamal 'of showing

distance from the standard dialects and the social groups typically associated with it [sic]'.[18] Lucious instantly brushes aside Jamal's suggestion,
answering 'Call it what you want, smartass', and resuming his speech.
Lucious's reply is a way for the series to reassure the viewers that knowing
one's Shakespeare is not necessary to follow the story. Lucious implies that,
for his part, he refuses to comply with the social norms that value familiarity with the classical literary canon, perhaps because he feels this would
be disloyal to his underprivileged social origins.

Lucious may also be reluctant to assimilate his decision with Lear's
catastrophically ill-advised handling of his own succession. He is later
shown quoting from Shakespeare (in 3.5) or invoking Shakespearean
models and counting on their cultural aura to serve his interests, for
instance in 2.12, an episode in which he dons armour to portray Richard
II in a video clip. These reappropriations feed his megalomania and need
for self-aggrandizement. On several occasions, Jamal's remarks offer counterpoints to these references. For instance, in 2.14, he regrets that 'this
family uses the term "heir" as if we were in a Shakespearean play',
foregrounding the contrast, even the opposition, between the Lyons'
world and the now apparently archaic world created by Shakespeare in
his plays. These shifts between fully embracing the Shakespearean reference and distancing oneself from it reflect the series's own explorations and
ambiguities in its efforts to display both 'overt' prestige as a reappropriation
of *King Lear* and 'covert' prestige as a hip-hop musical show and
a successful soap opera. The act of reinterpreting Shakespeare with black
characters is thus problematized, discussed and mirrored, while the series
ponders on the nature of this very act: is it supposed to be an empowering,
even subversive, appropriation of white European classical culture, or is it,
on the contrary, a re-affirmation of the domination of Shakespeare as the
'high cultural Other'[19] needed by African-American culture to gain
legitimacy?[20] The predominance of African Americans among the show's
viewers[21] would suggest that the series's references to the white playwright
are no hindrance to black audiences' engagement, which in itself testifies
both to the effectiveness of its appropriative strategies and to the pervasive
presence of Shakespeare in American culture across communities.

Another obvious twist brought to the Shakespearean model by the
series, which was also inspired by James Goldman's 1966 Broadway play
The Lion in Winter,[22] is the regendering of Lear's three daughters, as in
Akira Kurosawa's *Ran* (1985). Replacing the daughters with sons has
offered the show the opportunity to interrogate the constructions of
masculinity in hip-hop culture. The love test of the three daughters in

King Lear here becomes a test of masculinity. As Lucious tells his sons, clearly linking expectations intersecting race and gender, 'In order for it [the company] to survive, I need one of you Negroes to man up and lead it' (1.1). In this overmasculinized world, Lucious feminizes his sons when he disapproves of their actions, or mocks them – for instance, when he says to Hakeem in 3.3, as the brothers are all getting out of a van: 'Ain't you gonna follow your sisters?' The spectre of Lear's daughters always seems to be lurking in the background, ready to surface on any occasion. These sexist comments work as a way to undermine the greater challenge posed by sons rather than daughters to the father's authority in Lucious's patriarchal view: rivalry is not only among the male siblings but also between them and their father.

Lucious is particularly harsh on Jamal, for being gay and sensitive – in other words, too womanly in Lucious's heteronormative vision. Women also participate in these sexist conventions, as when young masculine-looking rap singer Freda Gatz declares to Hakeem in a rap battle in 2.8: 'I'm the son that your dad always wanted, look at daddy's little girl, girl.' This declaration blurs issues of gender even further and illustrates Freda's relationship with Lucious at that point of the series, when he treats her as his surrogate daughter/son. *Empire* has been praised for tackling the sensitive issue of homophobia in the hip-hop world, but the regendering of Lear's three daughters arguably emphasizes the predominance of masculinity in this realm. The 'heir' will necessarily be a man, and although there are strong female characters in the show, women do not seem to be able to run the company on their own.

Andre, Jamal and Hakeem are all at some point reminiscent of Regan and Goneril in the sense that they all in turn plot against their father or against each other. Characteristics of Lear's treacherous daughters are also redistributed among women in Lucious's entourage. *Empire* not only stages the 'return of the mother' (as *Boss* does) but also the entrance of a young fiancée (Anika) into the family pattern borrowed from *King Lear*, multiplying the possibilities for betrayals, alliances and love affairs. The boys' mother Cookie (Taraji P. Henson), who has spent the last seventeen years in prison, literally returns to claim her share of the company. She embodies the challenge to masculinity represented by the (absent) mother's sexuality in Shakespeare's play, while performing traditional maternal functions by offering potential protection to her children (differing from Meredith in this). Like Meredith, she becomes a variation of Goneril or Regan when she tries to get rid of her ex-husband in 1.12, as does Anika in 1.11, after leaving Lucious and becoming Hakeem's girlfriend.

These quasi-incestuous relationships are further complicated by the soap-opera dynamic of the show: Lucious legally becomes his granddaughter's father when he acknowledges Anika and Hakeem's baby as his own daughter. Furthermore, the jealousy and 'cat fights' – a staple of soap opera – between the main female characters of the show mimic what happens between the two sisters in the play, stressing in return the domestic aspects of Shakespeare's tragedy while trivializing them. The proliferation of figures of Lear's treacherous daughters enables the series to continue: the women get killed, not the men, so the king's children can continue to fight each other forever.

As the series progresses, its Learness that was so conspicuously fore-grounded in the pilot recedes as it is diluted in the innumerable stories that keep the soap-opera machine working. Fox's show teems with more or less direct evocations of Shakespeare's plays, be it in characterizations or through props and sets, intra-diegetic adaptations, verbal references in the dialogue, the names of the characters or the episode titles that are almost all 'some portion of a quote'.[23] Thus, the series is not so much a rewriting of a singular play as a remix of snippets from Shakespeare, practising a form of turntablism and sampling that mirrors the art of hip-hop music displayed in the musical numbers of the show.

Cordelia Revisited

Traces of Cordelia appear in *Empire*'s exploration and exploitation of Lucious's rejection of some of his sons, but none of the siblings is an obvious analogue of Cordelia. Hakeem, Lucious's youngest son and his favourite at the beginning of the show, is neither misunderstood nor wrongly treated by his father, contrary to Jamal, because of his homosexuality, and Andre, because he suffers from bipolar disorder. Moreover, Andre has married a 'stranger' (1.8) in Lucious's opinion, as his wife Rhonda is white. Andre is not a hip-hop artist like his brothers but the chief financial officer of Empire Entertainment. He and Rhonda live in a white suburb, while his brothers' luxury flats are in an urban environment, so that their way of life appears geographically (if not socially) more in line with hip-hop culture's street origins. In that sense, Andre can be viewed as an exiled Cordelia, in a reappropriation that draws upon the issues of racial relations and spatial segregation in the USA.

The figure of Cordelia is more apparent in *Boss* through the character of Emma, the Kanes' only daughter, a recovering drug addict who has become a priest. Emma is first seen working in a church's free clinic, looking after an uninsured elderly man. She seems to share Cordelia's altruistic qualities, illustrated in particular when Cordelia tends to her father with the help of a doctor. Emma appears as a Cordelia who has already been excluded from her family for political reasons: her father has not seen her in five years, because the Kanes decided that 'Her behavior could not be tolerated. She had to be cut loose' (1.2). Episode three brings a twist to the Shakespearean pattern when Kane reveals to Emma that he is terminally ill. She asks him why he wanted to see her:

> TOM   : I thought –
> EMMA   : What? That I'd take care of you? Go with you on your doctor
>   visits, sit by you in your hospital bed? I'm not that person.
>   You're not that person. . . . The only thing you care about is
>   you – what you want, what you need. I'm sorry, Dad. It's too
>   late. There's nothing here.
> TOM   : Emma, wait.
> EMMA   : What did you expect?

Emma's question also applies to the viewers' own expectations: did we expect, as Tom apparently did, a scene along the lines of the moving reunion between Lear and Cordelia? If so, then Emma's words stress that both Kane and she are entirely singular characters, not modern avatars of already defined figures. Emma's resistance to the Shakespearean model coincides with her resistance to her father's wishes. But even as she rejects the model of filial virtue embodied by Cordelia, her non-compliance is reminiscent of Cordelia's refusal to play the game orchestrated by her father at the beginning of the play, when Lear admits: 'I loved her most, and thought to set my rest/ On her kind nursery' (1.1.117–18). Emma's remark on her father's self-centredness also evokes Lear's psychological state and hunger for flattery in the first scene. By conflating evocations of two different moments of the play, the scene in *Boss* actually rewrites Shakespeare's father–daughter reunion, offering an alternative outcome in which the wronged daughter does not forgive nor wish to help her distressed father. This dialogue is reflexive of the series's relationship to Shakespeare, as a literary father figure whose authority is also defied at that point.

As the series's narrative progresses, however, Emma relents and agrees to reconnect with her father in an emotionally charged scene (1.4). Emma even agrees to secretly provide him with his prescription drugs, which she obtains illegally from her drug-dealing boyfriend Darius (1.4). The show seems to draw near the Lear–Cordelia model, only to diverge from it again a few episodes later, in a plot twist occurring in the penultimate episode (1.7). Kane, caught in a political scandal and in bitter need of a game-changer, once again sacrifices his relationship with Emma to ensure his political survival. Emma is sent to prison, not *with* her father like Cordelia in 5.3, but *by* her father. In the second season, she is allowed to live in the family home under house arrest and uses drugs again. Her evolution is typical of the moral greyness displayed by all the characters in the series, including Kane's victims: Emma is shown to be both manipulative and ungrateful towards Darius, unconsciously reproducing her father's selfish exploitation of other people that makes him a 'monster' (2.4) in her eyes. Emma's treatment of her black boyfriend Darius mirrors Kane's firing his African-American senior aide after getting infatuated with her and sup-porting her in her work for the black community of Chicago and, at the wider level, Kane's failing the black inhabitants of Lennox Gardens after winning their trust. Emma's character development deconstructs the figure of the 'good' daughter and throws light on Cordelia as an agent of preservation and perpetuation of her father's autocratic system.

'My Wits Begin to Turn' (3.2.65)

In *Boss*'s opening, Kane meets with his doctor secretly to hear her diagnosis. The theme of madness, a further element of Learness, is emphasized when the doctor matter-of-factly outlines the damage caused by Lewy body dementia. Like *Breaking Bad* (AMC, 2008–2013) before it, with the announcement of Walter White's cancer (1.1), *Boss* uses striking visual and sound devices (extreme close-ups, a long take, jump cuts, an off-screen voice) to present the delivery of the fatal news in an unsettling way, as a rendition of the main character's emotional state. The meeting place, a huge abandoned industrial building, is a derelict slaughterhouse whose fate seems to mirror Kane's own predicted decay, while its former function prompts him to reflect on the meaninglessness of human life, quoting Upton Sinclair's *The Jungle*: 'Thank you, Doctor. 20,000 men used to work here in this place slaughtering hundreds of thousands of hogs and cattle each day. "Life, for all its cares and its terrors is no such great thing after all", laborer or hog.' Like the heath, the abandoned meat factory is a no-man's land and Kane's considerations on the value of human life echo Lear's musings on humanity when he wanders with Poor Tom. Kane's drive to Millennium Park in downtown Chicago where a crowd attends his speech reverses Lear's centre-to-margin journey. In *Boss*, the private man and his secret weakness are revealed before the public figure is shown: this has the effect of arousing pity for Kane before his ruthlessness is demonstrated.

Other places can be viewed as reflections of the heath. At the beginning of season two, Tom is seen wandering in a desert landscape, protecting his face from the glaring sun. Far away in the background, cars are zooming past. Characteristically, the ontological status of this scene is left unclear: is it one of Kane's hallucinations or a memory? The vision of Kane in the arid, sun-drenched desert, an American transposition of the storm-lashed English heath, occurs again in the next episode when Kane is blinded by a flickering neon light in a hospital corridor. Metaphorical lightning recurs in 2.6: white flashes are a side effect of the experimental treatment Kane undergoes in a clinic in Canada while 'a storm is brewing' in Chicago as the relocation of the Lennox Gardens residents proceeds in an increasingly tense atmosphere. During this episode, Kane experiences an extreme version of Lear's 'O I have ta'en/ Too little care of this' (3.4.32–3) when he is harrowed by memories of his past misdeeds and their consequences on the people of Chicago. The pathos of Kane's plight is not because he is 'more sinned against than sinning' but because his greatest enemy is his own brain, and his secret battle against it is already lost. The betrayals he faces over the course of the two seasons never cause his downfall. Kane's mental troubles predate the plot hatched against him in season one and he finds himself spatially relegated to the margins of Chicago because of his disease, not as a result of the plotters' actions. However, the series retains the play's combination of personal and political matters in its own version of the heath scenes.

Empire starts with Lucious listening to an artist recording her song and interrupting her to advise her to draw on what she feels about her brother's death, 'show[ing him her] soul in this music'. This scene is interspersed with flashbacks of Lucious learning about his fatal neurodegenerative disease. The emotional soul music becomes a reflection not only of the singer's feelings but also of Lucious's, thereby performing the same function as the solilo-quies in Shakespeare's plays. The personal and public figures of Lucious are thus blurred from the beginning: he hides his disease from those around him but effectively uses it in his work as CEO of a record label.

At the end of season three, in a new twist, Lucious is almost killed, plotted against by his eldest son, and wakes up, suffering from amnesia, which literalizes Lear's loss of identity after his children's rebellion; but, contrary to Lear (and Mayor Kane), Lucious is not constructed as a character suffering from insanity. The notion of mental illness in *Empire* is largely transferred onto Andre and Leah, Lucious's supposedly deceased mother, who are linked by their bipolar disorder: the editing in 2.14, when the Lyon family watch

Lucious's video clip about his childhood, emphasizes this connection by juxtaposing shots of Leah about to shoot herself in the head in the clip and a flashback of Andre doing the same. The link between Leah and Lear is pointed at by the similar-sounding names and is another instance of the series's regendering of Shakespearean characters. Leah, in the true tradition of plot twists in soap operas, turns out to be still alive, exiled in a mental institution, which literalizes the idea of alienation and entrapment. Leah finally comes back in Lucious's life in 2.15, thanks to a Cordelia-like Andre. Lucious eventually becomes a repentant Regan or Goneril who has offered hospitality to his mother in season three. However, contrary to Kane's (and Lear's) political compunction, Lucious's remorse and introspection are never experienced beyond interpersonal relationships: the myth of the self-made man and social ascension 'from rags to riches' – which is central to the genre of the soap opera[24] – is neither challenged nor deconstructed.

If *Boss* is a 'post-television'[25] appropriation of *King Lear*, then *Empire* is a post-post-television reworking of Shakespeare's play. *Boss*, like other series imitating the 'HBO formula', strives to be 'not TV'.[26] The *Lear* intertext lends it the cachet of an 'old-fashioned story'[27] that reaches beyond the scope of modern-day Chicago. The series is thus given 'a weighty, universal content appropriate to genuine "art"'.[28] *Empire*, whose glamorous aesthetics is poles apart from the 'grittiness' and bleakness of *Boss* and other cable drama series,[29] appears as a reaction against 'post-television', unapologetically looking back to television before the rise of HBO et al. and paying tribute to prime-time soap opera – a very popular televisual genre that knew its heyday in the 1980s. *Empire*'s reconfigurations of *King Lear*, focusing on dysfunctional relationships and rivalries in a 'royal' family, are attuned to this nostalgia for television as a domestic medium. The Shakespearean parallels participate in the show's narrative and aesthetic excess by helping create larger-than-life characters and sensational situations. The show capitalizes on *King Lear*'s prestige but does not seem to take itself (and its Shakespearean inspirations) entirely seriously. In that sense, Lucious may even be seen as an ironical parody of all the white male anti-heroes of cable shows that have been compared to Shakespearean tragic heroes: Tony Soprano, Walter White, Frank Underwood . . . or Tom Kane.

Notes

1. R. Richmond, 'Emmys: Farhad Safinia, Creator of *Boss*', *Deadline*, 7 June 2012: http://deadline.com/2012/06/emmys-farhad-safinia-the-man-who-keeps-the-boss-machine-running-282987/ (accessed 29 November 2017).

2. E. Zuckerman, 'Danny Strong on *Empire: King Lear* Meets "Hip Hop" Meets *Dynasty*', *The Atlantic*, 13 May 2014: www.theatlantic.com/entertainment/ar chive/2014/05/danny-strong-on-empire-king-lear-meets-hip-hop-meets-dynasty/370067/ (accessed 7 August 2017).

3. J. Adalian, 'How 50 Cent and a Feminist Action Hero Are Finally Putting Starz on the Map', *Vulture*, 9 July 2015: www.vulture.com/2015/07/starz-outlander-power-populist-network.html (accessed 30 July 2017).

4. M. Leverette, B. L. Ott and C. L. Buckley (eds.), *It's Not TV: Watching HBO in the Post-Television Era* (New York: Routledge, 2008), 1.

5. J. McCabe and K. Akass, 'Sex, Swearing and Respectability', in J. McCabe and K. Akass (eds.), *Quality TV: Contemporary American Television and Beyond* (London and New York: I. B. Tauris, 2007), 62–76.

6. M. Zoller Seitz, '*Boss*: Is Kelsey Grammer's show the new *Wire*?', *Salon*, 21 October 2011: www.salon.com/2011/10/21/boss_is_kelsey_grammers_show_the_new_wire/ (accessed 30 July 2017).

7. See www.metacritic.com/tv/boss (accessed 29 November 2017).

8. J. Hibberd, 'Fox renews *Gotham, Empire* (After Only Two Episodes!)', *Entertainment Weekly*, 17 January 2015: http://ew.com/article/2015/01/17/got ham-empire-season-2/ (accessed 30 July 2017).

9. Zuckerman, 'Danny Strong on *Empire*'. The soap opera *Dynasty* aired on ABC from 1981 to 1989.

10. E. Steel and B. Sisario, '*Empire* May Provide Fox the Big Hit It Needs', *The New York Times*, 27 January 2015: www.nytimes.com/2015/01/28/business/me dia/empire-may-provide-fox-the-big-hit-it-needs.html (accessed 30 July 2017).

11. We thank Sarah Hatchuel for drawing our attention to this scene.

12. Henceforward 3.1.

13. This is the title of one of the bonus features on the DVD of the two seasons of *Boss* released in 2013 (Metropolitan Video).

14. See L. E. Boose, 'The Father and the Bride in Shakespeare', *PMLA* 97.3 (May 1982): 325–47; C. Kahn, 'The Absent Mother in *King Lear*', in M. Ferguson, M. Quilligan and N. Vickers (eds.), *Rewriting the Renaissance: the Discourses of Sexual Difference* (Chicago: University of Chicago Press, 1985), 33–49.

15. Kahn, 'The Absent Mother in King Lear', 40.

16. See O. Esteves and S. Lefait, *La Question raciale dans les séries américaines: The Wire, Homeland, Oz, The Sopranos, OITNB, Boss, Mad Men, Nip/Tuck* (Paris: Presses de Sciences Po, 2014), 139–59.

17. A. Sargent, '*Empire*: TV's Contemporary-Art Gallery', *The New Yorker*, 15 October 2015: www.newyorker.com/culture/culture-desk/empire-tvs-contemporary-art-gallery (accessed 30 July 2017).

18. J. Trotta, 'Dealers and Discourse: Sociolinguistic Variation in *The Wire*', in K. Beers Fägersten (ed.), *Watching TV with a Linguist* (Syracuse: Syracuse University Press, 2006), 57.

19. D. Lanier, 'Minstrelsy, Jazz, Rap: Shakespeare, African American Music, and Cultural Legitimation', *Borrowers and Lenders* 1.1 (Spring/Summer 2005): www.borrowers.uga.edu/782016/show (accessed 30 July 2017).

20. A. Thompson, *Passing Strange: Shakespeare, Race, and Contemporary America* (Oxford: Oxford University Press, 2011), 16–17.

21. R. Kissel, '*Empire*'s Growth Spurt Fueled by Young Women, Urban Markets', *Variety*, 26 February 2015: https://variety.com/2015/tv/news/empire-ratings-gr owth-women-urban-markets-1201442207/ (accessed 27 December 2018).

22. I. Chaiken, interview by B. Bogaev, 'Shakespeare Unlimited: How *King Lear* Inspired *Empire*', *Folger Shakespeare Library*, 22 March 2017: www.folger.edu /sites/default/files/Empire-Podcast-Transcript.pdf (accessed 30 July 2017).

23. *Ibid.*

24. See D. Hobson, *Soap Opera* (Oxford: Polity Press, 2003), 69.

25. Leverette, Ott and Buckley, *It's Not TV*.

26. HBO's most famous slogan was 'It's not TV, it's HBO' from 1997 to 2006.

27. B. Walter, 'Actor Kelsey Grammer Talks about his Hit Show Boss and its Similarity to King Lear', *The Edge*, 12 June 2013: www.theedgesusu.co.uk/cult ure/2013/06/12/actor-kelsey-grammer-talks-about-his-hit-show-boss-and-its-si milarity-to-king-lear/ (accessed 30 July 2017).

28. Lanier, 'Minstrelsy, Jazz, Rap'.

29. S. Mendelson, 'Why *Empire* is the True Heir Apparent to *Breaking Bad* And *Lost*', *Forbes*, 18 March 2015: www.forbes.com/sites/scottmendelson/2015/03/ 18/why-empire-is-an-heir-apparent-to-breaking-bad-mad-men-and-lost/#5a8 80dd350ba (accessed 29 November 2017).

WORKS CITED

Boose, L. E., 'The Father and the Bride in Shakespeare', *PMLA* 97.3 (May 1982): 325–47.

Chaiken, I., interview by B. Bogaev, 'Shakespeare Unlimited: How *King Lear* Inspired *Empire*', *Folger Shakespeare Library*, 22 March 2017: www .folger.edu/sites/default/files/Empire-Podcast-Transcript.pdf   (accessed 30 July 2017).

Esteves, O. and S. Lefait, *La Question raciale dans les séries américaines: The Wire, Homeland, Oz, The Sopranos, OITNB, Boss, Mad Men, Nip/Tuck* (Paris: Presses de Sciences Po, 2014).

Hobson, D., *Soap Opera* (Oxford: Polity Press, 2003).

Kahn, C., 'The Absent Mother in *King Lear*' in M. Ferguson, M. Quilligan and N. Vickers (eds.), *Rewriting the Renaissance: the Discourses of Sexual Difference* (Chicago: University of Chicago Press, 1985), 33–49.

Lanier, D., 'Minstrelsy, Jazz, Rap: Shakespeare, African American Music, and Cultural Legitimation', *Borrowers and Lenders* 1.1 (Spring/Summer 2005): www.borrowers.uga.edu/782016/show (accessed 30 July 2017).

Leverette, M., B. L. Ott and C. L. Buckley (eds.), *It's Not TV: Watching HBO in the Post-Television Era* (New York: Routledge, 2008).

McCabe, J. and K. Akass, 'Sex, Swearing and Respectability', in J. McCabe and K. Akass (eds.), *Quality TV: Contemporary American Television and Beyond* (London and New York: I. B. Tauris, 2007), 62–76.

Sargent, A., 'Empire: TV's Contemporary-Art Gallery', The New Yorker, 15 October 2015: www.newyorker.com/culture/culture-desk/empire-tvs-contemporary-art-gallery (accessed 30 July 2017).

Thompson, A. Passing Strange: Shakespeare, Race, and Contemporary America (Oxford: Oxford University Press, 2011).

Trotta, J., 'Dealers and Discourse: Sociolinguistic Variation in The Wire', in K. Beers Fägersten (ed.), Watching TV with a Linguist (Syracuse: Syracuse University Press, 2006), 40–65.

CHAPTER 14

Afterword: Godard's King Lear

Peter Holland

There is an old theatre warning about *King Lear*, worthy to be ranked alongside the advice to 'Get yourself a light Cordelia': 'When you're old enough to play King Lear, you're too old to play King Lear'.[1] It is a neat paradox but has not, of course, stopped many much younger men – and women – than Lear's 'fourscore and upward' (4.6.58) from playing the role. Paul Scofield was 40 when he played it for the RSC, 49 when Peter Brook's film was released; Kathryn Hunter was 40, too, while Yuri Yarvet was 51 when he was filming with Grigori Kozintsev, and Tatsuya Nakadai 53 for Akira Kurosawa's *Ran*. Two actors were rather nearer Lear's age: Norman Mailer was 64 and Burgess Meredith was 79 when Jean-Luc Godard's *King Lear* was shown at the Cannes Film Festival in 1987. Godard's extraordinary, demanding and unremittingly brilliant film, largely mocked and reviled, too often ignored, increasingly inaccessible,[2] can act as a kind of metafilmic analogy for the activity in the rest of this volume: its status not as a film of *King Lear* but as a film about the fragmentary possibility of making – or perhaps more accurately, *not* making – a film of *King Lear*, creating for itself a remarkably complex status as critical commentary on the materiality of what it is itself in the process of (not) creating. I offer some brief comments on its commenting as a way to begin to think back over, as well as forward and beyond, the accomplishments of this volume.

But did either Mailer or Meredith play King Lear in the film? After Godard signed the $1,000,000 agreement for the film with Menahem Golan of Cannon Films, a deal written on a napkin at Cannes in 1986, it was announced that Mailer would write the script and star. The script was written and Mailer did three hours' filming – five takes of the first shot – before flying off with his daughter Kate. In the shot, two takes of which are in the release print, Mailer plays, as the credits might have said, had there been any, 'Himself' or, as Godard calls him, 'The Great Writer'. Mailer's script was completely rewritten by Peter Sellars and Tom Luddy. Since Sellars plays William Shakespeare Junior the Fifth (hereafter 'WS Jr the

5th'), as he repeatedly and portentously describes himself in the film, Godard's *King Lear* has a screenplay co-written by Shakespeare, just not the usual Shakespeare of our work. Mailer, we might say, would have played Lear, had he stayed on as an actor. But Meredith plays Don Learo, the lead character in Mailer's script. As Kate Mailer wonders in the dialogue of the scene they filmed,

> ... Don Kenny, Don Glostro, Don Learo.
> MAILER   *[correcting her pronunciation]*: Don Learo.
> KATE: Learo. Why are you so interested in the Mafia?
> MAILER: I think the Mafia is the only way to do *King Lear*.

Mafia *Macbeth*s are not uncommon – for example, *Joe MacBeth* (1955) and *Men of Respect* (1990) – and, for *Lear*, there is the vexing case of *The Godfather, Part III* (1990), with its storm, madness and gender-inverted *pietà* (father with dead daughter, not mother with dead son). Certainly Don Learo has three daughters, with the older ones Gloria and Regina telexing in their messages of love. So, vestigially, there is a mafia *King Lear* narrative here, especially as Don Learo is writing his history of Bugsy Siegel and Meyer Lansky – except that the passages he dictates to his daughter (now Molly Ringwald rather than Kate Mailer) are taken verbatim from Arthur Fried's book *The Rise and Fall of the Jewish Gangster in America* (1980). Don Learo is, then, less writer than quoter in a film which includes innumerable quotations, most carefully and very helpfully identified in the unusually extensive entry on the film on Wikipedia.[3]

Perhaps, then, the way of considering Mailer as star is precisely as writer, in a film with other writers: Shakespeare, most obviously, plus Don Learo as well as the other Shakespeare who is (re)writing and reconstructing his ancestor's works in the film's overly emphasized post-Chernobyl world where art in particular has been lost. So Sellars' character is piecing together *King Lear* on behalf of Cannon's Culture Division and the Royal Library of Her Majesty the Queen and, by late in the film, has recovered 99% of it. After all, as Godard, *auteur* if not author, puts it in voiceover: 'It was not Lear with three daughters. It was Kate with three fathers: Mailer as a star, Mailer as a father and me as a Director.' This gender-inversion of *Lear*, as Coppola's *Godfather* will also soon create, might be seen as focusing on the construction, reconstruction and deconstruction of writing in general and writing *King Lear* in particular. As the film moves forward, passages of Shakespeare's play form heard but never seen materials, given in voices that are also at times gender-inverted or doubled, with Lear's lines spoken by a male and female voice, as well as being quoted, first by Don Learo with his daughter, but also quoted from, for instance, Kozintsev's 1970 film – in the midst of a film whose cast includes an appearance by a character identified as both Professor Kozintsev and Professor Quentin (Freddy Buache).

But, in its characteristically digressive mode, unstoppably resisting a linearity even of its own process of making the film that it itself is, this exploration of the writer is set off against the creation not only of words but also, perhaps even more so, of images. The relationship of words, music and image reaches something approaching a climax as Don Learo sits, gazing at the lake, with his back both to the camera and to the corpse of Cordelia (in a film self-described in a title-card as 'A Picture Shot in the Back'), though, since she is wearing the costume that belongs to her performance as Joan of Arc in a sequence that quotes the screenplay of Robert Bresson's *The Trial of Joan of Arc* (1962), she may not be Cordelia at all. As WS Jr the 5th watches the event with two of the film's 'goblins', Edgar and his girlfriend Virginia, the three comment on the astonishingly beautiful tableau that emerges – though they may also be commenting on the shot of a white horse galloping on the pebbled shore (think 'Like as the waves make to the pebbled shore' from Sonnet 60, as well as Virginia Woolf's *The Waves*, from which the soundtrack has just quoted):

VIRGINIA:	Edgar, Edgar. It's a pity there is not music of Nino Rota.
EDGAR:	OK, OK. Let's use then the words for once.
WSJR the 5th:	To accompany the dawn of our first image.

Barely a narrative at all – and certainly not one that follows a narrative arc of Shakespeare's play, beyond having some of its opening near the start and some of its ending near its end – this film is only (*only?!*) an aggregation of competing fragments of wildly various strands of event-sequences, creating, along the way, a genealogy of cinema, with the photographs of directors (Bresson, Pasolini, Eisenstein, Visconti, Welles and more) constituting a pantheon of patriarchy within which and against which Godard himself constructs and deconstructs the making of film itself. Strikingly and inevitably in its honesty, the whole film is unnervingly framed cinematically (or book-ended as print-text) by an intertitle announcing in its first text-image 'The Cannon Group Bahamas presents' and in its last '© 1987 Cannon Films, Inc. and Cannon International', that the rights of ownership in this act of making are always to be returned to the investment processes of capitalist financing, not to the makers.

Throughout, the acts of writing are both watched and heard, though hearing is made deliberately difficult with multiple simultaneous layers of sound: diegetic dialogue, different voiceovers and distortions of a Beethoven string quartet, not to mention the frequent cries of a seagull. Godard is, I think (unless he is quoting – and, if so, who from?), the first to find in Lear a pun on 'ear' as a voiceover puts it:

> For Learo, to hear is to see. 'A man may see how this world goes with no eyes. Look with thine ears'. This is what he tries to do, the king who calls himself Lear, E-A-R. In listening to his daughters he hopes to see their entire bodies stretched out across their voices . . . So that he can silence this silence, he listens as if he is watching television. And Cordelia? What she shows in speaking is not nothing but her very presence, her exactitude.

Godard forcefully uncouples speech and silence and image in setting out the gaps that keep emerging in his text, not least the one inserted into the middle of a word, where 'nothing' becomes, over and over again, both on intertitles and in speech, 'no thing', or as words that emerge inside one another so that 'clearing' becomes 'cLEARing' on another intertitle. At one moment WS Jr the 5th writes in the notebook which he is almost always seen holding 'Hear Lear' and then adds 'No Thing', but the words interspliced so as to produce the sequence 'Hear No Lear Thing', one word per line. What we hear is indeed no Lear thing. As Lear himself says, though not in this film, 'Does any here know me? This is not Lear' (1.4.185).

Whatever else the film makes difficult and magnificently troubling, it makes emphatically clear that this is not *King Lear* as narrative but instead, as various repeated intertitles suggest, 'An Approach', 'A Study', 'A Clearing', self-defining as a critical activity over the text that is glimpsed (or whatever the auditory equivalent might be) in its aural and visual snatches. Creating the fragments and putting them together for film is of course the activity of editing, a process whose mechanisms, we are told, have been lost in this world. WS Jr the 5th, in voiceover (and it is striking how much of the film's speech is in voiceover), recalls Edgar saying to him that Professor Pluggy, played by Godard himself in a wig of cables as if they were dreadlocks, has 'stayed inside his editing room now for twenty years'. And he continues: 'Editing. That sounded familiar. "What's that?" I asked. But the girl and the boy couldn't remember.'

Virtually at the end of the film, after an intertitle announcing 'The End' and after the opening intertitle about the Cannon Group is shown again, we watch editing as process rather than resulting product. Woody Allen, originally announced as playing the Fool in the film (a role that is to some

extent subsumed into Professor Pluggy's position as commentator as well
as that of WS Jr the 5th), appears at last, playing Mr Alien, whose name was
the last utterance of the (perhaps) dying Professor Pluggy. I have long
hoped that the character name is a result of a typo: Allen becoming Alien.
Allen/Alien is editing with safety pins and sewing film together with needle
and thread, literally suturing the film, then watching film on a Steenbeck
flatbed and speaking not *Lear* but Sonnet 60 with his words part-echoed by
WS Jr the 5th, who, moments before, is seen jumping onto an enormous
heap of unspooled film, a mass of celluloid quite literally on the cutting-
room floor.

After the end of filming came editing in that pre-digital age, just as it
does after writing in the creation of a collection of academic essays. The
three names on our title-page shift from being directors/producers (casting
the volume, creating the outline of a scenario, allowing the contributors to
co-create the volume as screenplay) to being editors/copy-editors. But they
also participate in the writing as contributors themselves, both of the
Introduction and of two of the chapters, just as Godard as Professor
Pluggy appears in his own film.

I do not want to overdo the analogy between film and book but some of
the chapters perform acts of critical analysis similar enough to Godard's for
the argument to work. When, for instance, Samuel Crowl considers how Fool
has appeared in the three great film versions (Brook, Kozintsev and
Kurosawa), Melissa Croteau examines Kurosawa's depiction of the hell that
humans have made of the world in *Ran* and Sarah Hatchuel traces the
problems in filming 'Dover Cliff', each is working on a part of the
Shakespeare text as much as Godard works with only parts of Shakespeare's
play, a text that he, unlike they, may never have read.[4]

While the film most like Godard's is, in some respects, Al Pacino's
Looking for Richard (1996), another film about not filming a Shakespeare
play, the interaction of making and product is also like *King Lear*'s haunting of the making of a theatre production of itself in season three of *Slings
and Arrows*, the subject of Lois Leveen's thinking about how Canada
becomes that which *Slings and Arrows* is producing. And, of course, if
the 'live from' phenomenon has been transforming the relationship
between theatre screen and audience in the last decade, as Rachael
Nicholas charts, Godard changed the relationship between the play and
filmmaking in ways even more radical in his redefinition of the place of
writing, editing, image-making in the Shakespeare movie.

Where we used only to be concerned with films that are unquestionably
'translations to screen' of Shakespeare's play – and might argue long about

whether *Ran* is or is not a Shakespeare film, noting as we did so the cultural variants, with *Ran* more likely to be seen as Shakespeare's in the Anglophone world than in Japan – now we are especially fascinated by spinoffs and citation. If Harold Brighouse's play *Hobson's Choice* (1916) toys with its likeness to *King Lear* as well as to *Cinderella*, then so too do the 1920, 1931 and 1954 film versions, the last and greatest of which Diana Henderson aligns with Sangeeta Datta's 2009 *Life Goes On*. Sometimes such rewritings/rethinkings make clear their links, like Jacob Gordin's *The Yiddish King Lear* (1892), filmed in 1934, and his gender-crossed version, *Mirele Efros* (1898), the former making its *King-Lear*-ness apparent in its title, the latter in its nickname, *The Yiddish Queen Lear*, as Jacek Fabiszak shows. Others are usefully seen as versions that renegotiate with their source-text in terms of genre: well-known adaptations like *The King of Texas* creating *King-Lear*-as-Western or less well-known ones like *Harry and Tonto* forming *King-Lear*-as-road-movie, the subjects of Pierre Kapitaniak's and Douglas Lanier's chapters. We are far past the erstwhile anxiety over fidelity but we start to push at limits when, as with *The Eye of the Storm*, in Victoria Bladen's account, the problem is Shakespeare/Not Shakespeare, not only as the division of scholars' recognitions of which side of the divide a work might be but also in critics' attempts to speak for audiences in defining whether the Learness is widely or narrowly perceived, whether it is a necessary part of the creation of meaning or an incidental feature. No-one watching *Slings and Arrows* could have failed to notice where *King Lear* is present in the narrative of production as well as in the repertory of the Stratford-Festival-lookalike theatre company. But Sylvaine Bataille and Anaïs Pauchet show how the writers of two US television series deliberately attempted to build the play fundamentally but also effectively invisibly into the underpinning of *Boss* and *Empire*.

In such accounts, the scholars are always aware of the problematics of visibility, the extent to which *Lear* is to be noticed as a controlling narrative, against which and through which the construction of a film's narrative is to be unfolded. In Kristian Levring's *The King Is Alive* (2000), one of the three films Courtney Lehmann tests out for their 'Trump Effect', the film's subject as a remembering but also a forgetting of *King Lear* becomes problematized in the multiplyings of Lears and Edgars and Cordelias, as Cartelli and Rowe so well described.[5] More than any of the other films discussed throughout this volume, *The King Is Alive* links strongly to Godard's *King Lear*. As WS Jr the 5th recovers *Lear*, so Henry sees the plight of the stranded tourists as like *Lear*, less as plot than as situation of humanity: 'Some fantastic striptease act of basic human needs. Is man no more than this? It's good old Lear again.'[6] Henry writes out *King Lear* from memory, not entirely accurately,[7] as WS Jr the 5th pieces out the text from his memory and those of others who, as it were, feed him the scraps of *Lear*.

Where next? Predicting the next stages of critical studies is a fairly fruitless task. My guess is that the influence of live theatre broadcasts will shift the pendulum back from the citings/sightings of *King Lear* in adaptations and spinoffs towards the materiality of the process of filming, for it is already apparent that the work on these cinecasts has a central concern with the camerawork and editing to an extent rare in the history of screened Shakespeare.[8] It may also result in a return to, as it were, more direct remediatizations of Shakespeare, back to Brook and Kozintsev, and outwards to recordings of theatre productions that have sat below the horizon of our field of view, such as Wu Hsing-Kuo's adaptation filmed in Taipei in 2006 or André Engel's *Le Roi Lear*, starring Michel Piccoli, filmed in 2007, both released on DVD. And, with luck, there may be a return to Godard's *Lear*, still for me one of the greatest achievements of Shakespeare on screen, the most thrilling study (or approach or clearing) of what it means to be filming a Shakespeare play at all.

Notes

1. The story is widely attributed but always somehow involving Sir John Gielgud: Harley Granville Barker to Gielgud, Donald Wolfit to Gielgud, Gielgud to Michael Hordern, Gielgud to an unnamed young actor, etc.
2. Lianne Habinek's article thanks 'Thomas Bartscherer for providing a copy of Godard's film', a kind of acknowledgement that is not common in Shakespeare film studies; L. Habinek, 'Getting to Page Four of *King Lear* with Jean-Luc Godard', *Shakespeare* (British Shakespeare Association) 9 (2013), 87. Currently copies of an Italian DVD, released in 2009, are available. It's also available on YouTube at www.youtube.com/watch?v=OL7Ii-6Rdpc (accessed 17 May 2019) in a version of the usual low-res kind available there.
3. See https://en.wikipedia.org/wiki/King_Lear_(1987_film) (accessed 17 March 2018).
4. See Habinek, 'Getting to Page Four', 76.
5. T. Cartelli and K. Rowe, 'Surviving Shakespeare: Kristian Levring's *The King Is Alive*' in their *New Wave Shakespeare on Screen* (Cambridge and Malden: Polity Press, 2007), 142–64.
6. My transcription from the 2002 DVD of *The King Is Alive*.
7. See my 'On the Gravy Train: Shakespeare, Memory and Forgetting', in P. Holland (ed.), *Shakespeare, Memory and Performance* (Cambridge: Cambridge University Press, 2006), 207–34.

8. See, for instance, many of the articles in P. Aebischer, S. Greenhalgh and
   L. E. Osborne (eds.), *Shakespeare and the 'Live' Theatre Broadcast Experience*
   (London: Bloomsbury, 2018).

WORKS CITED

Aebischer, P., S. Greenhalgh and L. E. Osborne (eds.), *Shakespeare and the 'Live'
    Theatre Broadcast Experience* (London: Bloomsbury, 2018).
Cartelli, T. and K. Rowe, 'Surviving Shakespeare: Kristian Levring's *The King Is
    Alive*' in their *New Wave Shakespeare on Screen* (Cambridge and Malden:
    Polity Press, 2007), 142–64.
Habinek, L., 'Getting to Page Four of *King Lear* with Jean-Luc Godard',
    Shakespeare (British Shakespeare Association) 9 (2013): 76–90.
Holland, P., 'On the Gravy Train: Shakespeare, Memory and Forgetting', in
    P. Holland (ed.), *Shakespeare, Memory and Performance* (Cambridge:
    Cambridge University Press, 2006), 207–34.

King Lear *on Screen: Select Film-bibliography*

José Ramón Díaz Fernández

The present chapter seeks to provide a selective reference guide to the screen adaptations of *King Lear*. This essay is divided into three sections listing films, television adaptations as well as derivatives and selected citations. In each section, adaptations are classified in chronological order followed by an alphabetical list of relevant critical studies, and a system of cross-references has been designed for those entries making reference to two or more screen adaptations. I have included theatrical productions such as Richard Eyre's *King Lear* (1998) in the television section if there are significant changes between the original stage design and the television programme, and in these cases I have only selected studies making specific reference to the recorded version. As far as the derivatives and citations are concerned, I have only listed those which have been discussed by critics. Unlike previous film-bibliographies in the series, the number of publications on *King Lear* on screen is so large that I have only included references written in English. For additional titles and/or bibliographical entries related to this play on screen, the reader may check the comprehensive online version of the present film-bibliography on the Cambridge University Press website. All electronic addresses were correct at the time of going to press.

1 FILM ADAPTATIONS

1.1 *King Lear.* **Dir. William V. Ranous (USA, 1909)**

1 Ball, Robert Hamilton, 'What, All in Motion? Shakespeare by Vitagraph (1908–1911)', in his *Shakespeare on Silent Film: a Strange Eventful History.* New York: Theatre Arts Books, 1968, 38–60.
2 Buchanan, Judith, '"An Excellent Dumb Discourse": British and American Shakespeare Films, 1899–1916', in her *Shakespeare on Film.* Harlow: Pearson Longman, 2005, 21–48.
3 Buchanan, Judith, 'Corporate Authorship: the Shakespeare Films of the Vitagraph Company of America', in her *Shakespeare on Silent Film: an Excellent Dumb Discourse.* Cambridge: Cambridge University Press, 2009, 105–46.

1.2   *Re Lear*. Dir. Gerolamo Lo Savio (Italy, 1910)

4 Babiak, Peter E. S., 'Silent Shakespeare', in his *Shakespeare Films: a Re-evaluation of 100 Years of Adaptations*. Jefferson: McFarland, 2016, 25–38.

5 Ball, Robert Hamilton, 'Strange Motions: the Continent (1908–1911)', in his *Shakespeare on Silent Film: a Strange Eventful History*. New York: Theatre Arts Books, 1968, 90–134.

6 Coursen, H. R., 'Silents', in his *Shakespeare in Space: Recent Shakespeare Productions on Screen*. New York: Peter Lang, 2002, 95–111.

7 Rothwell, Kenneth S., 'In Search of Nothing: Mapping *King Lear*', in *Shakespeare, the Movie: Popularizing the Plays on Film, TV, and Video*, ed. Lynda E. Boose and Richard Burt. London and New York: Routledge, 1997, 135–47.
See also 3.

1.3   *King Lear*. Dir. Ernest Warde (USA, 1916)

8 Ball, Robert Hamilton, 'These Visions Did Appear: During the War', in his *Shakespeare on Silent Film: a Strange Eventful History*. New York: Theatre Arts Books, 1968, 216–62.

9 Guneratne, Anthony R., 'Featuring the Bard: Frederick Warde's Shakespeare and the Transformation of American Cinema', in his *Shakespeare, Film Studies, and the Visual Cultures of Modernity*. New York and Basingstoke: Palgrave Macmillan, 2008, 95–113.

10 Rothwell, Kenneth S., 'Representing *King Lear* on Screen: from Metatheatre to "Meta-Cinema"', in *Shakespeare and the Moving Image: the Plays on Film and Television*, ed. Anthony Davies and Stanley Wells. Cambridge: Cambridge University Press, 1994, 211–33.
See also 2.

1.4   *King Lear*. Dir. Grigori Kozintsev (USSR, 1970)

11 Aebischer, Pascale, 'En-gendering Violence and Suffering in *King Lear*', in her *Shakespeare's Violated Bodies: Stage and Screen Performance*. Cambridge: Cambridge University Press, 2004, 151–89.

12 Ashby, Richard, 'Crowding out Dover "Cliff" in *Korol Lir*'. *Adaptation* 10 (2017): 210–29.

13 Babiak, Peter E. S., 'Kozintsev', in his *Shakespeare Films: a Re-evaluation of 100 Years of Adaptations*. Jefferson: McFarland, 2016, 84–98.

14 Baker, Christopher, 'Religion in Performance', in his *Religion in the Age of Shakespeare*. Westport and London: Greenwood, 2007, 95–126.

15 Buchman, Lorne M., 'Spatial Multiplicity: Patterns of Viewing in Cinematic Space', in his *Still in Movement: Shakespeare on Screen*. New York and Oxford: Oxford University Press, 1991, 12–32.

16 Buchman, Lorne M., 'Inside-Out: Dynamics of *Mise-en-scène*', in his *Still in Movement: Shakespeare on Screen*. New York and Oxford: Oxford University Press, 1991, 33–51.

17 Buchman, Lorne M., 'Houseless Heads: the Storm of *King Lear* in the Films of Peter Brook and Grigory Kozintsev', in his *Still in Movement: Shakespeare on Screen*. New York and Oxford: Oxford University Press, 1991, 52–63.

18 Buchman, Lorne M., 'Temporal Multiplicity: Patterns of Viewing in Cinematic Time', in his *Still in Movement: Shakespeare on Screen*. New York and Oxford: Oxford University Press, 1991, 107–25.

19 Buhler, Stephen M., 'Gaining in Translation', in his *Shakespeare in the Cinema: Ocular Proof*. Albany: State University of New York Press, 2002, 157–78.

20 Catania, Saviour, '"Darkness Rumbling": Kozintsev's *Karòl Lier* and the Visual Acoustics of Nothing'. *Literature/Film Quarterly* 36 (2008): 85–93.

21 Collick, John, 'Kozintsev's *Hamlet* and *Korol Ler*', in his *Shakespeare, Cinema and Society*. Manchester and New York: Manchester University Press, 1989, 128–48.

22 Coursen, H. R., 'Lear and Cordelia', in his *Shakespearean Performance as Interpretation*. Newark: University of Delaware Press, 1992, 129–39.

23 Davies, Anthony, '*King Lear* on Film', in *'Lear' from Study to Stage: Essays in Criticism*, ed. James Ogden and Arthur H. Scouten. Madison: Fairleigh Dickinson University Press, 1997, 247–66.

24 Dombrovskaia, Olga, '*Hamlet, King Lear* and Their Companions: the Other Side of Film Music', in *Contemplating Shostakovich: Life, Music and Film*, ed. Alexander Ivashkin and Andrew Kirkman. Farnham and Burlington: Ashgate, 2012, 141–64.

25 Etkind, Alexander, 'Mourning the Soviet Victims in a Cosmopolitan Way: Hamlet from Kozintsev to Riazanov'. *Studies in Russian & Soviet Cinema* 5 (2011): 389–409.

26 Gillespie, David, 'Adapting Foreign Classics: Kozintsev's Shakespeare', in *Russian and Soviet Film Adaptations of Literature, 1900–2001: Screening the Word*, ed. Stephen Hutchings and Anat Vernitski. London and New York: RoutledgeCurzon-Taylor and Francis, 2005, 75–88.

27 Griggs, Yvonne, 'On the Road: Reclaiming Grigori Kozinstev's *Korol Lir* (1970)', in her *Shakespeare's 'King Lear': the Relationship between Text and Film*. London: Methuen Drama, 2009, 62–79.

28 Gronsky, Daniel, 'Shakespeare in Translation'. *Film International* 11 (2004): 44–51.

29 Guntner, J. Lawrence, '*Hamlet, Macbeth* and *King Lear* on Film', in *The Cambridge Companion to Shakespeare on Film*, ed. Russell Jackson. 2nd edn. Cambridge: Cambridge University Press, 2007, 120–40.

30 Halio, Jay L., 'The Play in Performance', in his *'King Lear': a Guide to the Play*. Westport and London: Greenwood Press, 2001, 95–115.

31 Hodgdon, Barbara, 'Kozintsev's *King Lear*: Filming a Tragic Poem'. *Literature/Film Quarterly* 5 (1977): 291–8.

32 Hodgdon, Barbara, 'Two *King Lear*: Uncovering the Filmtext'. *Literature/ Film Quarterly* 11 (1983): 143–51.

33 Holland, Peter, 'Two-Dimensional Shakespeare: *King Lear* on Film', in *Shakespeare and the Moving Image: the Plays on Film and Television*, ed. Anthony Davies and Stanley Wells. Cambridge: Cambridge University Press, 1994, 50–68.

34 Jackson, MacDonald P., 'Screening the Tragedies: *King Lear*', in *The Oxford Handbook of Shakespearean Tragedy*, ed. Michael Neill and David Schalkwyk. Oxford: Oxford University Press, 2016, 607–23.

35 Jorgens, Jack J., '*King Lear*: Peter Brook and Grigori Kozintsev', in his *Shakespeare on Film*. 1977, rpt. Lanham and London: University Press of America, 1991, 235–51.

36 Keyishian, Harry, 'Performing Violence in *King Lear*: Edgar's Encounters in 4.6 and 5.3'. *Shakespeare Bulletin* 14.3 (Summer 1996): 36–8.

37 Kozintsev, Grigori, '*Hamlet* and *King Lear*: Stage and Film', in *Shakespeare 1971: Proceedings of the World Shakespeare Congress*, ed. Clifford Leech and J. M. R. Margeson. Toronto and Buffalo: University of Toronto Press, 1972, 190–9.

38 Kozintsev, Grigori, '*King Lear*': the Space of Tragedy: the Diary of a Film Director*. Trans. Mary Mackintosh. Berkeley: University of California Press, 1977.

39 Leaming, Barbara, '*King Lear*', in her *Grigori Kozintsev*. Boston: Twayne, 1980, 119–35.

40 Leggatt, Alexander, 'Grigori Kozintsev', in his *King Lear*. 2nd edn. Manchester and New York: Manchester University Press, 2004, 88–104.

41 Lehmann, Courtney, 'Grigori Kozintsev', in *Welles, Kurosawa, Kozintsev, Zeffirelli*, by Mark Thornton Burnett, Courtney Lehmann, Marguerite H. Rippy and Ramona Wray. London and New York: Bloomsbury, 2013, 92–140.

42 Leonard, Kendra Preston, 'King Lear', in her *Shakespeare, Madness, and Music: Scoring Insanity in Cinematic Adaptations*. Lanham: Scarecrow Press, 2009, 97–115.

43 Leonard, Kendra Preston, 'Edgar', in her *Shakespeare, Madness, and Music: Scoring Insanity in Cinematic Adaptations*. Lanham: Scarecrow Press, 2009, 117–26.

44 Margolies, David, '*King Lear*: Kozintev's Social Translation', in *Shifting the Scene: Shakespeare in European Culture*, ed. Ladina Bezzola Lambert and Balz Engler. Newark: University of Delaware Press, 2004, 230–8.

45 Moore, Tiffany Ann Conroy, '*King Lear* Revisited in the Brezhnev Era: Kozintsev's 1970 Film Adaptation', in her *Kozintsev's Shakespeare Films: Russian Political Protest in 'Hamlet' and 'King Lear'*. Jefferson and London: McFarland, 2012, 136–77.

46 Parker, R. B., 'The Use of *Mise-en-Scène* in Three Films of *King Lear*'. *Shakespeare Quarterly* 42 (1991): 75–90.

47 Radcliff-Umstead, Douglas, 'Order and Disorder in Kozintsev's *King Lear*'. *Literature/Film Quarterly* 11 (1983): 266–73.

48 Riley, John, 'Endgame (1964–1975): *Hamlet* to *King Lear*', in his *Dmitri Shostakovich: a Life in Film*. London and New York: I. B. Tauris, 2005, 94–107.

49 Rothwell, Kenneth S., 'Other Shakespeares: Translation and Expropriation', in his *A History of Shakespeare on Screen: a Century of Film and Television*. 2nd edn. Cambridge: Cambridge University Press, 2004, 160–91.

50 Rothwell, Kenneth S., '*King Lear*'. *Cineaste* 32.3 (Summer 2007): 80–2.

51 Ryle, Simon, 'Something from Nothing: *King Lear* and Film Space', in his *Shakespeare, Cinema and Desire: Adaptation and Other Futures of Shakespeare's Language*. New York and Basingstoke: Palgrave Macmillan, 2014, 36–84.

52 Sanders, Julie, 'Symphonic Film Scores', in her *Shakespeare and Music: Afterlives and Borrowings*. Cambridge and Malden: Polity Press, 2007, 135–58.

53 Schmalz, Wayne, 'Pictorial Imagery in Kozintsev's *King Lear*'. *Literature/Film Quarterly* 13 (1985): 85–94.

54 Sokolyansky, Mark, 'Grigori Kozintsev's *Hamlet* and *King Lear*', in *The Cambridge Companion to Shakespeare on Film*, ed. Russell Jackson. 2nd edn. Cambridge: Cambridge University Press, 2007, 203–15.

55 Thomas, Alfred, '"A Dog's Obeyed in Office": Subverting Authority in Shakespeare's *King Lear* and Grigori Kozintsev's *Korol' Lir*', in his *Shakespeare, Dissent, and the Cold War*. Basingstoke and New York: Palgrave Macmillan, 2014, 97–140.

56 Troncale, Joseph, 'The War and Kozintsev's Films *Hamlet* and *King Lear*', in *The Red Screen: Politics, Society, Art in Soviet Cinema*, ed. Anna Lawton. London and New York: Routledge, 1992, 193–210.

57 Welsh, James M., 'To See It Feelingly: *King Lear* through Russian Eyes'. *Literature/Film Quarterly* 4 (1976): 153–8.

58 Willson, Robert F., Jr, 'Lear and Dispossession: the Peopled Space of Kozintsev's *King Lear*'. *Shakespeare Bulletin* 6.3 (May/June 1988): 20–2.

59 Willson, Robert F., Jr, 'Yuri Yarvet's Lear: the Face of Tragedy', in *Images of Shakespeare: Proceedings of the Third Congress of the International Shakespeare Association, 1986*, ed. Werner Habicht, D. J. Palmer and Roger Pringle. Newark: University of Delaware Press, 1988, 251–7.

60 Womack, Kenneth, 'Assessing the Rhetoric of Performance Criticism in Three Variant Soviet Texts of *King Lear*'. *Yearbook of Comparative and General Literature* 41 (1993): 149–59.

61 Wood, Michael, 'The Languages of Cinema', in *Nation, Language, and the Ethics of Translation*, ed. Sandra Bermann and Michael Wood. Princeton and Oxford: Princeton University Press, 2005, 79–88.

62 Yutkevitch, Sergei, 'The Conscience of the King: Kozintsev's *King Lear*'. *Sight and Sound* 40 (1970–1971): 192–6.
    See also 7, 10.

1.5 *King Lear*. Dir. Peter Brook (Great Britain and Denmark, 1971)

63 Acker, Paul, 'Conventions for Dialogue in Peter Brook's *King Lear*'. *Literature/Film Quarterly* 8 (1980): 219–24.

64 Babiak, Peter E. S., 'Or Image of That Horror: the Apocalyptic Visions of Peter Brook and Akira Kurosawa', in *The Silk Road of Adaptation: Transformations across Disciplines and Cultures*, ed. Laurence Raw. Newcastle: Cambridge Scholars Publishing, 2013, 122–31.

65 Babiak, Peter E. S., 'Kott, Brook, Richardson and Polanski', in his *Shakespeare Films: a Re-evaluation of 100 Years of Adaptations*. Jefferson: McFarland, 2016, 114–23.

66 Berlin, Normand, 'Peter Brook's Interpretation of *King Lear*: "Nothing Will Come of Nothing"'. *Literature/Film Quarterly* 5 (1977): 299–303.

67 Brook, Peter, 'Filming *King Lear*', in his *The Shifting Point: Theatre, Film, Opera 1946–1987*. New York: Harper & Row, 1987, 203–6.

68 Buchman, Lorne M., 'Local Habitations: the Dialectics of Filmic and Theatrical Space', in his *Still in Movement: Shakespeare on Screen*. New York and Oxford: Oxford University Press, 1991, 84–106.

69 Buhler, Stephen, 'Transgressive, in Theory', in his *Shakespeare in the Cinema: Ocular Proof*. Albany: State University of New York Press, 2002, 125–56.

70 Cartmell, Deborah, 'Shakespeare, Film and Violence: Doing Violence to Shakespeare', in her *Interpreting Shakespeare on Screen*. Basingstoke: Macmillan, 2000, 1–20.

71 Chaplin, William, 'Our Darker Purpose: Peter Brook's *King Lear*'. *Arion* ns 1 (1973): 168–87.

72 Davies, Anthony, 'Peter Brook's *King Lear* and Akira Kurosawa's *Throne of Blood*', in his *Filming Shakespeare's Plays: the Adaptations of Laurence Olivier, Orson Welles, Peter Brook and Akira Kurosawa*. Cambridge: Cambridge University Press, 1988, 143–66.

73 Egan, Gabriel, 'Showing versus Telling: Shakespeare's *Ekphraseis*, Visual Absences, and the Cinema', in *Talking Shakespeare: Shakespeare into the Millennium*, ed. Deborah Cartmell and Michael Scott. Basingstoke and New York: Palgrave, 2001, 168–86.

74 Eidsvik, Charles, '*King Lear* and the Theater of Cruelty', in his *Cineliteracy: Film among the Arts*. New York: Random House, 1978, 257–62.

75 Gilman, Todd S., 'The Textual Fabric of Peter Brook's *King Lear*: "Holes" in Cinema, Screenplay, and Playtext'. *Literature/Film Quarterly* 20 (1992): 294–300.

76 Griggs, Yvonne, 'Peter Brook's *King Lear* (1971): "A Hollywood Showman's Nightmare?"', in her *Shakespeare's 'King Lear': the Relationship between Text and Film*. London: Methuen Drama, 2009, 41–62.

77 Harris, Laurilyn J., 'Peter Brook's *King Lear*: Aesthetic Achievement or Far Side of the Moon?' *Theatre Research International* 11 (1986): 223–39.

78 Holland, Peter, 'Peter Brook', in *Brook, Hall, Ninagawa, Lepage*, ed. Peter Holland. London and New York: Bloomsbury, 2013, 7–46.

79 Jackson, Russell, 'People', in his *Shakespeare and the English-speaking Cinema*. Oxford: Oxford University Press, 2014, 36–63.

80 Johnson, William, [Untitled.] *Film Quarterly* 25.3 (Spring 1972): 41–8.

81 Leggatt, Alexander, 'Peter Brook', in his *King Lear*. 2nd edn. Manchester and New York: Manchester University Press, 2004, 105–17.

82 Mullin, Michael, 'Peter Brook's *King Lear*: Stage and Screen'. *Literature/Film Quarterly* 11 (1983): 190–6.

83 Mullin, Michael, 'Peter Brook's *King Lear*: a Reassessment', in *Screen Shakespeare*, ed. Michael Skovmand. Aarhus: Aarhus University Press, 1994, 54–63.

84 Reddington, John, 'Film, Play and Idea'. *Literature/Film Quarterly* 1 (1973): 367–71.

85 Rothwell, Kenneth S., 'Classic Film Versions of Shakespeare's Tragedies: a Mirror for the Times', in *A Companion to Shakespeare's Works*, vol. 1: *The Tragedies*, ed. Richard Dutton and Jean E. Howard. Malden and Oxford: Blackwell, 2003, 241–61.

86 Rothwell, Kenneth S., 'Shakespeare Movies in the Age of Angst', in his *A History of Shakespeare on Screen: a Century of Film and Television*. 2nd edn. Cambridge: Cambridge University Press, 2004, 136–59.

87 Rozett, Martha Tuck, 'The Peter Brook-Paul Scofield *King Lear*: Revisiting the Film Version'. *Shakespeare Bulletin* 19.1 (Winter 2001): 40–2.

88 Rutter, Carol Chillington, 'Body Parts or Parts for Bodies: Speculating on Cordelia', in her *Enter the Body: Women and Representation on Shakespeare's Stage*. London and New York: Routledge, 2001, 1–26.

89 Saunders, John, '"The promis'd end? or image of that horror?": Two Different Ways of Looking at the Ending of *King Lear*', in *Critical Essays on 'King Lear'*, ed. Linda Cookson. Harlow: Longman, 1988, 120–9.

90 Saunders, J. G., '"Apparent Perversities": Text and Subtext in the Construction of the Role of Edgar in Brook's Film of *King Lear*'. *Review of English Studies* ns 47.187 (1996): 317–30.

91 'Shakespeare in the Cinema: a Film Directors' Symposium with Peter Brook, Sir Peter Hall, Richard Loncraine, Baz Luhrmann, [Trevor Nunn,] Oliver Parker, Roman Polanski and Franco Zeffirelli'. *Cineaste* 24.1 (1998): 48–55.

92 Shaw, William P., 'Violence and Vision in Polanski's *Macbeth* and Brook's *Lear*'. *Literature/Film Quarterly* 14 (1986): 211–13.

93 Teller, Joseph R., 'The (Dis)possession of Lear's Two Bodies: Madness, Demystification, and Domestic Space in Peter Brook's *King Lear*'. *Borrowers and Lenders: the Journal of Shakespeare and Appropriation* 5.1 (Spring/Summer 2010): www.borrowers.uga.edu/782421/show (accessed 17 May 2019).

94 Viguers, Susan, 'Costuming as Interpretation: the Elliott/Olivier and the Brook/Scofield *King Lear*'. *Shakespeare Bulletin* 12.2 (Spring 1994): 44–6.

95 Wilds, Lillian, 'One *King Lear* for Our Time: a Bleak Film Version by Peter Brook'. *Literature/Film Quarterly* 4 (1976): 159–64.
See also 7, 10, 11, 14, 17, 18, 22, 23, 29, 30, 32, 33, 34, 35, 36, 42, 43, 44, 46, 51.

1.6   *Ran*. Dir. Akira Kurosawa (Japan and France, 1985)

96 Babiak, Peter E. S., 'Kurosawa', in his *Shakespeare Films: a Re-evaluation of 100 Years of Adaptations*. Jefferson: McFarland, 2016, 69–83.

97   Baker, Rob, 'Fools on a Precipice'. *Parabola: The Magazine of Myth and Tradition* 11.4 (Nov. 1986): 90–5, 98.
98   Bannon, Christopher J., 'Man and Nature in *Ran* and *King Lear*'. *New Orleans Review* 18.4 (Winter 1991): 5–11.
99   Brown, Eric C., 'Akira Kurosawa'. *Shakespeare Bulletin* 34 (2016): 496–9.
100 Buchanan, Judith, 'Cross-cultural Narrative Rhymes: the Shakespeare Films of Akira Kurosawa', in her *Shakespeare on Film*. Harlow: Pearson Longman, 2005, 71–89.
101 Burnett, Mark Thornton, 'Akira Kurosawa', in *Welles, Kurosawa, Kozintsev, Zeffirelli*, by Mark Thornton Burnett, Courtney Lehmann, Marguerite H. Rippy and Ramona Wray. London and New York: Bloomsbury, 2013, 54–91.
102 Catania, Saviour, 'Wailing Woodwind Wild: the Noh Transcription of Shakespeare's Silent Sounds in Kurosawa's *Ran*'. *Literature/Film Quarterly* 34 (2006): 85–92.
103 Collick, John, 'Kurosawa's *Kumonosu jo* and *Ran*', in his *Shakespeare, Cinema and Society*. Manchester and New York: Manchester University Press, 1989, 166–87.
104 Conrad, Peter, 'Expatriating Lear', in his *To Be Continued: Four Stories and Their Survival*. Oxford: Clarendon Press, 1995, 95–152.
105 Cowie, Peter, 'The Literary Connection', in his *Akira Kurosawa: Master of Cinema*. New York: Rizzoli, 2010, 186–231.
106 Crowl, Samuel, 'The Bow Is Bent and Drawn: Kurosawa's *Ran* and the Shakespearean Arrow of Desire'. *Literature/Film Quarterly* 22 (1994): 109–16.
107 Davis, Darrell William, 'Other Manifestations of the Monumental Style', in his *Picturing Japaneseness: Monumental Style, National Identity, Japanese Film*. New York: Columbia University Press, 1996, 219–49.
108 Dawson, Anthony, 'Reading Kurosawa Reading Shakespeare', in *A Concise Companion to Shakespeare on Screen*, ed. Diana E. Henderson. Malden and Oxford: Blackwell, 2006, 155–75.
109 Diniz, Thaïs Flores Nogueira, '*King Lear*'s Filmic Adaptation: a Chaos?' *Canadian Review of Comparative Literature/Revue Canadienne de Littérature Comparée* 23 (1996): 775–80.
110 Dodson-Robinson, Eric, 'Karma, Revenge, Apocalypse: *Ran*'s Violent Victim-Agent through Japanese and Western Contexts'. *Shakespeare Bulletin* 31 (2013): 233–55.
111 Geist, Kathe, 'Late Kurosawa: *Kagemusha* and *Ran*'. *Post Script: Essays in Film and the Humanities* 12.1 (Fall 1992): 26–36.
112 Goodwin, James, 'Tragedy without Heroes', in his *Akira Kurosawa and Intertextual Cinema*. Baltimore and London: Johns Hopkins University Press, 1994, 165–216.
113 Griggs, Yvonne, 'Chaos on the Western Frontier: Akira Kurosawa's *Ran* (1985)', in her *Shakespeare's 'King Lear': the Relationship between Text and Film*. London: Methuen Drama, 2009, 79–99.
114 Grilli, Peter, 'Kurosawa Directs a Cinematic *Lear*', in *Akira Kurosawa: Interviews*, ed. Bert Cardullo. Jackson: University Press of Mississippi, 2008, 125–30.

115 Hapgood, Robert, '*Ran* from Screenplay to Film'. *Shakespeare Bulletin* 10.3 (Summer 1992): 37–8.

116 Hapgood, Robert, 'Kurosawa's Shakespeare Films: *Throne of Blood, The Bad Sleep Well*, and *Ran*', in *Shakespeare and the Moving Image: the Plays on Film and Television*, ed. Anthony Davies and Stanley Wells. Cambridge: Cambridge University Press, 1994, 234–49.

117 Hirano, Kyoko, 'The Director, Kurosawa: the Emperor of Japanese Cinema on Designing *Ran*'. *Theatre Crafts* 20.2 (Feb. 1986): 88–93.

118 Hirano, Kyoko, 'Making Films for All the People: an Interview with Akira Kurosawa', in *Akira Kurosawa: Interviews*, ed. Bert Cardullo. Jackson: University Press of Mississippi, 2008, 139–44.

119 Hoile, Christopher, '*King Lear* and Kurosawa's *Ran*: Splitting, Doubling, Distancing'. *Pacific Coast Philology* 22 (1987): 29–34.

120 Howlett, Kathy, 'Breaking the Frame: Akira Kurosawa's *Ran*', in her *Framing Shakespeare on Film*. Athens: Ohio University Press, 2000, 115–27.

121 Johansen, Ib, 'Visible Darkness: Shakespeare's *King Lear* and Kurosawa's *Ran*', in *Screen Shakespeare*, ed. Michael Skovmand. Aarhus: Aarhus University Press, 1994, 64–86.

122 Jortner, David, 'The Stability of the Heart amidst Fields of Green: an Ecocritical Reading of Kurosawa Akira's *Ran*'. *Post Script: Essays in Film and the Humanities* 20.1 (Fall 2000): 82–91.

123 Kane, Julie, 'From the Baroque to *Wabi*: Translating Animal Imagery from Shakespeare's *King Lear* to Kurosawa's *Ran*'. *Literature/Film Quarterly* 25 (1997): 146–51.

124 Kehr, Dave, 'Samurai *Lear*'. *American Film* 10.10 (Sept. 1985): 20–6.

125 Keller, Jocelyn and Wolfram R. Keller, '"Now is the time": Shakespeare's Medieval Temporalities in Akira Kurosawa's *Ran*', in *The Medieval Motion Picture: the Politics of Adaptation*, ed. Andrew James Johnston, Margitta Rouse and Philipp Hinz. New York and Basingstoke: Palgrave Macmillan, 2014, 19–40.

126 Kishi, Tetsuo and Graham Bradshaw, 'Shakespeare and Japanese Film: Kurosawa Akira', in their *Shakespeare in Japan*. London and New York: Continuum, 2005, 126–45.

127 Kott, Jan, '*Ran*, or the End of the World', in his *The Bottom Translation: Marlowe and Shakespeare and the Carnival Tradition*. Trans. Daniela Miedzyrzecka and Lillian Vallee. Evanston: Northwestern University Press, 1987, 143–51.

128 Kurosawa, Akira, Hideo Oguni and Ide Masato, *Ran*. Trans. Tadashi Shishido. Boston and London: Shambhala, 1986.

129 Leggatt, Alexander, 'Cross-cultural Dialogue: Akira Kurosawa's *Ran*', in his *King Lear*. 2nd edn. Manchester and New York: Manchester University Press, 2004, 169–99.

130 Linton, Joan Pong, 'Kurosawa's *Ran* (1985) and *King Lear*: Towards a Conversation on Historical Responsibility'. *Quarterly Review of Film and Video* 23 (2006): 341–51.

131 Manheim, Michael, 'The Function of Battle Imagery in Kurosawa's Histories and the *Henry V* Films'. *Literature/Film Quarterly* 22 (1994): 129–35.

132 McDonald, Keiko, 'The Noh Convention in *The Throne of Blood* and *Ran*', in her *Japanese Classical Theater in Films*. Rutherford: Fairleigh Dickinson University Press, 1994, 125–44.

133 Nardo, Anna K., 'Dialogue in Shakespearean Offshoots'. *Literature/Film Quarterly* 34 (2006): 104–12.

134 Nordin, Kenneth D., 'Buddhist Symbolism in Akira Kurosawa's *Ran*: a Counterpoint to Human Chaos'. *Asian Cinema* 16 (2005): 242–54.

135 Parker, Brian, '*Ran* and the Tragedy of History'. *University of Toronto Quarterly* 55 (1986): 412–23.

136 Perret, Marion D., 'Caveat Lector: the Screenplay of *Ran*'. *Shakespeare on Film Newsletter* 13.1 (Dec. 1988): 1, 6.

137 Phillips, Stephen J., 'Akira Kurosawa's *Ran*', in *'Lear' from Study to Stage: Essays in Criticism*, ed. James Ogden and Arthur H. Scouten. Madison: Fairleigh Dickinson University Press, 1997, 267–77.

138 Powers, John, 'Kurosawa: an Audience with the Emperor', in *Akira Kurosawa: Interviews*, ed. Bert Cardullo. Jackson: University Press of Mississippi, 2008, 131–8.

139 Prince, Stephen, 'Years of Transition', in his *The Warrior's Camera: the Cinema of Akira Kurosawa*. Revised and expanded edn. Princeton: Princeton University Press, 1999, 250–91.

140 Richie, Donald, '*Ran*', in his *The Films of Akira Kurosawa*. 3rd expanded edn. Berkeley and Los Angeles: University of California Press, 1996, 214–19.

141 Ryan, Bartholomew, 'Deception, Nature and Nihilism in Politics: *King Lear* and Kurosawa's *Ran*', in *Politics Otherwise: Shakespeare as Social and Political Critique*, ed. Leonidas Donskis and J. D. Mininger. Amsterdam and New York: Rodopi, 2012, 69–84.

142 Serper, Zvika, 'Blood Visibility/Invisibility in Kurosawa's *Ran*'. *Literature/Film Quarterly* 28 (2000): 149–54.

143 Serper, Zvika, 'The Bloodied Sacred Pine Tree: a Dialectical Depiction of Death in Kurosawa's *Throne of Blood* and *Ran*'. *Journal of Film and Video* 52.2 (Summer 2000): 13–27.

144 Serper, Zvika, 'Lady Kaede in Kurosawa's *Ran*: Verbal and Visual Characterization through Animal Traditions'. *Japan Forum* 13 (2001): 145–58.

145 Sheplock, Sarah, '"Contending with fretful elements": Shakespeare, Kurosawa and the *Benshi*. On Film Adaptation'. *Anglistica* 15.2 (2011): 1–14.

146 Takakuwa, Yoko, '(En)Gendering Desire in Performance: *King Lear*, Akira Kurosawa's *Ran*, Tadashi Suzuki's *The Tale of Lear*', in *Shakespeare and His Contemporaries in Performance*, ed. Edward J. Esche. Aldershot and Burlington: Ashgate, 2000, 35–49.

147 Thompson, Ann, 'Kurosawa's *Ran*: Reception and Interpretation'. *East-West Film Journal* 3.2 (June 1989): 1–13.

148 Willson, Robert F., Jr, '*Ran* and *King Lear*: Adaptation as Interpretation'. *Deutsche Shakespeare-Gesellschaft West: Jahrbuch* (1987): 114–16.

149 Wing, Susan L., '*King Lear* "Translated": a Cross-Cultural Psychoanalytic Reading of Kurosawa's Ran', in *Proceedings of the Seventh International Conference on Psychology and Literature*. Lisbon: Instituto Superior de Psicologia Aplicada, 1991, 169–75.

150 Yamamoto, Hiroshi, 'On Kurosawa's *King Lear*'. *Renaissance Bulletin* 12 (1985): 41–5.

151 Yong Li Lan, 'Spectacle and Shakespeare on Film', in *Shakespeare's World/World Shakespeares: the Selected Proceedings of the International Shakespeare Association World Congress, Brisbane, 2006*, ed. Richard Fotheringham, Christa Jansohn and R. S. White. Newark: University of Delaware Press, 2008, 182–92.

152 Yoshimoto, Mitsuhiro, '*Ran*', in his *Kurosawa: Film Studies and Japanese Cinema*. Durham, NC: Duke University Press, 2000, 355–8.

See also 19, 28, 29, 34, 42, 43, 46, 49, 51, 52, 61, 64.

1.7 *King Lear*. Dir. Brian Blessed (Great Britain, 1999)

See 34.

2 TELEVISION ADAPTATIONS

2.1 *King Lear*. Dir. Peter Brook (CBS, 1953)

153 Coursen, H. R., 'Editing the Script', in his *Watching Shakespeare on Television*. Rutherford: Fairleigh Dickinson University Press, 1993, 93–104.

154 Griffin, Alice, 'Shakespeare through the Camera's Eye 1953–1954'. *Shakespeare Quarterly* 6 (1955): 63–6.

155 Howard, Tony, 'When Peter Met Orson: the 1953 CBS *King Lear*', in *Shakespeare, the Movie: Popularizing the Plays on Film, TV, and Video*, ed. Lynda E. Boose and Richard Burt. London and New York: Routledge, 1997, 121–34.

156 Rippy, Marguerite H., 'Orson Welles', in *Welles, Kurosawa, Kozintsev, Zeffirelli*, by Mark Thornton Burnett, Courtney Lehmann, Marguerite H. Rippy and Ramona Wray. London and New York: Bloomsbury, 2013, 7–53.

157 Rosenberg, Marvin, 'Shakespeare on TV: an Optimistic Survey', in *Shakespeare on Television: an Anthology of Essays and Reviews*, ed. J. C. Bulman and H. R. Coursen. Hanover and London: University Press of New England, 1988, 85–91.

158 Wadsworth, Frank W., '"Sound and Fury"–*King Lear* on Television'. *Quarterly of Film, Radio, and Television* 8 (1954): 254–68.

See also 7, 10, 77, 89.

2.2 *King Lear*. Dir. Tony Davenall (Thames Television, 1974)

See 23.

2.3   *King Lear*. Dir. Jonathan Miller (BBC, 1975)

159   Miller, Jonathan, 'Subsequent Performances II: iv', in his *Subsequent Performances*. London and Boston: Faber and Faber, 1986, 119–53.

2.4   *King Lear*. Dir. Jonathan Miller (BBC, 1982)

160   Cook, Hardy M., 'Two *Lears* for Television: an Exploration of Televisual Strategies'. *Literature/Film Quarterly* 14 (1986): 179–86.
161   Coursen, H. R., 'Edmund's Nature', in his *Shakespearean Performance as Interpretation*. Newark: University of Delaware Press, 1992, 122–8.
162   Fenwick, Henry, 'The Production', in *'King Lear': the BBC TV Shakespeare*, ed. Peter Alexander et al. London: British Broadcasting Corporation, 1983, 19–34.
163   Leggatt, Alexander, 'Jonathan Miller and Michael Hordern', in his *King Lear*. 2nd edn. Manchester and New York: Manchester University Press, 2004, 118–31.
164   Lusardi, James P. and June Schlueter, *Reading Shakespeare in Performance: 'King Lear'*. Rutherford: Fairleigh Dickinson University Press, 1991.
165   Schlueter, June, 'Staging the Promised End', in her *Dramatic Closure: Reading the End*. Madison: Fairleigh Dickinson University Press, 1995, 115–23.
166   Willis, Susan, 'Jonathan Miller: Producer and Director', in her *The BBC Shakespeare Plays: Making the Televised Canon*. Chapel Hill and London: University of North Carolina Press, 1991, 107–34.
167   Worthen, William B., 'The Player's Eye: Shakespeare on Television'. *Comparative Drama* 18 (1984): 193–202.
       See also 7, 10, 22, 23, 34, 36, 70, 89.

2.5   *King Lear*. Dir. Michael Elliott (Channel Four, 1983)

168   Davies, Anthony, 'Revisiting the Olivier *King Lear* on Television', in *Shakespeare on Screen: Television Shakespeare: Essays in Honour of Michèle Willems*, ed. Sarah Hatchuel and Nathalie Vienne-Guerrin. Mont-Saint-Aignan: Publications des Universités de Rouen et du Havre, 2008, 79–90.
169   Gibińska, Marta, 'Olivier's *King Lear* and the Problem of Naturalistic Mimesis in Modern Media', in *Reception of the Classics in Modern Theatre: Proceedings of Kraków-Bochum Symposium in Theatre Studies, Kraków, 21–23 May 1991*, ed. Marta Gibińska. Cracow: Towarzystwo Autorów i Wydawców Prac Naukowych Universitas, 1991, 57–72.
170   Kimbrough, R. Alan, 'Olivier's *Lear* and the Limits of Video', in *Shakespeare on Television: an Anthology of Essays and Reviews*, ed. J. C. Bulman and H. R. Coursen. Hanover and London: University Press of New England, 1988, 115–22.
171   Leggatt, Alexander, 'Laurence Olivier', in his *King Lear*. 2nd edn. Manchester and New York: Manchester University Press, 2004, 132–43.

172 Mebane, John S., 'Olivier's *King Lear* and the "Feminine" Virtues in Shakespearean Tragedy'. *Shakespeare Yearbook* 3 (1992): 143–66.

173 Millard, Barbara, 'Husbanded with Modesty: Shakespeare on TV'. *Shakespeare Bulletin* 4.3 (May/June 1986): 19–22.

174 Occhiogrosso, Frank, '"Give Me Thy Hand": Manual Gesture in the Elliott-Olivier *King Lear*'. *Shakespeare Bulletin* 2.9 (May/June 1984): 16–19.

175 Orbison, Tucker, 'The Stone and the Oak: Olivier's TV Film of *King Lear*'. *CEA Critic* 47.1–2 (Fall and Winter 1984): 67–77.

176 Rothwell, Kenneth S., 'Laurence Olivier Directs Shakespeare', in his *A History of Shakespeare on Screen: a Century of Film and Television*. 2nd edn. Cambridge: Cambridge University Press, 2004, 47–68.
See also 7, 10, 22, 23, 33, 34, 36, 70, 94, 160, 161, 164, 165, 167.

2.6 *King Lear.* Dir. Richard Eyre (BBC, 1998)

177 Coursen, H. R., 'Shakespeare on Television: Four Recent Productions', in his *Shakespeare in Space: Recent Shakespeare Productions on Screen*. New York: Peter Lang, 2002, 53–70.

178 Leggatt, Alexander, 'Ian Holm and Richard Eyre', in his *King Lear*. 2nd edn. Manchester and New York: Manchester University Press, 2004, 144–68.

179 Rothwell, Kenneth S., 'Shakespeare in Love, in Love with Shakespeare: the Adoration after the Millennium', in his *A History of Shakespeare on Screen: a Century of Film and Television*. 2nd edn. Cambridge: Cambridge University Press, 2004, 248–74.
See also 11, 30, 70.

2.7 *King Lear.* Dir. Trevor Nunn and Chris Hunt (Channel Four, 2008)

180 Coursen, H. R., 'Three Recent Productions', in his *Contemporary Shakespeare Production*. New York: Peter Lang, 2010, 160–72.

2.8 *King Lear.* Dir. Richard Eyre (BBC, 2018)

3   DERIVATIVES AND CITATIONS

3.1 *Le Roi Lear au village.* Dir. Louis Feuillade (France, 1911)

181 Rowe, Katherine, 'Medium-Specificity and Other Critical Scripts for Screen Shakespeare', in *Alternative Shakespeares 3*, ed. Diana E. Henderson. London and New York: Routledge, 2008, 34–53.
See also 5.

3.2   *House of Strangers*. Dir. Joseph L. Mankiewicz (USA, 1949)

182   Coursen, H. R., '*King Lear*', in his *Shakespeare Translated: Derivatives on Film and TV*. New York: Peter Lang, 2005, 115–31.
183   Griggs, Yvonne, 'Displacing the Patriarchal Family: Joseph Mankiewicz's *House of Strangers* (1949)', in her *Shakespeare's 'King Lear': the Relationship between Text and Film*. London: Methuen Drama, 2009, 121–6.

3.3   *Tokyo Story*. Dir. Yasujiro Ozu (Japan, 1953)

184   Oya, Reiko, 'Filming "The Weight of This Sad Time": Yasujiro Ozu's Rereading of *King Lear* in *Tokyo Story* (1953)'. *Shakespeare Survey* 66 (2013): 55–66.

3.4   *Broken Lance*. Dir. Edward Dmytryk (USA, 1954)

185   Griggs, Yvonne, '*King Lear* as Western Elegy: Edward Dmytryk's *Broken Lance* (1954)', in her *Shakespeare's 'King Lear': the Relationship between Text and Film*. London: Methuen Drama, 2009, 100–10.
186   Kliman, Bernice W., '*Broken Lance* Is Not *Lear*'. *Shakespeare on Film Newsletter* 2.1 (Dec. 1977): 3.
187   Pendleton, Thomas A., 'The Return of *The Broken Lance*'. *Shakespeare on Film Newsletter* 3.1 (Dec. 1978): 3.
188   Willson, Robert F., Jr, 'Selected Offshoots: Shakespeare at War, on Broadway, in the Mob, in Space, and on the Range', in his *Shakespeare in Hollywood, 1929–1956*. Madison and Teaneck: Fairleigh Dickinson University Press, 2000, 74–129. *See also* 104, 182.

3.5   *Theatre of Blood*. Dir. Douglas Hickox (Great Britain, 1973)

189   Ardolino, Frank, 'Metadramatic Grand Guignol in *Theater of Blood*'. *Shakespeare on Film Newsletter* 15.2 (Apr. 1991): 9.
190   Gearhart, Stephannie S., '"Only he would have the temerity to rewrite Shakespeare": Douglas Hickox's *Theatre of Blood* as Adaptation'. *Literature/Film Quarterly* 39 (2011): 116–27.
191   Holdefer, Charles, 'Bad Shakespeare: Adapting a Tradition', in *Screening Text: Critical Perspectives on Film Adaptation*, ed. Shannon Wells-Lassagne and Ariane Hudelet. Jefferson and London: McFarland, 2013, 197–206.
192   Hutchings, Peter, 'Theatres of Blood: Shakespeare and the Horror Film', in *Gothic Shakespeares*, ed. John Drakakis and Dale Townshend. London and New York: Routledge, 2008, 153–66.
193   Loiselle, André, '*Cinéma du Grand Guignol*: Theatricality in the Horror Film', in *Stages of Reality: Theatricality in Cinema*, ed. André Loiselle and Jeremy Maron. Toronto: University of Toronto Press, 2012, 55–80.
194   Lowe, Victoria, '"Stages of Performance": Adaptation and Intermediality in *Theatre of Blood* (1973)'. *Adaptation* 3 (2010): 99–111.

195 Pendleton, Thomas A., 'What [?] Price [?] Shakespeare [?]' *Literature/Film Quarterly* 29 (2001): 135–46.
196 Tibbetts, John C., 'Backstage with the Bard: Or, Building a Better Mousetrap', in *The Encyclopedia of Stage Plays into Film*, ed. John C. Tibbetts and James M. Welsh. New York: Facts on File, 2001, 541–70.
  See also 70.

3.6   *Harry and Tonto.* Dir. Paul Mazursky (USA, 1974)

197 Schoenbaum, S., 'Looking for Shakespeare', in *Shakespeare's Craft: Eight Lectures*, ed. Philip H. Highfill. Carbondale: Southern Illinois University Press for George Washington University, 1982, 156–77.
198 Wasson, Sam, 'Harry and Tonto', in his *Paul on Mazursky*. Middletown: Wesleyan University Press, 2011, 77–88.
199 Wasson, Sam, 'Josh on Mazursky', in his *Paul on Mazursky*. Middletown: Wesleyan University Press, 2011, 89–92.

3.7   *36 Chowringhee Lane.* Dir. Aparna Sen (India, 1981)

200 Burt, Richard, 'All That Remains of Shakespeare in Indian Film', in *Shakespeare in Asia: Contemporary Performance*, ed. Dennis Kennedy and Yong Li Lan. Cambridge: Cambridge University Press, 2010, 73–108.
201 Cassity, Kathleen J., 'Emerging from Shadows: the "Unhomed" Anglo-Indian of *36 Chowringhee Lane*'. *International Journal of Anglo-Indian Studies* 6 (2001): home.alphalink.com.au/~agilbert/chowri-1.html (accessed 17 May 2019).
202 García-Periago, Rosa M., 'English Shakespeares in Indian Cinema: *36 Chowringhee Lane* and *The Last Lear*'. *Borrowers and Lenders: the Journal of Shakespeare and Appropriation* 9.2 (Fall/Winter 2015): www.borrowers.uga.edu/1634/show (accessed 17 May 2019).

3.8   *The Dresser.* Dir. Peter Yates (Great Britain, 1983)

203 Greenberg, Harvey R., '*The Dresser*: Played to Death'. *Psychoanalytic Review* 72 (1985): 347–52.
204 Meyer-Dinkgräfe, Daniel, 'From Theatre to Film: Ronald Harwood's *The Dresser*'. *Shakespeare Bulletin* 8.3 (Summer 1990): 37–8.
  See also 133.

3.9   *King Real and the Hoodlums.* Dir. John Fox (Great Britain, 1983)

205 Bennett, Susan, 'Production and Proliferation: Seventeen Lears', in her *Performing Nostalgia: Shifting Shakespeare and the Contemporary Past*. London and New York: Routledge, 1996, 39–78.

206 Kershaw, Baz, 'King Real's King Lear: Radical Shakespeare for the Nuclear Age'. *Critical Survey* 3 (1991): 249–59.

3.10   *King Lear*. Dir. Jean-Luc Godard
(USA and Switzerland, 1987)

207 Bennett, Susan, 'Godard and Lear: Trashing the Can(n)on'. *Theatre Survey* 39 (1998): 7–19.
208 Diniz, Thaís Flores Nogueira, 'Godard: a Contemporary *King Lear*', in *Foreign Accents: Brazilian Readings of Shakespeare*, ed. Aimara da Cunha Resende. Newark: University of Delaware Press, 2002, 198–206.
209 Donaldson, Peter S., 'Disseminating Shakespeare: Paternity and Text in Jean-Luc Godard's *King Lear*', in his *Shakespearean Films/Shakespearean Directors*. Boston and London: Unwin Hyman, 1990, 189–225.
210 Donaldson, Peter S., 'Shakespeare and Media Allegory', in *Shakespeare and Genre: from Early Modern Inheritances to Postmodern Legacies*, ed. Anthony R. Guneratne. New York and Basingstoke: Palgrave Macmillan, 2011, 223–37.
211 Griggs, Yvonne, '"Meantime we shall express our darker purpose": Jean-Luc Godard's *King Lear* (1987)', in her *Shakespeare's 'King Lear': the Relationship between Text and Film*. London: Methuen Drama, 2009, 156–70.
212 Guneratne, Anthony R., 'Six Authors in Search of a Text: the Shakespeares of Van Sant, Branagh, Godard, Pasolini, Greenaway, and Luhrmann', in his *Shakespeare, Film Studies, and the Visual Cultures of Modernity*. New York and Basingstoke: Palgrave Macmillan, 2008, 211–49.
213 Guneratne, Anthony R., 'Four Funerals and a Bedding: Freud and the Post-Apocalyptic Apocalypse of Jean-Luc Godard's *King Lear*', in *Apocalyptic Shakespeare: Essays on Visions of Chaos and Revelation in Recent Film Adaptations*, ed. Melissa Croteau and Carolyn Jess-Cooke. Jefferson and London: McFarland, 2009, 197–215.
214 Guneratne, Anthony, 'A Certain Tendency in Post-New Wave French Shakespearean Cinema: from Early Truffaut to Late Godard via Orson Welles', in *Shakespeare on Screen in Francophonia*, special issue, ed. Melissa Croteau, gen. ed. Patricia Dorval and Nathalie Vienne-Guerrin. Université Montpellier III, Institut de Recherche sur la Renaissance, l'Âge Classique et les Lumières (IRCL), 2016. shakscreen.org/post-new_wave_french_cinema/ (accessed 17 May 2019).
215 Habinek, Lianne, 'Getting to Page Four of *King Lear* with Jean-Luc Godard'. *Shakespeare* (British Shakespeare Association) 9 (2013): 76–90.
216 Harrison, Keith, 'Bakhtinian Polyphony in Godard's *King Lear*', in his *Shakespeare, Bakhtin, and Film: a Dialogic Lens*. Cham: Palgrave Macmillan, 2017, 141–62.
217 Impastato, David, 'Godard's *Lear* . . . Why Is It so Bad?' *Shakespeare Bulletin* 12.3 (Summer 1994): 38–41.

218 Maerz, Jessica M., 'Godard's *King Lear*: Referents Provided upon Request'. *Literature/Film Quarterly* 32 (2004): 108–14.

219 Morrey, Douglas, 'Smiling with Regret: 1984–90', in his *Jean-Luc Godard*. Manchester and New York: Manchester University Press, 2005, 165–95.

220 Murray, Timothy, 'The Crisis of Cinema in the Age of New World Memory: the Baroque Legacy of Jean-Luc Godard', in his *Digital Baroque: New Media Art and Cinematic Folds*. Minneapolis and London: University of Minnesota Press, 2008, 85–110.

221 Petříková, Linda, 'Against Adaptation: Jean-Luc Godard's *King Lear*'. *Litteraria Pragensia* 20.39 (July 2010): 41–54.

222 Robinson, Marc, 'Resurrected Images: Godard's *King Lear*'. *Performing Arts Journal* 11.1 (31) (Jan. 1988): 20–5.

223 Rosenbaum, Jonathan, 'The Importance of Being Perverse: Godard's *King Lear*', in his *Placing Movies: the Practice of Film Criticism*. Berkeley: University of California Press, 1995, 184–9.

224 Walworth, Alan, 'Cinema *Hysterica Passio*: Voice and Gaze in Jean-Luc Godard's *King Lear*', in *The Reel Shakespeare: Alternative Cinema and Theory*, ed. Lisa S. Starks and Courtney Lehmann. Madison and Teaneck: Fairleigh Dickinson University Press, 2002, 59–94.

See also 7, 19, 51, 205.

3.11 *The Godfather, Part III*. Dir. Francis Ford Coppola (USA, 1990)

225 Griggs, Yvonne, 'Mafia Father Figures: Francis Ford Coppola's *The Godfather* Trilogy (1972, 1974, 1990)', in her *Shakespeare's 'King Lear': the Relationship between Text and Film*. London: Methuen Drama, 2009, 126–33.

See also 182.

3.12 *Romani Kris*. Dir. Bence Gyöngyössy (Hungary, 1997)

226 Burnett, Mark Thornton, 'Capital, Commodities, Cinema: Shakespeare and the Eastern European "Gypsy" Aesthetic'. *Shakespeare Jahrbuch* 150 (2014): 146–60.

3.13 *A Thousand Acres*. Dir. Jocelyn Moorhouse (USA, 1997)

227 Ezell, Pamela, '*A Thousand Acres*: *King Lear* for the Heartland'. *Creative Screenwriting* 5.2 (1998): 16–19.

228 Griggs, Yvonne, '*King Lear* as Melodrama: Jocelyn Moorhouse's *A Thousand Acres* (1997)', in her *Shakespeare's 'King Lear': the Relationship between Text and Film*. London: Methuen Drama, 2009, 143–54.

229 Keller, James R., 'Dreaming of the Pure Vegetable Kingdom: Ecofeminism and Agriculture in *A Thousand Acres* and *Antonia's Line*', in his *Food, Film and Culture: a Genre Study*. Jefferson and London: McFarland, 2006, 94–108.

230 Lehmann, Courtney, 'A Thousand Shakespeares: from Cinematic Saga to Feminist Geography or, The Escape from Iceland', in *A Companion to Shakespeare and Performance*, ed. Barbara Hodgdon and W. B. Worthen. Malden and Oxford: Blackwell, 2005, 588–609.

231 Marquardt, Anne-Kathrin, 'Unlearning Tradition: William Shakespeare's *King Lear*, Jane Smiley's and Jocelyn Moorhouse's *A Thousand Acres*', in *Rewriting Shakespeare's Plays for and by the Contemporary Stage*, ed. Michael Dobson and Estelle Rivier-Arnaud. Newcastle: Cambridge Scholars Publishing, 2017, 11–29. *See also* 133.

3.14   *The King Is Alive.* Dir. Kristian Levring (Denmark, 2001)

232 Bottinelli, Jennifer J., 'Watching *Lear*: Resituating the Gaze at the Intersection of Film and Drama in Kristian Levring's *The King Is Alive*'. *Literature/Film Quarterly* 33 (2005): 101–9.

233 Buchanan, Judith, 'Leaves of Brass and Gads of Steel: Cinema as Subject in Shakespeare Films, 1991–2000', in her *Shakespeare on Film*. Harlow: Pearson Longman, 2005, 220–60.

234 Burnett, Mark Thornton, 'Spirituality/Meaning/Shakespeare', in his *Filming Shakespeare in the Global Marketplace*. Basingstoke and New York: Palgrave Macmillan, 2007, 107–28.

235 Burt, Richard, 'Alluding to Shakespeare in *L'Appartement, The King Is Alive, Wicker Park, a Time to Love*, and *University of Laughs*: Digital Film, Asianization, and the Transnational Film Remake'. *Shakespeare Yearbook* 17 (2010): 45–78.

236 Calbi, Maurizio, 'Shakespearean Retreats: Spectrality, Survival, and Autoimmunity in Kristian Levring's *The King Is Alive*', in his *Spectral Shakespeares: Media Adaptations in the Twenty-First Century*. New York and Basingstoke: Palgrave Macmillan, 2013, 39–61.

237 Cartelli, Thomas and Katherine Rowe, 'Surviving Shakespeare: Kristian Levring's *The King Is Alive*', in their *New Wave Shakespeare on Screen*. Cambridge and Malden: Polity Press, 2007, 142–64.

238 Chumo II, Peter N., '*The King Is Alive*: Screenplay by Kristian Levring'. *Creative Screenwriting* 8.4 (July/Aug. 2001): 20–2.

239 Ferguson, Ailsa Grant, 'The Dance of Death: *Dogme#4: The King Is Alive* and *King Lear*', in her *Shakespeare, Cinema, Counter-Culture: Appropriation and Inversion*. New York and London: Routledge, 2016, 58–86.

240 Griggs, Yvonne, '"Radical art phalanx" versus "a clever flag of PR convenience": Kristian Levring's *The King Is Alive* (2000)', in her *Shakespeare's 'King Lear': the Relationship between Text and Film*. London: Methuen Drama, 2009, 171–85.

241 Harrison, Keith, 'Shakespeare Shaping in Dogme95 Films, and Bakhtin's Theory of Tragedy', in his *Shakespeare, Bakhtin, and Film: a Dialogic Lens*. Cham: Palgrave Macmillan, 2017, 163–86.

242 Holland, Peter, 'On the Gravy Train: Shakespeare, Memory and Forgetting', in *Shakespeare, Memory and Performance*, ed. Peter Holland. Cambridge and New York: Cambridge University Press, 2006, 207–34.

243 Jess, Carolyn, '"The Barbarous Cronos": (Post)Colonialism, Sequelization, and Regenerative Authority in Kristian Levring's *The King Is Alive* (2000)'. *Shakespeare in Southern Africa* 15 (2003): 11–20.

244 Jess, Carolyn, 'New-ness, Sequelization, and Dogme Logic in Kristian Levring's *The King Is Alive*'. *New Cinemas: Journal of Contemporary Film* 3 (2005): 3–16.

245 Jess-Cooke, Carolyn, '"The Promised End" of Cinema: Portraits of Apocalypse in Post-Millennial Shakespearean Film', in *Apocalyptic Shakespeare: Essays on Visions of Chaos and Revelation in Recent Film Adaptations*, ed. Melissa Croteau and Carolyn Jess-Cooke. Jefferson and London: McFarland, 2009, 216–27.

246 Kelly, Richard, '"Is this the promised end?": Kristian Levring & *The King Is Alive*', in his *The Name of This Book Is Dogme95*. London and New York: Faber and Faber, 2000, 209–17.

247 Lehmann, Courtney, 'The Passion of the W: Localizing Shakespeare, Globalizing Manifest Density from *King Lear* to Kingdom Come'. *Upstart Crow* 25 (2005): 16–32.

248 Livingston, Paisley, 'Artistic Self-Reflexivity in *The King Is Alive* and *Strass*', in *Purity and Provocation: Dogma 95*, ed. Mette Hjort and Scott MacKenzie. London: British Film Institute, 2003, 102–10.

249 Nochimson, Martha P., '*The King Is Alive*'. *Film Quarterly* 55.2 (Winter 2001): 48–54.

250 Roman, Shari, 'Dogme 95 and the New Guard: Original Dogme: Kristian Levring', in her *Digital Babylon: Hollywood, Indiewood & Dogme 95*. Hollywood: ifilm Publishing, 2001, 71–8.

251 Scott-Douglass, Amy, 'Dogme Shakespeare 95: European Cinema, Anti-Hollywood Sentiment, and the Bard', in *Shakespeare, the Movie, II: Popularizing the Plays on Film, TV, Video, and DVD*, ed. Richard Burt and Lynda E. Boose. London and New York: Routledge, 2003, 252–64.
See also 51, 133, 179, 196, 247.

3.15 *My Kingdom*. Dir. Don Boyd (Great Britain, 2001)

252 Griggs, Yvonne, 'Gangster *Lear* as Morality Tale: Don Boyd's *My Kingdom* (2001)', in her *Shakespeare's 'King Lear': the Relationship between Text and Film*. London: Methuen Drama, 2009, 133–43.

253 Lehmann, Courtney, 'The Postnostalgic Renaissance: the "Place" of Liverpool in Don Boyd's *My Kingdom*', in *Screening Shakespeare in the Twenty-First Century*, ed. Mark Thornton Burnett and Ramona Wray. Edinburgh: Edinburgh University Press, 2006, 72–89.
See also 247.

3.16   *King of Texas*. Dir. Uli Edel (USA, 2002)

254 Aldama, Frederick Luis, 'Race, Cognition, and Emotion: Shakespeare on Film'. *College Literature* 33.1 (Winter 2006): 197–213.
255 Coursen, H. R., 'Shakespeare on Television', in *Sh@kespeare in the Media: from the Globe Theatre to the World Wide Web*, ed. Stefani Brusberg-Kiermeier and Jörg Helbig. 2nd, revised edn. Frankfurt: Peter Lang, 2010, 169–78.
256 Osborne, Laurie E., 'A Local Habitation and a Name: Television and Shakespeare'. *Shakespeare Survey* 61 (2008): 213–26.
See also 179, 182, 247.

3.17   *Second Generation*. Dir. Jon Sen (Channel Four, 2003)

257 Dengel-Janic, Ellen and Johanna Roering, 'Re-Imaging Shakespeare in *Second Generation* – A British-Asian Perspective on Shakespeare's *King Lear*', in *Drama and Cultural Change: Turning around Shakespeare*, ed. Matthias Bauer and Angelika Zirker. Trier: Wissenschaftlicher Verlag Trier, 2009, 211–19.
258 Marino, Alessandra, 'Multicultural Shakespeare: Italian and British TV Series of the 9–11 pm Slot. "Brand" Shakespeare and TV Adaptations'. *Anglistica* 15.2 (2011): 15–26.
259 Marino, Alessandra, 'Cut'n'mix *King Lear: Second Generation* and Asian-British Identities', in *Shakespeare and Conflict: a European Perspective*, ed. Carla Dente and Sara Soncini. Basingstoke and New York: Palgrave Macmillan, 2013, 170–83.

3.18   *Wicker Park*. Dir. Paul McGuigan (USA, 2004)

See 235.

3.19   *Slings and Arrows* (Season Three). Dir. Peter Wellington (Canada, 2006)

260 Fedderson, Kim and J. Michael Richardson, '*Slings & Arrows*: an Intermediated Shakespearean Adaptation', in *OuterSpeares: Shakespeare, Intermedia, and the Limits of Adaptation*, ed. Daniel Fischlin. Toronto: University of Toronto Press, 2014, 205–29.
261 Osborne, Laurie E., 'Serial Shakespeare: Intermedial Performance and the Outrageous Fortunes of *Slings & Arrows*'. *Borrowers and Lenders: the Journal of Shakespeare and Appropriation* 6.2 (Fall/Winter 2011): www.borrowers.uga.edu/783090/show (accessed 17 May 2019).
262 Pittman, L. Monique, 'Tracing *Hamlet* in *Slings and Arrows*: Fathers Haunt the Theater', in her *Authorizing Shakespeare on Film and Television: Gender, Class, and Ethnicity in Adaptation*. New York: Peter Lang, 2011, 177–206.
263 Royster, Francesca T., 'Comic Terror and Masculine Vulnerability in *Slings and Arrows: Season Three*'. *Journal of Narrative Theory* 41 (2011): 343–61.
See also 256.

3.20   *The Last Lear.* Dir. Rituparno Ghosh (India, 2007)

264 Chakravarti, Paromita, 'Reading Intertextualities in Rituporno [sic] Ghosh's *The Last Lear:* the Politics of Recanonization'. *Shakespearean International Yearbook* 12 (2012): 115–29.

265 Chakravarti, Paromita, 'Interrogating "Bollywood Shakespeare": Reading Rituparno Ghosh's *The Last Lear*', in *Bollywood Shakespeares*, ed. Craig Dionne and Parmita Kapadia. New York and Basingstoke: Palgrave Macmillan, 2014, 127–45.

266 Mukherjee, Ankhi, 'hamarashakespeare.com: Shakespeare in India', in her *What Is a Classic?: Postcolonial Rewriting and Invention of the Canon.* Stanford: Stanford University Press, 2014, 182–213.
     See also 202.

3.21   *Life Goes On.* Dir. Sangeeta Datta (Great Britain, 2009)

267 Földváry, Kinga, 'Postcolonial Hybridity: the Making of a Bollywood *Lear* in London'. *Shakespeare* (British Shakespeare Association) 9 (2013): 304–12.

3.22   *The Eye of the Storm.* Dir. Fred Schepisi (Australia, 2011)

268 Rayner, Jonathan, 'Meditative Tangents: Fred Schepisi's *The Eye of the Storm* (2011)'. *Australian Studies* 4 (2012): https://www.austlit.edu.au/austlit/page/6130749 (accessed 17 May 2019).

3.23   *Margaret.* Dir. Kenneth Lonergan (USA, 2011)

269 Walker, Elsie, 'Adaptation as Re-reading, Line by Line'. *Literature/Film Quarterly* 41 (2013): 86–91.

3.24   *Dahsha [Perplexity].* Dir. ʿAbd al-Raḥīm Kamāl (Egypt, 2014)

270 Ibraheem, Noha Mohamad Mohamad, 'ʿAbd al-Raḥīm Kamāl's *Dahsha*: an Upper Egyptian *Lear*'. *Critical Survey* 28.3 (Winter 2016): 67–85.

3.25   *Westworld* (HBO, 2016–)

271 Winckler, Reto, 'This Great Stage of Androids: *Westworld*, Shakespeare and the World as Stage'. *Journal of Adaptation in Film & Performance* 10 (2017): 169–88.

Index